Research Series on the Chinese Dream and China's Development Path

Series Editors
Yang Li, Chinese Academy of Social Sciences,
Peilin Li, Chinese Academy of Social Sciences,

Drawing on a large body of empirical studies done over the last two decades, this Series provides its readers with in-depth analyses of the past and present and forecasts for the future course of China's development. It contains the latest research results made by members of the Chinese Academy of Social Sciences. This series is an invaluable companion to every researcher who is trying to gain a deeper understanding of the development model, path and experience unique to China. Thanks to the adoption of Socialism with Chinese characteristics, and the implementation of comprehensive reform and opening-up, China has made tremendous achievements in areas such as political reform, economic development, and social construction, and is making great strides towards the realization of the Chinese dream of national rejuvenation. In addition to presenting a detailed account of many of these achievements, the authors also discuss what lessons other countries can learn from China's experience.

Project Director

Shouguang Xie, President, Social Sciences Academic Press

Academic Advisors

Fang Cai, Peiyong Gao, Lin Li, Qiang Li, Huaide Ma, Jiahua Pan, Changhong Pei, Ye Qi, Lei Wang, Ming Wang, Yuyan Zhang, Yongnian Zheng, Hong Zhou

More information about this series at https://link.springer.com/bookseries/13571

Hongwu Liu · Jianbo Luo

Sino-African Development Cooperation

Studies on the Theories, Strategies, and Policies

Hongwu Liu
Zhejiang, China

Jianbo Luo
Beijing, China

Translator: Simin Tan

Editor: Zhaojuan Chen

Published with support of Zhejiang People's Publishing House

ISSN 2363-6866   ISSN 2363-6874 (electronic)
Research Series on the Chinese Dream and China's Development Path
ISBN 978-981-16-5483-1   ISBN 978-981-16-5481-7 (eBook)
https://doi.org/10.1007/978-981-16-5481-7

Jointly published with Social Sciences Academic Press
The print edition is not for sale in China (Mainland). Customers from China (Mainland) please order the print book from: Social Sciences Academic Press.

© Social Sciences Academic Press and Springer Nature Singapore Pte Ltd. 2021
This work is subject to copyright. All rights are reserved by the Publishers, whether the whole or part of the material is concerned, specifically the rights of reprinting, reuse of illustrations, recitation, broadcasting, reproduction on microfilms or in any other physical way, and transmission or information storage and retrieval, electronic adaptation, computer software, or by similar or dissimilar methodology now known or hereafter developed.
The use of general descriptive names, registered names, trademarks, service marks, etc. in this publication does not imply, even in the absence of a specific statement, that such names are exempt from the relevant protective laws and regulations and therefore free for general use.
The publishers, the authors, and the editors are safe to assume that the advice and information in this book are believed to be true and accurate at the date of publication. Neither the publishers nor the authors or the editors give a warranty, express or implied, with respect to the material contained herein or for any errors or omissions that may have been made. The publishers remain neutral with regard to jurisdictional claims in published maps and institutional affiliations.

This Springer imprint is published by the registered company Springer Nature Singapore Pte Ltd.
The registered company address is: 152 Beach Road, #21-01/04 Gateway East, Singapore 189721, Singapore

Series Preface

Since China's reform and opening began in 1978, the country has come a long way on the path of Socialism with Chinese characteristics, under the leadership of the Communist Party of China. Over 30 years of reform, efforts and sustained spectacular economic growth have turned China into the world's second largest economy, and brought many profound changes in the Chinese society. These historically significant developments have been garnering increasing attention from scholars, governments, and the general public alike around the world since the 1990s, when the newest wave of China studies began to gather steam. Some of the hottest topics have included the so-called "China miracle", "Chinese phenomenon", "Chinese experience", "Chinese path", and the "Chinese model". Home-grown researchers have soon followed suit. Already hugely productive, this vibrant field is putting out a large number of books each year, with Social Sciences Academic Press alone having published hundreds of titles on a wide range of subjects.

Because most of these books have been written and published in Chinese, however, readership has been limited outside China—even among many who study China for whom English is still the lingua franca. This language barrier has been an impediment to efforts by academia, business communities, and policy-makers in other countries to form a thorough understanding of contemporary China, of what is distinct about China's past and present may mean not only for her future but also for the future of the world. The need to remove such an impediment is both real and urgent, and the *Research Series on the Chinese Dream and China's Development Path* is my answer to the call.

This series features some of the most notable achievements from the last 20 years by scholars in China in a variety of research topics related to reform and opening. They include both theoretical explorations and empirical studies, and cover economy, society, politics, law, culture, and ecology, the six areas in which reform and opening policies have had the deepest impact and farthest reaching consequences for the country. The authors for the series have also tried to articulate their visions of the "Chinese Dream" and how the country can realize it in these fields and beyond.

All of the editors and authors for the *Research Series on the Chinese Dream and China's Development Path* are both longtime students of reform and opening and recognized authorities in their respective academic fields. Their credentials and expertise lend credibility to these books, each of which having been subject to a rigorous peer-review process for inclusion in the series. As part of the Reform and Development Program under the State Administration of Press, Publication, Radio, Film, and Television of the People's Republic of China, the series is published by Springer, a Germany-based academic publisher of international repute, and distributed overseas. I am confident that it will help fill a lacuna in the studies of China in the era of reform and opening.

Shouguang Xie

About this Book

In this volume, we look at China-Africa partnerships in contemporary times, and the global impact and significance of such partnerships. In the introduction, we outline the core issues that will be addressed in this volume from the perspective of the transformation of the contemporary global system and the reshaping of modernity in mankind. We also look at the bodies of knowledge, concepts, and theoretical assumptions relevant to these issues. We discuss theories on China-Africa partnerships, existing academic disciplines, and methodologies. This discussion involves areas such as the theoretical background of China-Africa partnerships, and disciplinary and methodological issues. Certain strategic questions in comtemporary China-Africa partnerships are discussed. Here, we look at the historical background and evolution of China's strategies vis-à-vis Africa, its choice of targets, and impact on the world. We look at government policies concerning contemporary China-Africa partnerships. Specific areas that are examined include policy selections, pathway adjustments, improvements made to certain measures, and institutional building.

Introduction

Both China and Africa have been, over different historical periods and in many areas, at the forefront of human civilization. Along the upper and lower reaches of the north-flowing Nile, through the vast expanses of West Sudan and the Ethiopian Highlands, and on both sides of the Yangtze River and Yellow River that run from west to east across eastern continental Asia, the peoples of Africa and China have created their own dazzling civilizations, and formed distinct systems of knowledge and ideas.

The rich legacies of the two civilizations, including their unique knowledge and mindset, still manifest their impact today. When we try to probe deeper into the nature and roots of modernity and reassess the values of older civilizations by adopting a broad historical perspective, we will see that at once ancient and modern, the civilizations of China and Africa are set to unleash hitherto-unseen creative powers, and help reshape modernity.

A global perspective is needed if we are to fully understand the historical significance and global implications of the China-Africa partnership today.

Radical Changes in the Global System and the Reshaping of Modernity

From a historical perspective, the evolution of civilization has always led to transformations in the form of society. Given the diversity of social forms and the vast temporal span of human history, the evolution of civilization is bound to be a tortuous and heterogeneous process. The transformation from agrarian society to industrial society in modern times marks yet another milestone in the history of civilization. The relative tranquility and equality characteristic of the slow-paced agrarian society were replaced by intensified social interactions and rapid innovations. Modern civilization has led to unprecedented growth in people's understanding of nature and ability to control their destiny. However, for the first time in history, they have also been brought face-to-face with the many challenges and conflicts brought about by modernity.

For various reasons, the breakthroughs that had led to the transition from agrarian society to industrial society first occurred in Western Europe.

For centuries, the West has led and dominated development in the modern world. Certainly, the creative power that the West first unleashed has made important contributions to modern civilization. However, one consequence of a modern global system of development centered on the West is civilizational collapse and regress in the early stages of modern development in China, Africa, and Latin America after they came in contact with capitalism, imperialism, and the industrialized West. In these places, there has been a painful process of social disintegration and the marginalization of the development of the local peoples. This is also an important reason why the development of humankind and modernity around the world was riddled with perversion, turbulence, and conflict.

Modernity has brought on major changes in global history, and the West has played a critical role in this process. However, the modern history of the world is perhaps not the "world system" completely centered on the West as described by Immanuel Wallerstein.[1] The process of modern growth that began in the West was only one part of an even more complex and longer process of history and growth. It is a stage and cannot possibly be the entire story in itself. In truth, since the onset of modern times, with the sustained dominance of the West, other peoples in the rest of the world have continued to defend their histories and cultures and at the same time, bore the changes brought forth by modernity in their own ways. They have sought independence amidst encounters and interactions, and stubbornly sought ways of modern development compatible with their specific conditions and needs. This is how they have participated in the process of modern global civilization. Today, the non-Western world's hard work has paid off, and it has begun to accrue its own experiences of modern development as well as grow in terms of confidence. As the non-Western world rises politically, economically, and culturally, what is emerging is a new world where peoples and civilizations interact on an equal footing.

On the historical level, following the advances of a Western-dominated world system for several hundred years, the establishment and development of mutually

---

[1] Wallerstein's theory has found many subscribers among Chinese scholars in recent years. However, we believe that Wallerstein's West-centric world systems theory cannot adequately explain the complexity of various civilizational systems from the advent of modern times to the present day. This is because, the theory overlooks the fact that even as Western dominance of the world reached its apogee in the late nineteenth century and the early twentieth century, the non-Western world never did become a fully passive player subject to the complete domination of the West. In fact, although since the beginning of modern times Western systems of knowledge have become highly developed, they have never become "global" or "universal" systems of knowledge and ways of thinking shared by all of humanity. With core concepts like "civilization", "progress", "development", "democracy", "freedom", and "human rights", Western beliefs and experiences are, to a certain extent, rooted in "localized knowledge" accrued in places like Europe and America. It is only that such knowledge has been spread far and wide due to the political and economic strength of the West in modern times and has thus gained the "halo" of universality. However, Wallerstein's theoretical framework is the result of extending his approach from the West to Africa and the rest of the non-Western world. Thus, Wallerstein's perspective is still marginally better than those who are fixated on Western-centrism. As such, we are of the opinion that contemporary Chinese scholars can also draw on certain implications from Wallerstein's theory.

respectful relations between China and Africa on an equal footing today against the backdrop of the Asian and African renaissance has special symbolic meaning. It reflects the basic form of global inter-civilizational relations and international relations, which are to a certain degree moving towards a "multi-polar" model where diverse cultures interact on equal terms. Although this process is difficult, tumultuous, and protracted, it shows clearly that the Western-centric experience of modernity and the discourse process is but a particular stage of the development of modernity among the whole of humanity. Naturally, the history and modernity of humanity will not terminate with the rise and completion of Western civilization, and will instead continue to move forward with the renaissance and rise of Asia and Africa.[2]

However, compared to the Western world which has had over hundreds of years' experience of modernity, Asian and African countries have achieved successful development for but decades; thus, their experience and value have yet to be widely understood and recognized, and the Western-centric model of the world has yet to be fully eradicated. Generally speaking, in past colonial times, the influence of Western counties over the development of non-Western countries occurred mostly on the material level, in the areas of technology, behavior, and systems. Today, apart from the material, new influences are being expressed on the level of culture, through ways of thinking, knowledge, and ideas. In the last two to three centuries, by the systematic building of the humanities and social sciences the West has established its own modern system of discourse, which includes not only scientific ways of thinking and theories that are universally valid but also many cultural elements and beliefs about values that are specific to the West. However, in the last one or two hundred years, despite the West having an absolute advantage in terms of knowledge and discursive power around the globe even at its peak following the end of the Cold War in the 1980s, it has not been able to fully describe either modernity or the future prospects of, and challenges to the development of mankind, for the lack of necessary comparisons, supplementation, and corrections from the study of the experiences of non-Western countries and due to ideological reasons. Furthermore, globally the "post-Western era" has already emerged, and the modern Western system of knowledge, accustomed to seeing itself at the center, is in fact already being confronted by challenges that it has never seen before.

In truth, although the Western system of knowledge and ways of thinking mainly based on Western history and experiences has become highly developed since the advent of modern times, currently there is no single brand new non-Western system of knowledge and ways of thinking that can fully challenge or even replace it. Nevertheless, we still believe that this Western system of knowledge and ways of thinking has yet to provide a complete narrative of modernity, which is a condition that concerns the destiny of mankind as a whole, and that the knowledge and tools accumulated to date are insufficient in explaining, and counteracting, new developments and modern growth in a "post-Western era" that is already with us today and which may see

---

[2] Liu, Hongwu (2007). The historical value and global significance of the establishment of new strategic partnerships between China and African countries. *Foreign Affairs Review*, 2007 (1), 12–18.

major developments in the future. As a matter of fact, "Western knowledge" will face increasing challenges posed by new development pathways, development experiences, and developmental issues in relation to Asia and Africa. If the corresponding changes and innovations do not occur with the Western system of knowledge and ways of thinking, a sustained global ways of thinking conflict of ideas would be inevitable. This is a key reason for the challenges in knowledge[-building] and innovation which humanity is facing today, and it is also the root of the various conflicts in beliefs and attitudes between the Western and non-Western worlds.

For a long time, Western civilization has been described as universal in its value and all-encompassing in its scope, while other civilizations were neglected or even belittled. Industrial civilization has been setup in contrast to traditional civilizations, and capitalism and the capitalist system have been touted as superior. Such expression of ways of thinking and knowledge has led to, to a very large extent, the perversion of the nature of modernity by Western ways of thinking that misled many people. This state of affairs, and the biases and chaos it has caused, has in fact already impeded the healthy development of modern human civilization that is becoming increasingly complex by the day and which also faces an increasing number and types of challenges. As mankind develops along a diverse array of models, the modernity of mankind is in an era that is developing swiftly. If we are to continue to use the limited knowledge and experiences of the West to explain the world around us and to continue to use Western ways of seeing as the only measure for modernity, then mankind will never be able to counter the complex challenges of today or move towards a new high point in history. It is on this point that we say that we must look towards the needs of a much longer kind of human development today and henceforth, and that much of the Western systems of knowledge and experiences that have dominated the world for a long time will have to be cleaned up, corrected, and discarded. Universal models that concern matters like modern civilization, development, progress, justice, freedom, democracy, and human rights should also contain input from the rich trove of accumulated experiences of the long-standing Asian and African worlds as well as the development experiences of these worlds. There should be an addition of an even more diverse array of "Asian and African knowledge" (such as "Chinese episteme", "African knowledge", "Indian knowledge", and "Arabian knowledge") or any other wisdom that can be used to improve the system of human knowledge and experiences. Then, we will be able create new global knowledge, ways of thinking, experiences, and sentiments, through integration. Only through this sort of absorption and integration can the system of knowledge and ways of thinking of humanity serve as a source of strength, adequately express all of mankind's accumulated experiences and value needs to date, and support and help mankind in overcoming various issues and challenges posed by modernity.

Here, we use the concepts of "Chinese episteme" and "Asian and African knowledge" and their modern sense due to our basic understanding of the structure of human history and new appreciation for the internal structure of modernity. From a broad point of view of human civilization and history, the nurturing and growth of modernity should be regarded as a much greater process than the experience of Western Europe over the last few hundred years, whose spatial-temporal scope is really rather limited. The origins and core of modernity consist of more than the parts that modern Western thinkers like Georg Hegel, Max Weber, Fernand Braudel, Francis Fukuyama, etc., see or are interested in. In terms of history, although the West was the first to achieve breakthroughs in modernization and people's obtaining modernity, certain aspects which are still today considered as fundamental elements of modern civilization have already been developed over the long course of the evolution of agrarian society. These core elements have a far longer lasting effect and significance. Both the ancient Chinese civilization and ancient African civilizations had reached rather advanced states and have, at different points in history, had a deep impact on the growth and development of Western civilization. Even in the early part of the rise of the West in modern times, China's institutions and systems, cultures, political form, governance and system of bureaucracy, and knowledge and sentiments, as well as her silver and commodities, were all instrumental in bringing the West out of the Dark Ages. Furthermore, the rise of the West in early modern times is perhaps unimaginable had it not had rapacious access to the rich material and spiritual resources of the dark-skinned peoples of Africa and the American Indians.[3] Thus, the process of modern growth—wherein the West was the first to achieve breakthroughs—should be regarded as a result of a long period of civilizational development among mankind for thousands of years. It is but a stage in the development of modernity. This stage had been kickstarted, and dominated, by the West. No matter the importance of this part, it cannot replace the entire course of the growth of modernity, neither is it the highest point, and end-point of the growth of modernity, the point at which the further growth of modernity in other parts of the world is terminated. This is our understanding of why China-Africa cooperation today will necessarily have promising prospects and global significance, an understanding drawn upon a broader understanding of the history of the world.

Since early modern times, the West, which was the first to rise, created what were some "self-evident" truths or theories in the gradual course of dominating the world in discursive and ideological terms. These "self-evident" core beliefs can be classified into two groups that are in turn mutually supporting: the first is related to the simple understanding of modernity as a process that only began in the West. Here, Western civilization is described as a special case in world history and the West, as the only region in the world that had given rise to modern civilization. Within the logic of such a belief, other world civilizations—no matter how old they are, or how glorious they were in their heyday—had neither the capabilities nor the consciousness to transition to modern civilization. In many strands of modern Western ways of thinking, the emergence of modern civilization in the West is purely an exception in world history and something that would never have happened in any non-Western society. Other world cultures and societies had no choice but to learn from Western civilization, transplant Western institutions, and imitate Western

---

[3] The Agricultural Revolution that occurred as a result of food crops imported from the Americas (potato, corn, sweet potato, etc.) has played a key role in augmenting population growth in early modern Europe and the beginning of the Industrial Revolution. See Liu Hongwu (1992). On the reasons Western Europe rose ahead [of the rest of the world]. *Ideology Frontline*, 1992 (2).

systems if they wanted to enter modern civilization. This Western-centric belief, a kind of power and ideology itself, strengthened in the nineteenth century and beyond, reached its apogee and even became the monopolistic ideology for a time following the end of the Cold War in the 1970s. This ideology has woven a dazzling "halo" of civilization and legitimacy for the Western world and has played a significant role in the West's long-time domination of the world. Another similarly blinkered belief is the understanding that modern civilization stands in diametric opposition to traditional civilizations and that modern civilization is an all-new phenomenon that happened all of a sudden. This creates artificial walls between traditional agrarian civilization and modern industrial civilization when the two actually share relations of continuity, and relegates mankind's civilizational creations and knowledge over millennia and associated systems, ways of thinking, technologies, etc., to the bin of "archeology". In the same vein, within the logic of such a belief the Asian and Africa worlds, or even the entire non-Western world, are categorized into the scope of "traditional civilizations" and their knowledge and ways of thinking, regarded as useless to modern development and thus disregarded. As such, the non-Western world lost its power and legitimacy to exist in the modern world.

With a historical perspective like this, we believe that international relations and partnerships between developing countries in the new era today, including China-Africa cooperation, can help to enhance the collective developmental power of developing countries and promote a development and cultural renaissance in these countries. Further, such partnerships also have another historical purpose: to participate in a revamped understanding and description of the origins and evolution of modernity from the very beginning, and to participate in the shaping of a global discourse of modernity, so as to dismantle the narrow discourse of modernity that is centered on the West. The whole world has to work together to integrate the traditions and contemporary knowledge and experience of the Asian and African peoples or the non-Western world into various value systems that are universal to mankind and which concern matters such as human reason, democracy, freedom, and human rights, such as modern political systems, economic systems, ways of thinking and culture, ethical standards, and principles. In this way, the understanding and scope of modernity can be broadened and the structure and basis of modern civilization, enriched. And only in this way can mankind be better equipped to tackle various issues and challenges that have arisen as a result of modernity and promote the healthy development of modern civilization around the globe.

The Strategic Value and Historical Significance of China-Africa Development Partnerships

Over the course of this process, undoubtedly China-Africa development relations will be of high strategic significance in many areas as described below.

First of all, China-Africa development relations create for China the space for its global development strategy with the greatest historical significance as well as historical and cultural basis. The creation of this space will then facilitate the demonstration of how China, an emerging developing country, plays a unique role in promoting global development.

For developing countries, development is the greatest priority as well as the ultimate expression of the national interest. For China, development is of special significance for the rejuvenation of civilization. China is the world's largest developing country and has the longest history as a unified country. During the agrarian civilizational period, the Chinese civilization in the eastern part of Asia was generated and developed independently. It is also for this reason that the development and existence of this civilization was limited to East Asia. In Africa, especially in southern Africa south of the Sahara, civilizations also developed in a comparatively more isolated manner for geographic reasons. Although there are significant differences in the history and cultures of China and Africa, the two are similar in that their civilizations used to be in existence in a small corner of the world, and that has, to a certain extent, had an impact on how these civilizations interacted with other civilizations and how these civilizations developed prior to the advent of modernity.

The Chinese civilization, fostered over several thousand years, bears distinctive creativity and historical potential. Modern civilization is an open and globalized civilization. The scale of Chinese society and the history of Chinese civilization have determined that today China must transcend the previous spatial-temporal limits as it opens itself up to the world and embraces the world. It must, on a global basis, open up and obtain the space for inter-civilization interaction and further development. Contemporary China can no longer be like the West of the past and realize the expansion of the physical space needed for the continued existence and development of the Chinese civilization by means of colonization, coercion, or war. The non-peaceful approach to development is not in line with the norms of the international order today. More importantly, such an approach runs counter to China's civilization and traditions since antiquity and to China's goal of peaceful development in contemporary times. As such, China needs to take a new approach and the power of its civilization to carve out a new way of national development and to create new space for the development of global relations. The correct strategic choice in this case that would be in line with China's specific circumstances and her fundamental interests would be to participate in global development and to win the greatest possible amount of space for global development during this process.

Like China, Africa—the continent with the largest number of developing countries—has tremendous and sustainable developmental needs with its vast territory, rich resources, diverse and age-old histories and cultures, and underdeveloped societies and economies. Therefore, the establishment of long-term strategic development relations between the world's largest developing country and the world's largest developing continent and the establishment of the world's largest organic development entity through the combined creative energies of two major civilization groups based on the principles of equality, mutual support and mutually beneficial initiatives, and with continued joint efforts, will realize joint development for these two major civilizations in both regions as well as the modern renaissance of these two civilizations. Such development is highly significant and bears long-term impact for China, Africa, the world at large, and also for history and the future.[4]

China is a developing country and will be a competitive country in the future. Under normal circumstances, China would need to ensure that it maintains good foreign relations on four levels: with key global countries, with neighboring countries, with countries in the region, and with countries around the world. From the narrative above, we can see that Chinese relations and partnerships with Africa are situated at the fourth or global level, and have a special, fundamental position. Given how special China-Africa relations are, China's leaders over the years have been very clear about the importance of China-Africa relations, both during the past and the present, and no matter if relations at other levels had been more pressing. Today, as China's civilization renaissance and pathway to becoming a competitive country become increasingly clear, the significance of China-Africa relations to China's long-term development strategy has also become more precise and salient. For Africa, the strategic meaning of China-Africa relations has also become more pronounced. In the past 30 years, the achievements made in China-Africa development relations have demonstrated to Africa China's new external partnerships with the greatest potential and development prospects. Moreover, with China's participation and hard work, Africa's competitiveness on the global stage has also been significantly improved. In summary, poverty can only be eradicated with the joint efforts of a few generations, and for China and Africa which are working to complete the task of economic and social development, the significance of sincere, long-term cooperation between both parties cannot be in any way overstated.

Second, China-Africa development partnerships will provide an important external and international platform for the realization of China's strategy of peaceful development as well as provide a unique international stage for building of a "national identity" and "national image" for contemporary China with greater political legitimacy and moral appeal.

Today, China being somewhere between the state of a developing country and a developed one bears the characteristics of both categories. China may perhaps, in the course of interacting and cooperating with the Western developed countries and developing countries, play a more active and diversified role as a bridge for greater global development. Conversely, with China being in such a unique position, it has greater strategic leeway in terms of its positioning, the definition of its interests, strategic choices, and development. At the same time, however, it may also face more challenges and pressures on a greater number of fronts. Precisely because of the unique position between that of a developing country and that of a developed one, China may present more saliently the contradictions and dilemmas pertaining to the interests of mankind in contemporary development that are universal in nature.

---

[4] Liu, Hongwu (2008). Contemporary China-Africa relations and the wave of renaissance in Asian and African civilizations: questions on the special characteristics and significance of contemporary China-Africa relations. *World Economics and Politics*, 2008 (9), 29–37.

Against such a backdrop, how China can best handle its various relationships with developed and developing countries which have an array of interests and beliefs is a major strategic issue that would require contemporary China to think over strategically, make meticulous plans for, and be patient in implementing and demonstrating. This would perhaps also involve the building of a more stable external development platform with multiple strategic fulcrums.

From a long-term point of view, China's developmental objective should of course be to eventually become a developed country, or at least a comparatively strong and developed country that is able to break free of poverty, backwardness, and a position of weakness. Here, the authors believe that China does not have to be shy about stating its strategic goals. Although today China continues to call itself—and still is—a developing country, China's identity and role are changing. At the same time, the "developing country" is also changing both as a conceptual symbol and an existence in reality. Therefore, the issue is not whether China wants to become a (comparatively) developed country but what kind of a (comparatively) developed country China should become. The question is whether the process of China becoming a (comparatively) developed country takes place simultaneously with China's promoting the development of developing countries as a whole or a process wherein China would bring to the entire developing world new developmental opportunities, models, and platforms, as well as new room for development. The key to whether China can eventually become a (comparatively) developed country in the world is that China should position itself as a rising country that can promote the joint and harmonious development of mankind, and a constructive power that would bring developmental opportunities and hope to the world of the future, especially to developing countries. Hence, China's correct, and only, developmental choice would be the path of the rising power that does not sacrifice the interests of other countries and peoples and which instead brings hope and opportunities to others. Any other choice would lead to China facing massive resistance and containment from external parties in the course of its development and rise.

We should understand the strategic meaning and value of China-Africa developmental partnerships, which are not simply a "worthy endeavor" but a necessity, from such strategic perspective. For China, promoting comprehensive developmental partnerships with dozens of countries on the African continent is both for its national interests and part of its international responsibilities. Undoubtedly, such strategic partnerships involving both one's interests and responsibilities can completely bring both China and its African partners tremendous opportunities. We say that just as China and the US have a high degree of complementarity in the area of economic and technological cooperation, it is the same for China and Africa in many areas of partnership. In our opinion, in global strategy, once China establishes shared economic and developmental interests and strategic partnerships with the world's wealthiest and most advanced countries as well as the least developed countries on the globe, it would be able to realize its own goal of peaceful development and establish a strong and open international stage. This hypothesis is turning into reality...

After 30 years of successful development, China is currently surpassing Japan to become the world's second-largest economy. In the coming two to three decades, China will continue to maintain relatively high economic growth and may even come close to, or even eclipse, America in terms of the size of its economy. The changes in the size of the Chinese economy will undoubtedly have an impact in the world's existing political and economic structures. In the real international political and economic world, where conflicts of interest exist, China's development is viewed as a kind of challenge. Suspicion of China's development in the international arena is unavoidable. Indeed, internationally we are already seeing negative opinions about "containing China", "conflict", "the China threat", "the Chinese collapse", "guarding against China", etc. We should understand and handle such talk with the facts at hand.

Suspicion about China's goal and process of peaceful development mainly comes from Western countries, which are used to a Western-centric world order. China should not be too bothered by such criticism. However, there are some issues that have arisen from China's swift growth and development, and those that are uncertain and anxious about the future world order will naturally zoom in on. These are issues that China should tackle seriously. In addition, China's geographic location and her regional environment also mean that her strategy of peaceful development is confronted with challenges which are deeply rooted in history and take the form of conflicts of interests with surrounding countries and powers from within and outside the region. As China advances progressively into the center of world politics and economics, it takes on greater global responsibilities, exerts greater international influence, and faces greater and more global challenges. All these require China to depart from its accustomed way of thinking about international issues in an ad-hoc manner and to develop with a global perspective an international strategy and countermeasures that would express China's strategy of peaceful development.

As mentioned earlier, Africa is a long way away from China but shares strong relationships with China both in history and at present in terms of politics and economics. It exerts a distinctive influence in global political and economical affairs, and is able to demonstrate and put into practice for China the strategy of peaceful development. Through a variety of means—political and economic, historical, and cultural—we can work actively to establish China's image as a global power that is civilized and responsible, thus mitigating pressures and conflicts that have arisen as a result of complex interests and developments around the world. Such an approach can help to provide a stage for international activity that is sufficiently broad and which can produce global impact over a sustained period. If we are to look at the ancient Chinese political concept and model of "tianxia" (lit. "under the Heaven"), we will see that if we are to establish a theory of international relations and corresponding strategies that bear contemporary Chinese characteristics as well as the characteristics of realism and constructivism, we will be able to express a highly innovative strategy of China-Africa partnership that serves practical needs. Clearly, such efforts in the arena of international relations are not only one-sided actions on China's part but also an internal logic based on global development and at the same time a choice to engage in the building of a global system of culture through communication and cooperation with African countries and other stakeholders. In summary, compared to China-US relations, China's relations with Africa can also provide China with comparative effect and global influence and yet at the same time the continent lies on the other side of international cooperation and contestation in terms of interests. China should draw on the great wisdom of its people and history and seek to understand and handle the opportunities and challenges presented by spatial and temporal relations in international relations within the distinctive "country-region" cooperation structure.

Third: China-Africa relations and the studies of such relations will open up more space for China to think about its international relations and the corresponding theories. Further, such relations and studies will also provide a special theoretical incubator and practice platform for the nurturing of contemporary "Chinese episteme" and "Chinese ways of thinking" and in the process build up the reputational foundation and discursive legitimacy of Chinese episteme and ways of thinking.

In general, China-Africa partnerships comprise both Chinese partnerships with individual African countries as well as the partnership between China as a major country in the world and an entire continent. As such, such a development-focused partnership between a major country and an entire continent involves major civilizations or international relationships, and may see involvement, intervention, and interaction by other major countries, and the strategy that may be extended from this partnership bears massive potential in terms of both strategic breadth and depth as well as across time and space. Therefore, the many dimensions of contemporary Chinese foreign relations will necessarily constitute an arena of practice and ways of thinking with great historical importance. Contemporary Chinese scholars should have a clear picture of this, and understand, from the level of national strategy and changes in the global landscape, that the African continent and its development bear special significance for China so as to work hard on the subject of China-Africa relations.[5]

China is an ancient Oriental country with a distinctive outlook on international relations and profound theoretical and ideological traditions. Historically, China has undergone the Warring States Period and the tumultuous Spring and Autumn Period. Prior to the nineteenth century, the regional inter-state system that existed in East Asia centered on Chinese civilization was one of the most important international systems in pre-modern history. Since the early modern period, China was first passively engulfed into the Western-centric modern international system and then participated in this system as an active and open player. In over several thousand years of history,

---

[5] The Chinese state has paid increasing amounts of attention to African studies in recent years. The China-Africa Joint Research Exchange Program was initiated in 2009 at the 4th Forum on China–Africa Cooperation (FOCAC) Ministerial-level Meeting. The same year, the Ministry of Education established for the first time on the national level a key research program in the social sciences focusing on China-Africa relations. In 2010, the China Scholarship Council established its Research on International and Regional Issues scholarship program, with African Studies listed as one of the areas of interest under the program. Institutions focusing on African studies within China have also seen significant growth and development.

the people of China have engaged with her neighbors and other countries and peoples around the world in a myriad of ways: war and peace; regional domination and the experience of being invaded; integration and dissolution, even confrontation; and closing off from the outside world and opening up. With a complex history of foreign relations which encompasses military and political affairs, economics and society, and ways of thinking and culture, China has become one of the most experienced countries in global history in terms of ways of thinking and practical experience on international relations.

However, by modern and contemporary standards, and when considering people's state of survival and development as well as changes around the globe over time, it is clear that China still has a fair bit to catch up on with the West in terms of theories on international relations. China has a deep well of national ways of thinking to draw upon from pre-modern times, and has also itself drawn upon Western ways of thinking (including from the former Soviet Union) at various junctures, and the Chinese people have for over a hundred years accumulated many experiences both negative and positive. However, perhaps due to historical changes or the lack of full absorption or the lack of native original theories and systems, China today has yet to be able to connect its profound history with its practical experience. Indeed, China has yet been able to produce theories of international relations and the corresponding social-science theories that can serve as an effective guide for it to participate in global changes and challenges with ease, engage in the building of international ways of thinking and systems, and communicate more effectively with the outside world.

As China continues to develop, and participate more and more in international affairs and international ways of thinking, and particularly as it gradually breaks free of Western domination in social-science discourse in modern times, the conditions for it to produce its original theory and global ways of thinking are also becoming increasingly mature. Just like the competition in the Olympic Games, Chinese intelligentsia is also becoming more determined to, and confident of, dismantling the West's deep-rooted knowledge and discursive domination of the social sciences which has been in place for over a hundred years. Chinese scholars know very well that developing countries will not be able to realize true equality in international society and in international relations if they are unable to participate and compete in the building of knowledge and scientific discourse. China-Africa partnerships and the corresponding theoretical studies can become a special ways of thinking incubator and a special area of study that can serve as the source of knowledge and ways of thinking for theories of international relations, foreign relations, and international cooperation and aid with Chinese characteristics as well as for the formation of original theories in other social-science fields. Further, this special area of study can also lead to the formation of "Chinese episteme" and "Chinese ways of thinking"—that are highly contemporary but at the same time also draw on the deep heritage of ancient Chinese culture—as well as enrich and enhance the discursive power obtained and lay down a broad foundation.

In summary, in the fast-changing era when various beliefs and attitudes among people continue to collide on a global basis, behind the creation of academic and research is actually a tremendous amount of national interests that affect the basic survival and developmental capacity of the people as well as the country's core competitiveness. In this regard, Chinese scholars should have a clear idea of what "Chinese episteme" and "Chinese ways of thinking" are, know how to build up the discursive strength of such knowledge and ways of thinking, and bear responsibility towards the building up of such knowledge and ways of thinking.

Here, "Chinese episteme" or "Chinese ways of thinking" is not a figment of the imagination or a romantic fancy but the distillation of Chinese civilization since antiquity. It is a system of knowledge and system of ways of thinking that expresses the essence and core of Chinese civilization and continues to innovate as modern China continues on its path of rejuvenation and development. Just as in the past we have often talked about such concepts as "Western knowledge" and "Western ways of thinking", "Chinese episteme" or "Chinese ways of thinking" exists in reality. With thousands of years of heritage behind such "Chinese episteme" or "Chinese ways of thinking", China is able to present its particular spirit in its contemporary governance, foreign relations, and survival and development in the world today. From a broad perspective, that contemporary China's Africa policy and China's development strategies and philosophy for cooperation with Africa show Chinese characteristics can be attributed to the internal support of such "Chinese episteme" and "Chinese ways of thinking", which also play an important role in presenting and maintaining these policies, strategies, and attitudes.

This traditional knowledge must confront the new challenges that come with developments in contemporary China. It must necessarily be an open system that improves with the times. Such a system should obtain merits from practices of development and rejuvenation of contemporary China, including its contemporary relations with African countries. Then, new theoretical summarizations should be made while maintaining the lineage of Chinese culture and tradition in order to establish the position of "Chinese episteme" and "Chinese ways of thinking" within today's global system of knowledge and ways of thinking and to claim the discursive position and power of ways of thinking that such knowledge and ways of thinking deserve.[6]

As contemporary China becomes increasingly involved in the global system, it would require increasing efforts to fight for, and protect its national interests in the global sphere through cooperation and interaction. In light of this, the building of the legitimacy of contemporary China's national politics, the moral influence, as well as the enhancing of the discursive position of Chinese episteme and ways of thinking, Chinese experiences and models, and Chinese intelligence and sentiments in order to facilitate communication have become especially important. But the building of effective ways of thinking, knowledge, and discursive power for such a system cannot come out of thin air. It must have a platform of its own as well as the room for practice, as well as its own innovative fields and opportunities. China-Africa relations and other relevant fields are precisely one key area that China can work actively on to grow and a special opportunity that China must not lose grasp of.

---

[6] Liu, Hongwu (2004). *The Road Home: college textbook for the humanities* (1st ed.). Beijing: Tsinghua University Press, p. 187.

In this regard, apart from the room for China to develop internationally as afforded by China-Africa relations mentioned above, and apart from the theoretical and innovation issues related to strategic platforms for China's international development, the following points are also worthy of consideration.

First, with China and Africa being independent major civilizations, China-Africa relations involve a broad spectrum of issues which require in-depth investigation. A good number of issues are not unilateral and non-localized, and are complex, interrelated to other issues, and perennial. Such complex issues require both specialist study as well as in-depth research that systematically integrates multiple fields of study. The needs for the latter are greater, and here, there are more gaps to be filled in as well. However, there is also greater room for breakthroughs. Once a breakthrough has been made, it will significantly advance development and innovation in Chinese social sciences.

Second, African studies began much later in China than they did in the West and certain other Asian countries. However, China has its unique strengths nevertheless. These strengths include (i) the facilitation of practices and support of experience developed quickly over 30 years in China-Africa relations; (ii) the profound historical theory and experience of a major civilization; (iii) the ability to compare and contrast against existing Western literature in the area; and (iv) unlike other researches in international affairs and relations, African development studies and the relevant theoretical studies of international affairs have yet to be dominated by Western discourse as completely. Furthermore, in many ways African issues can help to illuminate the biases and flaws inherent in Western knowledge and discourse. African studies can thus be regarded to a greater extent as an epistemologically pristine field that can serve as a "new theoretical frontier" and can make special contributions to the development of knowledge in the non-Western world.[7]

We believe, therefore, that in this age of globalization, it may be possible for Chinese scholars to overcome the historical monopoly of Western episteme, wean ourselves of theoretical dependence on it, and create our own space for the development of knowledge and ideas by drawing from our own epistemological methodology and bringing together the past and the future, the Chinese and African perspectives. This would lead to the emergence of a home-grown cross-cultural meta-theoretical discourse of knowledge and distinctly Chinese and original ideas about globalization and modernity.[8]

---

[7] Liu, Hongwu (2009). African Studies: the new 'borders' of Chinese academia. *Ministry of Foreign Affairs China-Africa Cooperation Online Forum*, 12 October 2009. http://www.fmprc.gov.cn/zflt/chn/jlydh/xzhd/t619846.htm.

[8] Liu, Hongwu (2008). On the experiences gained from thirty years of China-Africa relations and a theoretical response. *West Asia and Africa*, 2008 (11), 13–18.

Contents

1 **The Historical Background and Evolution of China-Africa Partnerships** 1
   1.1 The Historical Logic of, and Basis in Reality for, Contemporary China-Africa Partnerships 1
   1.2 The Early Days of China-Africa Partnerships and Relations 5
   1.3 Issues in China-Africa Relations in the Late 1970s 10
   1.4 Changes Made by China to Its Africa Policies in the Early 1980s, and Effects 13
   1.5 China-Africa Relations in the 1990s, and Challenges to These Relations 19

2 **The Establishment of Forum on China-Africa Cooperation and a New Chapter in China-Africa Cooperation** 29
   2.1 The Establishment of the FOCAC in 2000 and the Enhancement of China-Africa Relations on All Fronts 30
   2.2 The Core Mission and Global Significance of Contemporary China-Africa Relations 37
   2.3 The Impact of the Swift Development of China-Africa Relations on the Relationship Between China and Western Nations 39
   2.4 Sino-Africa Development Relations Beneficial to Efforts to Resolve Global Developmental Issues Once and for All 42

3 **The Global Impact and Future Trajectory of China-Africa Partnerships** 47
   3.1 "Out of Africa" or "Into Africa We Go"? 48
   3.2 Resolving Developmental Issues and Universal Human Values 50
   3.3 A Re-acquaintance with the Historic Civilizations of Asia and Africa 55
   3.4 The East's View of History, and the Future Trajectory of China ... 57

4 Chinese Aid to African Countries: Evolution, Motives, and Outcomes 61
- 4.1 Changes in Developmental Concerns over Time, and Changes in Chinese Aid to Africa over Various Stages 62
- 4.2 New Models of Chinese Aid to Africa in the New Period, and Outcomes 66
- 4.3 The Basic Spirit and Characteristics of China Aid to Africa over 50 Years 71
- 4.4 A Few Ways of Thinkings on China's Future Strategy for Aid to Africa 74

5 Changes in the Geopolitics of Africa, and Issues Pertaining to Three-Way Cooperation Among China, Africa and the West 79
- 5.1 High Levels of Attention Paid to China-Africa Relations by the West in Recent Years 79
- 5.2 Why Western Countries Are Paying Close Attention to China-Africa Relations 83
- 5.3 Differences in Opinion and Policy Regarding Africa Between China and Western Countries 86
- 5.4 Cooperation Between China and the West in Promoting Development in Africa: In Search of Possibilities and Methods 95

6 China's "Going to Africa" Policy in Post-crisis Era: Adjustments and Improvement 103
- 6.1 New Understanding of the Significance of "To Africa" Strategy After the Financial Crisis 103
- 6.2 Difficulties in Chinese Enterprises' "Go Global" Efforts After the Financial Crisis 105
- 6.3 Adjustment of Chinese Enterprises' "To Africa" Strategy After the Economic Crisis 107

7 China-Africa Cooperation and Cultivating China's Soft Power 111
- 7.1 Essence and Style of Diplomatic Policy: Important Foundation for China's Soft Power in Africa 112
- 7.2 Cultural Influence: An Important Manifestation of China's Soft Power in Africa 115
- 7.3 Exemplary Effect of Development Model: A Key Element for Expanding China's Soft Power in Africa 119
- 7.4 Multilateral Cooperation Mechanism: Effective Way to Enhance China's Soft Power in Africa 121

8 African NGOs and China's Public Diplomacy in Africa 123
- 8.1 African NGOs Pay Attention to China-Africa Relations 123
- 8.2 Truth About China's African Policy and China-Africa Cooperation 128
- 8.3 China's Strategic Planning for Public Diplomacy in Africa 131
- 8.4 China's Policies and Measures in Public Diplomacy to Africa 132

9 African Integration and China's African Policy of Multilateral Cooperation 137
9.1 Progress and Historical Achievements of African Integration 138
9.2 Birth and Development of Multilateral Exchanges Between China and Africa 146
9.3 How to Further Promote China's Multilateral Diplomacy to Africa? 149

About the Authors

Hongwu Liu is a Changjiang Scholar of Africa Studies appointed by the Ministry of Education of China, Qianjiang Scholar of the Zhejiang provincial government, Director of the Institute of African Studies, doctoral supervisor, and deputy head of the academic committee at Zhejiang Normal University. Liu is Vice President of the Chinese African Studies Association, deputy chairman of the Chinese Society of African Historical Studies, Vice President of the Chinese Society for African History, and council member of the Chinese-African People's Friendship Association. Liu, who studied in Nigeria and Tanzania at University of Lagos in Nigeria in 1990, and at University of Dar es Salaam in Tanzania in 2003 has conducted field investigation over 30 countries in Africa. He has been Senior Scientist for a number of major research projects supported by the National Social Science Fund and on Ministry of Education Philosophy and Social Sciences Key Research Projects. He is the author of more than ten monographs, and Editor-in-Chief of the *Series of African Studies of Zhejiang Normal University*, the *Annual Report on the Development of Africa*, and *African Studies*, among others. He has won many national awards for excellence in research and teaching. In 2009, Liu was one of the winners of "China-Africa Friendship Awards—Ten Chinese Most Admired by the People of Africa" given by the Chinese People's Association for Friendship with Foreign Countries and the Chinese-African People's Friendship Association.

Jianbo Luo is Professor and department director at the Institute for International Strategic Studies of the Central Party School of the Communist Party of China. Luo has visited Africa, the United States, India, and ROK on academic exchanges and study trips. He was head of the National Social Science Fund project titled "Issues of Development with the African Union and African countries" (since completed). He is the author of *African Integration and China-Africa Relations*, *The African Union and African Integration*, and dozens of papers.

Chapter 1
The Historical Background and Evolution of China-Africa Partnerships

From the perspective of a long historical period, China's renaissance in the twentieth century as well as the hard-earned rise of the African continent in the twenty-first century will undoubtedly be regarded as the historical developments of greatest global importance and influence. The gradual development and expansion of trans-oceanic partnerships built up by China and African countries through joint hard work is a special component of the hard work put in by both China and African countries in the areas of foreign relations and international cooperation as they seek their modern renaissance and development. Thus, the historical and global significance of China-Africa partnerships can only be better understood and examined in the context of global changes and the transformation of the global system.

1.1 The Historical Logic of, and Basis in Reality for, Contemporary China-Africa Partnerships

When we examine the evolution of China-Africa relations we see that since the founding of the People's Republic of China in the mid-twentieth century China-Africa relations have held a special place in China's foreign relations. Many a time, China-Africa relations have served as a "pivoting point" for China's relations with the external world.[1] Hence, China-Africa relations are a special factor that can affect the structure of China's relations with Western countries and change China's strategic position in the international arena. Over the last few decades, China-Africa relations have been steadfast, to the point that China has been called an "all-weather friend" by Kenneth Kaunda, the first President of Zambia. China-Africa relations have played

---
[1] Liu, Hongwu (2008). China-Africa relations: a pivoting point for the three-way relationship between China, Africa and Europe. *Investing in Africa*, 22 Feb 2008. http://www.invest.net.cn/News/ShowInfo.aspx?ID=22838.

© Social Sciences Academic Press and Springer Nature Singapore Pte Ltd. 2021
H. Liu and J. Luo, *Sino-African Development Cooperation*, Research Series on the Chinese Dream and China's Development Path,
https://doi.org/10.1007/978-981-16-5481-7_1

an indispensable and unique role in enhancing China's foreign-relations environment and international position over various periods. The peoples of China and Africa have also felt the tremendous value of China-Africa relations through various stages. The new principles of honesty, openness and equal footing between partners in international relations as established by China-Africa relations have provided a highly-effective model of South-South cooperation and even more importantly, more hope for a better future for the chaotic and uncertain world. As Meles Zenawi, then-Prime Minister of Ethiopia (chair of the African Union) said on 5 Nov 2006 at the opening ceremony of the Forum on China-Africa Cooperation Beijing Summit, China practices the principles of equal sovereignty between countries and mutual non-interference. This has given Africa the opportunity to build with China a partnership that is based on mutual trust. 50 years ago, the two sides began building strategic partnership while fighting colonialism and apartheid, and struggling for sovereignty. 50 years on today, the two sides were reiterating the China-Africa strategic partnership. There is no better occasion to do so. The people of Africa have deep hopes for the new China-Africa partnership. All along, they have paid attention to, and supported, China's tremendous achievements, and have been greatly inspired by these achievements.[2]

Zenawi's speech is representative of the perspective of contemporary African politicians. Looking from a broader perspective based on the development of the modern world, we believe that fundamentally contemporary China-Africa relations have been able to progress through decades of change and adjustments due to the fact that such relations have been rooted in, from the very beginning, the pursuit of national self-strengthening on the part of the Asian and African peoples, and that such relations contain the long-time hard work and hopes of non-Western peoples seeking modern development in the twentieth century.[3]

Since the advent of modern times, China had seen her fortunes decline, as well as much humiliation by outsiders, and had lost her independent voice in foreign relations. Africa's plight can be described as similar to, if not worse than, China's plight. However, the founding of the People's Republic of China in the mid-twentieth century and the subsequent founding of a number of independent African countries have made the dream of changing this state of affairs possible. In the 1950s and 1960s, China and African countries discovered each other at the same time as they sought rejuvenation and development in modern times. As the Chinese saying goes, "the bird makes its calls in order to seek out its friends".[4] These two worlds, which had been oppressed and humiliated by the West since modern times, discovered upon initial contact that there were peoples in far-flung locales who were ready to

---

[2] Zenawi, Meles (6 Nov 2006). PM Zenawi's address at the opening ceremony of the Forum on China-Africa Cooperation Beijing Summit. *People's Daily*.

[3] Liu, Hongwu (2007). China-Africa relations: the significance of the history of civilizations. *West Asia and Africa*, 2007 (1), 16.

[4] *Shijing: Lesser Court Hymns*.

treat them as equals and extend assistance with full sincerity.[5] In the time since, the modern partnership between China and African countries began to develop along an all-new model that has also since undergone complex changes and enhancements.

From the perspective of diverse world cultures and equal conversations, the establishment and development of mutually-respectful and equal relationships such as those between China and African countries after hundreds of years of "center-periphery" domination by the West bear special symbolic meaning. This is because such relations reflect the basic form of global inter-civilizational exchange and international relations and how it is moving towards a multi-dimensional and 'web' or network form where relations are conducted between diverse civilizations in an equal manner. Although this process is difficult, tumultuous and long, it shows clearly that the Western-centric experience of modernity and discursive dominance is but a particular stage of the development of modernity among mankind as a whole. Naturally, the advance and development of world history will not end with the rise and completion of the Western civilization; instead, it will continue to progress along with the rejuvenation and rise of the Asian and African worlds. Today, after more than half a century of hard work and arduous trial-and-error, Asia and Africa are moving forward more quickly than ever and new, significant changes are occurring. Such fundamental structural changes mean that a new, deeply-meaningful era in world history is quietly upon us.[6]

In the three decades since China began its reform and opening-up (1978–2008), the value of trade between China and African countries grew over a hundred times from over USD700 million to USD106.8 billion. In 2008, nearly 1,000 Chinese enterprises from all over China had made investments in dozens of African countries in various industries. In Jan-Jun 2009 alone, over 50 events related to China-Africa trade—investment events, investment fora, project launches, and academic events—were held in China and Africa. China-Africa trade relations and China's role and strategy in Africa have, in recent years, become a hot research topic internationally.

In fact, the swift changes in China-Africa relations are but a window—a highly eye-catching one that offers great views—in the gradual changes that have been occurring over the last few decades in the non-Western world or Asian and African worlds. Significant changes are occurring in the relations between the Asian and African worlds and developing countries. Between 2000 and 2007 Africa's exports to Asia as a proportion of its total exports doubled from 14 to 28%. From a global perspective, since 2000 trade and investment from China, India and Southeast Asia has increasingly become the engine of economic growth in Africa. The economic relationships between various Asian and African countries are becoming increasingly close. Structurally, from a global perspective, these changes are also leading to historic changes in the relations between China and developed countries. Between

---

[5] Liu, Hongwu (2006). The Call from Far, Far Away, From across the Oceans: historical understanding, and real-life cooperation between the two major civilizations of China and Africa. *The Journal of International Studies*, 2006 (4) (no. 102), 32.

[6] Liu, Hongwu (2007), The historical value and global significance of the new China-Africa strategic partnership. *Foreign Affairs Review*, 2007 (1), 12.

2000 and 2006, the share of developing economies in the global economy also grew from 36 to 41%. It is generally believed that in the near future the share of "developing countries" in the traditional sense of the world, combined, will exceed that of developed countries (or Western countries) combined.

All these developments indicate that the global system is changing in a profound and significant way in political and economic terms as a result of the rejuvenation and development of non-Western countries. Although the road towards the modern rejuvenation and development of the Asian and African countries, the global South or the non-Western world as a whole is a long and arduous one, progress has been made along this path much more quickly in recent years. As economic relations between Asia and Africa strengthen quickly, a growing "new border" that is full of life and driving global economic growth is emerging between China and Africa, between India and Africa, between Africa and the Middle East, and even more broadly, between East Asia and Southeast Asia, between East Asia and South Asia, and between East Asia and the Middle East and Africa. A "modern Silk Road" that will lead to the world of the future is emerging. In our opinion, contemporary China-Africa relations are precisely part of this "new border" and are the most promising 'pioneer' and 'builder' of this "modern Silk Road".

When the Cold War concluded, the theory of the "end of history" was popular in the West for a while. It was believed that Western civilization was the apogee of human civilization, and that there could be no further change or development thenceforth. However, history is a process of constant change that creeps up on one. Over the last few decades, China-Africa relations have developed as massive changes were going on in Chinese society. These relations, and, in particular, the partnerships between both parties in the areas of trade, investment and other economic areas, and the results of such partnerships, have already significantly broadened the room for man to imagine modern human development as well as the room for more choices. The wealth of experience and developmental outcomes accrued are proof positive that history has yet to "end" and will pave its own way forward with the modern rejuvenation of the Asian and African worlds. In the past 30 years, China has experienced tremendous changes while absorbing the merits from and coping with complex challenges in the outside world, and has also had a profound impact on the outside world. Today, China's interactions and relations with the outside world are more complex than they have ever been historically. And this is a change that is still occurring at a great speed. For a millennia-old civilization like the Chinese civilization, the developments and changes that have occurred in the last 60 or 30 years can be described as "the kind of change that occurs once in thousands of years".[7] This has given China's intellectual elites new opportunities and challenges to re-acquaint themselves with distinctive characteristics of Chinese civilization and the relationship between Chinese civilization and the outside world. We should also work to further

---

[7] In 1895, China was defeated in the First Sino-Japanese War and was forced to sign the Treaty of Shimonoseki. Liang Qichao, lamenting the development, termed the defeat and its consequences "the kind of change that occurs once in thousands of years" for China. A century later, China has achieved a fundamental change in its global status through unceasing hard work. Of course, this is a change that has enhanced rather than undermined China's global position.

our understanding of contemporary China-Africa relations and our understanding of the value and significance of China-Africa partnerships in this new era.

1.2 The Early Days of China-Africa Partnerships and Relations

In order for us to better understand the special characteristics and strategic significance of China's partnerships and relations with African countries in the last 60 years, we will need to first review the historical background and early days of such partnerships and relations so that we will be able to understand how China-Africa relations have been maintained through decades of complex developments on the international scene and have even advanced through the years into the twenty-first century, where an even broader new world awaits.

In recent years, some Western media outlets have criticized China's African policies, claiming that China had "suddenly" appeared in Africa as it had wanted access to Africa's resources. However, this is far from the truth. China's engagement with Africa is not a "sudden" development, and neither is her engagement for the purpose of obtaining Africa's resources. Contemporary partnerships and relations between China and African countries have been in the making for decades. However, they have been significantly enhanced in recent years. Moreover, partnerships in the area of natural resources are but a part of China-Africa partnerships.

The People's Republic of China began to establish official relations with African countries in the 1950s. The establishing of such relations were part of the Chinese and African countries' efforts in the foreign-relations arena in the twentieth century in order to achieve national rejuvenation and strengthening. Those in the West are often unable to understand the characteristics and process of such relations, for they are not in the shoes of the protagonists. Hence, they tend to interpret China-Africa relations through the lens of their earlier historical experiences in expansion and conquest, terming China's efforts as "imperialist" and "colonialist". As such, often they have not been able to explain the present circumstances of China-Africa relations, as well as predict the future of such relations.

Since the advent of modern times, China had seen her fortunes decline, as well as much humiliation by outsiders, and had lost her independent voice in foreign relations. Africa's plight can be described as similar to, if not worse than, China's plight. However, the establishment of the People's Republic of China and the liberation of the African continent have made the dreams of both parties to change this state of affairs a possibility. At that time, both China and African countries had discovered each other at the same time as they sought out national rejuvenation and modern development.[8] As the Chinese saying goes, "the bird makes its calls in order to seek

---

[8] Larkin, Bruce D. (1971). *China and Africa, 1949–1970, The foreign Policy of The People's Republic of China.* University of California Press, p. 1.

out its friends".[9] These two worlds, which had been oppressed and humiliated by the West since modern times, discovered upon initial contact that there were peoples in far-flung locales who were ready to treat them as equals and extend assistance with full sincerity.[10]

China had already begun to pay attention to the liberation of the African peoples at the early days after its establishment.[11] The first Asian-African Conference in Bandung in April 1955 provided the opportunities for direct Asia-Africa contact. During the Conference, Chinese Premier Zhou Enlai, and Deputy Premier and Foreign Minister Chen Yi met with Gamal Abdel Nasser, and also talked with representatives from Ghana, Libya, Sudan, Liberia, and Ethiopia, etc. These efforts yielded results quickly: a year later on 30 May 1956, Egypt became the first country to establish diplomatic relations with China. The chapter on China-Africa relations had begun. In October 1959, Guinea became the first African country south of the Sahara to establish official relations with China. China-Africa relations developed quickly in the two decades that followed. By 1979, China had established official relations with as many as 44 African countries.

The establishment of friendly relations with dozens of African countries have significantly changed China's foreign-relations environment in general. During this period, over 120 heads-of-state and heads-of-government from over 40 countries visited China. Over 210 senior officials of ministerial-grade and above also visited China on more than 300 occasions. Several Chinese leaders and more than 10 Chinese officials of ministerial-grade and above have visited over 40 African countries. Meanwhile, China conducted a large number trade, cultural, sports, educational and military exchanges with African countries, with nearly 1,000 African students visiting China for academic purposes. There are also dozens of Chinese medical teams in Africa. A total of more than 50,000 Chinese technicians worked in the tropical jungles building the Tanzam Railway. In addition, there are many Chinese students travelling to Africa to learn the Swahili and Hausa languages. Within a short period, from the perspective of China's foreign-relations history, the exchanges and bonds between the two worlds of China and Africa, though far away from each other in geographic terms, have been strengthened, which reminds us of the thriving international relationship between the Tang Dynasty and other countries in history.

From the perspective of the history of contemporary human relations, the particularity of China-Africa relations lies in the fact that such relations are rooted in both parties' pursuit of national rejuvenation in modern times.[12] The leaders of China and Africa have had their unique perspectives on the nature, significance and effect of

---

[9] *Shijing: Lesser Court Hymns.*

[10] Liu, Hongwu (2006). The Call From Far, Far Away, From Across the Oceans: historical understanding, and real-life cooperation between the two major civilizations of China and Africa. *The Journal of International Studies,* 2006 (4) (no. 102), 32.

[11] Larkin, Bruce D. (1971). *China and Africa, 1949–1970, The foreign Policy of the People's Republic of China.* University of California Press, p. 4.

[12] Liu, Hongwu (2007). China-Africa relations: the significance of the history of civilizations. *West Asia and Africa,* 2007 (1).

1.2 The Early Days of China-Africa Partnerships and Relations

such a relationship. Julius Nyerere, former President of Tanzania, was an influential African nationalist leader who had visited China on a total of 14 occasions. He has said that contemporary Africa is dotted with small countries that are poor and weak and are not highly regarded by the West. The only way for African countries to have a global voice, he said, was to be united. However, internal unity among African countries was not strong enough: Africa also needed to establish friendly relations with countries that treated it as equals, like China, and countries that would engage in mutual aid with Africa and lend a voice to Africa on the global stage.[13] For China, support for the liberation of the African peoples and for anti-Western imperialism efforts can help it to break through the foreign-relations embargo imposed by the West, improve its foreign-relations environment, and show its special strategic significance as a swiftly rejuvenating country to African and other Asian countries.[14]

In fact, at the very start of China-Africa relations the concept of "foreign aid" had already become the center of China-Africa engagement. However, China has always had its own understanding of the nature and significance of "assistance to Africa". Chinese leaders have always told their African counterparts that it has not been just a case of 'China helping Africa'; Africa was helping China too. They have also emphasized that Chinese aid for Africa was rendered on a basis of mutual assistance, equality, and sincerity. During the 1963 visit to 10 African countries, Chinese Premier Zhou Enlai unveiled to the world China's "Eight Principles for Rendering Assistance to Africa":

1. The Chinese government shall provide African countries with aid in adherence to the principles of equality and mutual benefit. The Chinese government believes that aid is a two-way matter and that China is also being aided by African countries.
2. Aid from China does not come with any conditions. China strictly respects the national sovereignty and dignity of the aid recipient.
3. The Chinese government provides aid at preferential terms and tries as much as possible not to impose further burden on the aid recipient.
4. Aid from the Chinese government is not meant to create reliance on China on the part of the aid recipient but to help the latter to enhance its abilities to develop autonomously.

---

[13] Nyerere, J.K. (23 May 1979), South-South Dialogue and Development in Africa, *Uhuru* (Dar es Salaam).

[14] Between end-1963 and early 1964, during the Chinese Premier's visit to 10 African countries, China declared for the first time its strategy and policies with regard to China-Africa relations: 1. China was in support of African countries' struggles against imperialism and colonialism old and new, as well as their struggles for the independence of their peoples; 2. China was in support of African countries' adherence to the peaceful and neutral policy of non-alignment; 3. China was in support of African countries' wish to realize unification and unity through their preferred approaches; 4. China was in support of African countries resolving conflicts through peaceful negotiation; and 5. China advocated that the sovereignty of African countries should be respected by all other countries, and opposed violation of such sovereignty and interference from any party.

5. Projects for which the Chinese government is providing the aid recipient with assistance should require small investments and show results quickly. Such projects should also help increase the income of the government of the aid-receiving country so that it would be able to amass funds.
6. The Chinese government shall provide good-quality equipment and material resources that it manufactures and negotiate pricing based on prices in the international market. The Chinese government also guarantees the quality of equipment and material resources supplied.
7. The Chinese government guarantees that personnel of the aid-receiving country will be able to master all technologies relevant to the technical assistance provided.
8. Experts sent to the aid-receiving country from China may only enjoy benefits that are provided to local experts and are not eligible for any special treatment.

The proposing and implementation of these eight principles indicate that the Chinese government has, from the very beginning, sought to establish relations with African countries which are based on the specific cultural characteristics of both sides and on actual strategic needs. Such relations have been established on the basis of mutual respect, equality, and mutual benefit. In particular, the principle of non-interference in the domestic affairs of the aid-receiving country became a corner stone of China-Africa relations early on. The leaders of China have emphasized on many occasions that aid from China is neither charity nor a sign of benevolence but mutual aid between friends, and that China would never interfere in the domestic affairs of African countries or try to wrest political rights in the name of aid.

In 1956, Egypt became the first African country to receive aid from China. By the late 1970s, Chinese aid to African countries had reached a significant scale with its particular characteristics and impact. In the first half of the 1970s, Chinese aid to other countries amounted to 5.88% of total public finance expenditure. The proportion was the highest in 1973 at 6.92%.[15] By 1978, China had provided aid worth more than USD2.4 billion to a total of 36 African countries, making up 50% of the aid China was extending to non-Communist countries and 70% of the aid to more than 50 Third World countries.[16] China was aiding Africa in more than 200 projects in the fields of agriculture, meteorology, health, sports, and education, etc. In particular, the Chinese government invested a total of USD455 million, a significant sum for its economy, in order to build the Tanzam Railway, an 1,860-km-long railway line that extended from the coast of east Africa to the copper-ore producing areas of Zambia through dense jungle and mountainous areas.[17] This railway, which has been termed by our African friends as the "Freedom and Friendship Railway", laid a long-lasting

---

[15] Shi, Lin. (1989) *ed. The Foreign Economic Partnerships of Contemporary China.* Beijing: Social Sciences Academic Press, p. 69.

[16] Yu, George T. Working on the Railroad: China and the Tanzania-Zambia Railway. *Trans.* Shen, P. In The Centre for African Studies of Peking University (2000) *ed., China and Africa.* Beijing: Peking University Press, p. 274.

[17] The amount announced by the Chinese government was RMB900 million (the RMB to USD exchange rate at that time was around 1.5:1). See: Liu, Guijin. His Excellency Ambassador Liu

foundation for China-Africa relations. The railway has an "epic-like symbolic value" and heralded the beginning of non-Western South-South partnership in the history of modern global and international relations.[18]

By the end of the 1970s, China's economic aid to Africa had not only reached a certain scale but had also exhibited its particular characteristics and impact. The new relationship model advocated by China in the context of the historical conditions then was especially attractive to African countries that had been humiliated by the experience of colonialism by the West.[19] As such, the majority of African countries flocked to establish friendly relations with China soon after gaining independence. These weak African countries had once worked to restore China's legitimate place at the United Nations. When they had finally managed to "carry" China into the United Nations they saw the development as a victory of their own.

By 1978, when China began to implement the reform and opening-up policy, although the Chinese economy was in severe difficulty, aid to African countries continued to be a key part of China-Africa relations. When we look at 1978 alone, we see that on 1 April China signed a three-way outline agreement on the building of a vehicular bridge over the Chari River with Chad and Cameroon in Chad's capital N'Djamena. According to these minutes, the Chinese government would, in the following five years, provide funding to the government of Chad to help the latter build a road that would connect the Chad border with the northwestern border of Cameroon. Apart from the engineering and technical personnel, material resources and equipment that the Chinese government would send to Chad and Cameroon, the partnership also involved monetary aid amounting to approximately RMB2 million. On 31 July the same year, a Chinese government delegation held three-way talks with Tanzania and Zambia on the matter of the Tanzam Railway in the Tanzanian capital of Dar es Salaam. After three days of complex negotiations, the heads of the three national delegations signed an agreement on the technical cooperation protocol for Phase II of the Tanzam Railway, a technical cooperation agreement on a training school for the Tanzam Railway, and an outline agreement on the Tanzam Railway technical partnership. According to these agreements, the Chinese government would continue to provide funding and technical support for the operations of the Tanzam Railway, and at the same time establish a railway vocational school in Tanzania for the training of management and technical personnel from both countries. The agreement was to be renewed by signature every two years. On 14 September, a World Health Organization study team comprising representatives from seven African Francophone countries—Cameroon, the Central African Republic, Gabon, Upper Volta, Mali, the Niger and Chad—arrived in Beijing for talks on cooperation in the area of health between China and African countries. A joint United Nations Development

---

Guijin's Speech at the Institute for Security Studies in South Africa. *Ministry of Foreign Affairs China-Africa Cooperation Online Forum.* http://www.focac.org/chn/zyzl/hywj/t280368.htm.

[18] Nyerere, J.K. (23 May 1979), South-South Dialogue and Development in Africa, *Uhuru* (Dar es Salaam).

[19] In recent years, some in Western media have called China's policy of non-interference with African countries in her dealings as a mercantilist policy. Clearly, this is due to a lack of understanding of the history of China-Africa relations.

Program and the World Meteorological Organization "Meteorology in Service of Agriculture" study team arrived in China on 16 September. The team, which spent a month in China, comprised meteorology personnel from nine African countries.

We can see that cooperation and exchange between China and African countries took place at a high frequency in various areas in the late 1970s. In the 1970s alone a total of 24 African countries established official diplomatic relations with China. Considering that China was in the throes of the Cultural Revolution then, that China managed to establish relations with so many African countries is undoubtedly highly significant. To some Western scholars, China at that time had already regarded Africa as a part of its "united international front" and has benefited immensely from this front.

1.3 Issues in China-Africa Relations in the Late 1970s

China-Africa relations that began in the 1950s have been a great source of political wealth for China and Africa. However, for both China and Africa the road to national rejuvenation is inevitably a long one. The African continent had entered modern civilization at a comparatively lower historical starting point and achieved comparatively lower economic development within the framework of traditional society. On the other hand, modern China had to surmount a good number of obstacles due to a delay in its development beginning from early modern times. As such, in the early days of China-Africa relations in the 1960s and 1970s the characteristics of South-South cooperation between less-developed countries and regions were highly salient. Thus, the form, content and scale of China-Africa exchanges and cooperation at that time were also highly characteristic of the era. Hence, although China-Africa relations developed swiftly in the 1960s and 1970s, both parties had benefited immensely from this relationship. However, some issues remained in China-Africa relations due to historical factors. These were structural issues that plunged the relationship between both sides into considerable difficulty. In fact, by the late 1970s the passion in China-Africa relations had seemingly fizzled, with the material basis and political conditions for the maintenance of this relationship significantly weakened. This led to rethinking by both parties about their respective developmental paths and the flaws in the relationship.

From the perspective of the broader international landscape, in the late 1970s and the early 1980s Western countries had embarked on a new round of scientific and technological revolution, and economic development. Although Asian and African countries had achieved considerable economic development in the preceding two decades, the gap with Western economies was widening. Both China and the African countries were facing tremendous pressures to reform their political and economic systems. However, the difficulties and pressures faced by China were seemingly greater. In 1978, following the tumult of the Cultural Revolution, the Chinese economy was in a process of slow recovery. China had no choice but to focus on its domestic situation and on economic and political reforms. Hence, it made adjustments to its foreign policy, including its policy towards African countries.

At the beginning, these changes were made without clear objectives in mind. Thus, there was also a fairly longer period of experimentation and adjustments.

First, on the political level, China needed to tweak its policy with regard to China-Africa partnerships in response to changes in the times. This was caused by changes in China's understanding and judgment of the international landscape, and changes in the way its people ways of thinking about war and revolution. China was beginning to focus more on the pursuit of peace and development. After peace and development became China's top two priorities in its approach to the global situation, the tenor of China-Africa relations also shifted from a focus on the liberation of countries to the peace and development that China sought.

In fact, by the 1980s, China began to work more actively on its policy of peaceful foreign relations and sought to establish normal diplomatic relations with every country in the world. This change led to the result that China gradually broke ideological and political shackles on foreign relations, and China began to work on establishing relations with even more African countries. After gaining independence, African countries had adopted various ways of developing their political systems and economies. Some had tilted towards socialism and established close relations with China, the Soviet Union and Eastern Europe, while others went the way of capitalist systems and cultivated close relations with Western Europe and American countries. For a long time, China has had good relations with the majority of African countries, all with the status of Third World and developing country. However, due to the limitations and influence of certain factors at the time, and to a certain degree in the 1960s and 1970s relations between China and African countries were hinged on ideological concerns or the East/West divide. Hence, in terms of relationship, China was comparatively more distant from African countries that were more pro-West or had opted for the capitalist market system. In particular, during the Cultural Revolution, China's relations with countries that had implemented the market economy or multi-party political system such as Kenya, Nigeria, the Côte d'Ivoire, Lesotho, Malawi, the Niger, Burkina Faso, and Tunisia, was on the cool side or even worsened. Although the responsibility for worsened relations did not lie entirely with China, her emphasis on political affiliation did indeed have an impact on the building and development of normal relations between China and these African countries. In addition, in terms of interactions between political parties, due to the influence of ideology at that time the Communist Party of China essentially did not have any contact or interactions with democratic parties and organizations in African countries which advocated parliamentary elections and approved of the market economy. The Party had instead limited its contact to political parties that advocated socialism or Marxism. In the early part of the Cultural Revolution, China's foreign policy *vis-à-vis* African countries had even deviated. It was believed that Africa would become socialist, and thus China provided support for the political activities of political parties and organizations that were more vociferous in calling for the implementation of Marxism in various countries. Although China soon moved away from this relatively extreme approach, how close it was to an African country continued to be determined by ideology. This was one characteristic of China-African relations at that time and had brought a negative impact on the relationship between China and African countries.

Second, China also had to make certain policy adjustments in the area of the economy with African countries. After the founding of the People's Republic of China, China trade and economic relations with the outside world were severely limited as it had opted for a planned-economy system where foreign trade had been under the purview of the state. Furthermore, various embargoes and blockades had been imposed on China by the Western countries at that time. As such, foreign trade had made up a very small part of Chinese economic life for a long time. It was against this backdrop that the China's trade relations with African countries were retarded. Although China had begun to build economic and trade relations with African countries in the 1950s and trade volume between both parties had grown over time, relations were predominantly of the political and foreign-relations stripe. Apart from very limited amounts of normal trade occurring on the international market, at that time economic relations between China and African countries were mostly of a mutual-assistance nature. Generally, the choice of aid recipient and scale of aid provided were not predicated on one's interest as in normal global trade but on how close a particular African country was to China or how similar it was to China in ideological terms. The majority of aid programs were political endeavors that were performed without regard for economic cost. One salient feature of China-Africa relations was that economic relations were subordinated to political relations.

Or rather, given the conditions of the time, that China had established with African countries relations of economic aid which were strongly tinged with political concerns was not entirely a choice made by China but a choice related to the fact that the world was caught up in the Cold War at that time and at the global system in itself was highly politically-tinged. The foreign policies of Western countries at that time were also highly ideologically-driven. In particular, these countries' economic aid and development programs in Asia came with clear political motives and a Cold War background. However, as in general the Western countries had already achieved some degree of maturity with their market economies and had comparative separation between political and economic relations, the majority of their private enterprises and the trade that such enterprises engaged in were distinct from the economic aid led by the state. Such trade was more in line with market principles and the principle of economic interest. On the other hand, at that time the Chinese economy was under the planned-economy system and politics and economics were highly integrated at that time. There was no economic actor that was independent of the political system. Under the planned economy system, China's external economic relations were necessarily subordinated to political imperatives. This also made China's external economic relations easier to implement and maintain. In this context, the politically-driven economic relations that were established between China and African countries where China provided African countries with economic aid and support were both a product of the times and also in line with the expectations and demands of China-Africa relations on both the part of China and her African counterparts. We should note that China—from the very beginning—had adhered to the principles of equality and non-interference with its aid to Africa. China has never made use of such aid to force its political will upon Africa. All along, China has shown much respect and consideration of the wishes of her African partners. This was strongly expressed in the Eight Principles of African aid proposed in the early 1960s, and this approach of non-interference in domestic affairs and respecting African countries were more important than even the aid itself in establishing friendly China-Africa relations.

However, in the late 1970s and the early 1980s, as peace and development gradually became the focus of the Chinese government's basic understanding of the global landscape, developing the economy and modernization also became the top priority of the Chinese government. As such, the economy gradually gained an autonomous position and was no longer merely a tool for the furthering of political goals. It was against such a backdrop that the Chinese government began to consider changes to its Africa aid policies and methods. On one hand, the goals of economic aid were adjusted; second, the Chinese government began to consider ways to enhance the benefits of economic aid; third, the Chinese government sought to reform the ways in which economic aid was delivered; and fourth, the Chinese government saw that there was a need to integrate economic aid with the economic development of both China and Africa. Hence, the Chinese government began to think about how to revamp its Africa aid policies with due consideration to China's capabilities and the actual needs of African countries.

With this process of change, by the late 1980s China-Africa relations entered a new phase of development where changes and adjustments were conducted over the long term.

1.4 Changes Made by China to Its Africa Policies in the Early 1980s, and Effects

Between 20 December 1982 and 17 January 1983 Chinese Premier Zhao Ziyang visited a total of 11 African countries. This visit was a key effort by China to break new ground in China-Africa relations on the basis of existing relations following the tumult of the Cultural Revolution and after China had returned to the path of seeking modernization. As Zhao had put it when he had met African ambassadors posted to China prior to his visit: "This is a major foreign-relations move by the government of China."

Compared to the first visit by a Chinese premier to Africa in the 1920s, China and Africa in the early 1980s had seen a good number of changes both in political terms and in their external environments. For both Africa and China, revolution and struggle were no longer the key task at hand. The need to build the economy and social development became increasingly urgent issues for both parties.

From the African perspective, after the independence of Zimbabwe in 1980 the African continent had more or less been fully liberated. This was a historic advance for the continent. However, on the other hand, the African countries were seeing greater challenges in the areas of economic development and the livelihood of their people. Some African countries had seen their economic conditions worsen in the two decades since independence, with the peoples of certain countries worse off than they were before independence… That year, the Organization of African Unity (OAU) held a special meeting on economic development issues in the Nigerian capital of Lagos, where they passed the ambitious Lagos Plan of Action aimed at promoting economic development and economic integration in Africa. This was the first plan that African leaders had committed to under the OAU framework for the improvement of economy and society in Africa, and although many ideas in the plan were never realized the plan was a sign that African countries had already placed economic development as their top priority. In the subsequent few years, the OAU and the United Nations also issued a number of other programmatic documents on economic rejuvenation and development in Africa. Several countries also began to make structural adjustments to their respective economies and market reforms led by the World Bank and the International Monetary Fund (IMF).[20]

From the Chinese perspective, in the early 1980s China had already emerged from its ideologically-driven economic policies, and the spirit of rationality as well as its practical attitude was making a return. One of the results of these developments is that China began to seek economic and wealth creation. At that time, this change was termed as "the shift in the country's work focus to the building of the economy". To create the corresponding external environment for such political and economic reforms domestically, China also started to adjust its foreign policies. In terms of its Africa policies, China needed to examine its relations with African countries in this new environment, and development new bilateral relations based on the pursuit of economic development while strengthening existing relations. Hence, Zhao's visit was particularly significant at a turning point in China-Africa relationships.

Similar to the visit by the Chinese premier 20 years prior, in a trip that lasted nearly a month long Zhao visited a total of 11 countries: Egypt, Algeria, Morocco, Guinea, Gabon, Zaire, the Republic of Congo, Zambia, Zimbabwe, Tanzania, and Kenya. During his visit, the Chinese premier engaged on a number of issues in China-Africa relations with the leaders of these 11 countries. Zhao also visited local luminaries and old friends who had made important contributions to the development of China-Africa relations as well as a number of economic and technical aid projects by China underway in Africa at that time. At that juncture in history, China was swiftly opening up to the outside world and needed to explain to African countries friendly to her what was happening with China. China was also seeking new ways of developing

---

[20] Following the issuing of the Lagos Plan of Action, in July 1985, the Priority Programme for Economic Recovery 1986–1990 was also passed at the 21st OAU Summit. In May 1986, the United Nations Programme of Action for African Economic Recovery and Development 1986–1990 was passed at the 13th Special Session of the United Nations General Assembly.

friendly relations with African countries in this new situation. For China, China-Africa relations at the time were generally stable on the political level. Although certain adjustments were needed, it was at the economic level that adjustments were urgently needed. In particular, changes and reforms were urgently needed in the ways in which China extended economic and technical aid to Africa. China hoped to change the ways in which it extended economic and technical aid to Africa and improve upon the outcomes of such aid while maintaining and strengthening its existing relationships with African countries. These changes were necessary due to the transformation of the Chinese economy and political system and were as well the result of lessons drawn from past aid. In the 1960s and 1970s, China's foreign aid won her the friendship and support of a large number of developing countries. However, certain countries had returned China's kindness with evil, leading to the breakdown of bilateral relations. In addition, objectively speaking, as the Chinese economy at that time was undergoing an arduous transition China needed to prioritize its own developmental needs and thus was unable to fully satisfy all aid requests from African countries. Therefore, China needed to explain to these African countries and to seek their understanding.

Zhao made an official statement on the trajectory and principles of changes made to China's foreign aid policy at a press conference in Dar es Salaam held on 13 January, towards the end of this trip. He stated that the Chinese government hoped to continue providing African countries with aid as much as it could, and on that basis, extend China-Africa economic and technical cooperation in order to transform pure aid approaches into effective economical and technical partnerships that benefit both parties and thereby making China-Africa relations the driving force for economic development and modernization in both China and Africa. During this address, Zhao stated the four principles of Chinese aid policy for Africa in this new period, which were: equality and mutual benefit, a focus on aid outcomes, aid in multiple forms, and joint development.[21]

It is worth noting that since the 1980s the term "partnership" has been used to replace the term "aid" with increasing frequency by China when speaking about its economic relations with African countries. China has sought to emphasize mutually-beneficial partnerships rather than one-directional aid from China. This is because

---

[21] The Chinese Premier spoke in detail on these four principles during his address: 1. Adherence to the principles of unity, amity, equal standing, and mutual benefit; respect for the sovereignty of the opposite party, non-interference in each other's domestic affairs, no political conditions to be attached to aid and no special rights to be granted. 2. Deals are to be established based on the actual needs and what is possible on the part of both parties, with each party harnessing its strengths and potential. Projects are to require little investment, short term and produce results quickly for economic benefit. 3. Economic and technical partnerships between both parties may take several forms and should suit local conditions. Partnerships may take the form of the provision of technical services, the training of technical and management personnel, science and technology exchanges, the contracting of project works, joint production, and joint ventures, etc. With all partnerships undertaken, China would adhere to the terms of the agreement, ensure the quality of deliverables, and be moral. 4. The aim of the aforementioned partnerships is to harness the complementary strengths of each party and mutual assistance so that both parties would be able to enhance their abilities to survive independently and to promote the development of their national economies.

on one hand China has always believed its relations with African countries to be equal and mutually beneficial and that its aid is also two-way. On the other hand, this also indicates that China, a developing country, had developed new attitudes and expectations in terms of her objectives for, and the significance of, her efforts to develop economic and technical partnerships with African countries.

First of all, compared to the eight principles of aid outlined by Zhou Enlai on his visit to Africa in the 1960s, the Chinese government's Africa policies in the early 1980s had maintained consistency with existing policy while at the same time underlined the need for rationality and practicality in bilateral economic and technical partnerships rather than partnerships based mostly only shared ideology or ideals.

Second, the Chinese government took pains to emphasize that bilateral economic and technical partnerships must be two-way and mutually beneficial. The ultimate objective of these partnerships is to promote economic and social development in both China and Africa and to enhance the developmental capabilities of both parties. Because both China and the African countries were developing countries, development was of topmost priority. Chinese aid to Africa and China-Africa economic and technical partnerships should help to promote development on both sides.

Third: China also emphasized the need for aid projects to have high operability, and that project implementation must be within existing capabilities. Further, the Chinese government also emphasized the need to consider the actual needs and conditions for both parties in order to achieve salient economic benefits with aid projects. Only this way would economic partnerships between both parties be sustainable.

Fourth, China should also adopt multiple formats with its aid to African countries, and thus develop more ways apart from its accustomed approaches of uncompensated aid and cash assistance. The Chinese government began to encourage Chinese enterprises to develop a multitude of economic activities in Africa, including works contracting, labor partnerships, technical services, business training, science and technology exchanges, jointly-operated plants, and joint-venture businesses, etc., as these new modes of cooperation can achieve greater aid benefits. The final principle among these four principles, "joint development", encapsulates China's basic attitudes towards, and expectations of, future China-Africa relations.

In truth, this sort of understanding and expectation of China-Africa economic relations is actually consistent with the domestic reforms and adjustments occurring with China's politics and economics at that time. Since the 1980s, the changes that China has made in its foreign policies have increasingly been linked with domestic reforms in the political and economic sectors. Shifting the focus of China-Africa relations from politics to economics and the move from selfless assistance (regardless of cost) to mutually-beneficial economic and technical partnerships were an expression of changes in China's politics and economy in its Africa policy. As the Egyptian newspaper *Al Akhbar* put it, the situation in China has stabilized and a new chapter in history has commenced. A New China has opened up its arms and heart to the entire world.

Relations between China and Africa changed gradually since the 1980s in accordance with the four principles of China-Africa relations stated in the 1980s. Significant advances and development were achieved in many areas.

Changes in, and the reform of, aid directed at African countries continued to be implemented with aid outcomes significantly improved. In terms of scale, during the 1980s China provided assistance to nearly 30 African countries in the form of complete sets of equipment and project assistance on over a hundred projects in the areas of agriculture, irrigation, power generation, traffic, telecommunications, public and residential building, and the building of sports and cultural facilities, etc. In order to improve on aid outcomes, China negotiated with various African countries on the reform of aid approaches, and formats became more diversified. Drawing lessons from past experience, both parties began to place greater focus on post-project management and maintenance. Further, in accordance with the principles tabled, China began to reduce its cash gifts and cash assistance to African countries and started instead to advocate for the shift to economic and technical cooperation and for interest-free loans and gifts to be replaced by building projects. At the same time, to increase the impact of projects, China and African countries also reformed post-project management processes following negotiation. With these new changes, China was to send technical and management professionals to Africa to participate in project operations and management. Alternatively, Chinese personnel were to act as trustees or service providers in the management of completed projects. In certain countries, there were also attempts to transform Chinese aid into investments in the recipient country with projects operated and managed by joint ventures established by Chinese enterprises. These reform measures were consistent with reforms of the enterprise management system then occurring in China. With these reform measures, positive results were achieved in certain African countries. Certain projects, like the Tanzam Railway, the concrete plant in Rwanda, the textile plant in Burundi, and the textile plant in Benin, produced excellent economic benefits and realized profits. These projects also became an important source of tax collection for the respective governments. In addition, certain enterprises that were poorly managed and which saw heavy losses were also turned around. This development was highly praised by many African countries, which regarded these enterprises models for China-Africa cooperation in a new era.

Together with the reforms it provided aid to Africa, in the 1980s China also saw her economic and trade relations with Africa develop. Beginning in the early 1980s, certain Chinese state-owned enterprises (SOEs) began to seek development opportunities in the international market as they sought to reform themselves. In Africa, they began to be involved in areas such as labor partnerships and works contracting. The Chinese government provided loans or outright gifts to some of these labor partnerships and contracting works. In other cases, Chinese enterprises had won international works contracting tenders put out by the World Bank and Western countries that were providing loans for these projects. By the late 1980s, Chinese enterprises were involved in over 1,000 contracting works and labor contracts in more than 40 African countries. Thousands of Chinese technical professionals and laborers were sent to Africa. We should say that Chinese enterprises had begun to enter Africa with lower-tier projects like works contracting and labor contracts. However, this process bore special significant for the future development of China-Africa trade relations. Because of this process, Chinese enterprises and companies were able to familiarize themselves with the economic and investment environment in these countries earlier and hence win a large share of infrastructural and engineering works projects before the West and win markets and market reputation in African countries. In fact, at that time the Western countries generally discriminated against Africa, and Western enterprises and funds were pulled out of the continent. At the same time, Chinese enterprises had begun to enter the international market by way of Africa. For many Chinese multinational companies that had gained international success many years down the road, Africa was their entryway into the world market and where they learned to adapt to the fierce competition of the global economy. Works contracting and labor services undertaken by Chinese enterprises in the 1980s led to a growth in exports of Chinese machinery and equipment and transport products to Africa. Furthermore, these efforts have allowed Chinese enterprises to train its employees and managers and thus lay a strong foundation for the swift rise in Chinese trade with, and corporate investment in, Africa in the new century.

Apart from works contracting and labor services, in the 1980s China also saw a fair bit of development in its trade with Africa. The Chinese government signed intergovernmental trade agreements with eight countries, including Togo, Zimbabwe, Angola, the Côte d'Ivoire and Djibouti, on separate occasions. By the late 1980s, China had established trade relations with almost all countries and regions on the African continent, and had signed intergovernmental trade agreements with 40 African countries. Total trade volume between China and African countries rose in 25.1% in value from USD817 million in 1979 to USD1.022 billion in 1988. At that time, trade between China and African countries comprised mainly of trade in primary products, industrial and agricultural raw materials and machinery and equipment. However, the proportion of trade in finished goods and semi-finished goods had already risen to about half of the total. Key African imports from China were: agricultural machinery, hand tools, machinery and equipment sets, chemical raw materials, apparel, textiles, rice, tea and other daily household goods. On the other hand, China's main imports from Africa comprised cotton, cocoa beans, coffee beans, gum arabic, sugar, chemical fertilizers, steel, and ships and marine equipment, etc.

China and Africa also saw tremendous development in their political and foreign relations in the 1980s. First of all, China's relations with countries that it had been traditionally friendly with, like Tanzania, Zambia, Egypt, Zaire, Benin, Ghana, Guinea, Mali and Gabon, were strengthened in this period. Cooperation between both parties on the international stage became stronger and the frequency of political interactions intensified. Guinea's President Ahmed Sékou Touré visited China twenty years later, while Tanzanian President Julius Nyerere visited China on two occasions in the 1980s. Newly-appointed President of Ghana Jerry Rawlings, and Gabon President, etc., also visited China on separate occasions. The repeat visits of the first generation of post-independence African leaders show that the friendly relations established between China and African countries in the 1960s had continued into the new era. In particular, Rawlings's visit helped to restore and develop the friendly relations that were established in the era of Mao Zedong and Kwame Nkrumah. This visit was highly significant in a symbolic sense for China's foreign relations post-'opening up' and reforms. Second, in the 1980s the development of relations between China and African countries also saw the Chinese making adjustments to her Africa policies. The influence of ideological factors was diluted, and China established, restored, or improved relations with African countries that were pro-West or pro-Soviet Union, like Ethiopia, Kenya, Senegal, Madagascar, Angola, Lesotho, and the Côte d'Ivoire. Many of these countries were key players in Africa and had strong influence, and the restoration and development of relations between China and these countries indicated that China's Africa policies were becoming more mature and rational by the day. By the late 1980s, China's relations with African countries had reached new heights, with relations established with 47 out of the then-51 countries on the continent.

In addition, China-Africa interactions and cooperation in the areas of science, education, cultural activity and health were also fairly frequent in the 1980s. Over the span of ten years, more than 80 cultural groups representing African countries visited China, and more than ten African performing arts groups also performed in China. On China's part, it had also sent more than 20 performing arts groups to perform in Africa, as well as established Chinese-funded Chinese cultural centers in Mauritius and Benin. During this period, as many as 2,000 African individuals traveled to China for studies in areas including medicine, agriculture, construction, textiles, electric machines, transportation, mining, and languages. At the same time, over a hundred Chinese experts and teachers also traveled to Africa in this period to teach the Chinese language, mathematics, physics, and chemistry at universities and high schools in over ten African countries. Certain Chinese students and academics also traveled to universities in Africa to study the African languages and humanities subjects. China-Africa healthcare cooperation continued to be of a significant scale in the 1980s, with dozens of Chinese medical teams sent to more than 20 African countries. These teams serviced rural and remote areas, bringing basic healthcare services to the people of Africa. These medical personnel, who were able to save many patients, earned a strong reputation for themselves in African countries and were called "the model of South-South cooperation".

1.5 China-Africa Relations in the 1990s, and Challenges to These Relations

In the late 1980s and early 1990s, with dramatic changes in the Soviet Union and the ending of the Cold War, the international landscape was dramatically changed. The external environment for China-Africa relations became extremely different. Following the incident of 4 June 1989, China was plunged into severe difficulty due to domestic political turmoil and sanctions by Western countries. China, which had already adopted the reform and opening up policy for a decade, faced the threat of losing all the progress it had made. At this unique moment, just like twenty years prior, China received invaluable help from friendly African countries in its efforts to break through the cordon set up by the West, to restore its image internationally, and to return to international society.

Following the political storms of 4 June 1989, Western countries imposed a series of sanctions on China in the international arena, and international media was saturated with negative reportage on China. China's image took a severe hit internationally. However, the countries of Africa did not appear to have been affected by the opinions of the Western countries, let alone give in to dissuasions by the West. They continued to engage in normal political, economic and cultural interactions with China based on their own understanding and expectations. In December 1989, amidst a wave of sanctions imposed on China by Western countries, Egyptian president Hosni Mubarak issued an invitation for Chinese President Yang Shangkun to visit Egypt. Egypt was a highly influential player in both Africa and the Arabic world, and shared close relations with the Western countries. It was also the first country to establish diplomatic relations with the People's Republic of China. The subsequent visit by Yang to Egypt, the first after the 4 June incident, had the effect of mitigating Western suppression and restoring China's image internationally at a highly challenging time for China's foreign relations.

During Yang's visit to Egypt, he was warmly welcomed by local government officials and businessmen. He also spoke on the Chinese government's attitudes towards its domestic politics and foreign relations on multiple occasions, serving as a voice for China speaking towards international society after the tumult of the 4 June incident. At this particular moment when China was facing severe challenges and difficulties in the area of foreign relations, the special strategic significance of China-Africa relations in terms of mitigating China's circumstances in the international arena and of enhancing her international position had come through. The first foreign head of state, prime minister and foreign minister to visit China after the 4 June incident all came from African countries. In 1989, the heads of state of Burundi, Uganda, Togo, Mali, and Burkina Faso visited China. In 1990, the heads of state of Egypt, Equatorial Guinea, the Central African Republic, Sierra Leone, Chad, and the Sudan visited China. Between 1990 and 1998, a total of 53 African heads of state, 15 African prime ministers, and over a hundred African government ministers visited China. During this period, the frequent visits and political interactions between China and African countries at high levels of government significantly improved China's foreign-relations environment and ecology. Since the 1990s, China's foreign minister has made his or her first overseas of the year to an African nation. This has almost become customary in Chinese foreign policy. Africa clearly has an important place in Chinese foreign policy.

In fact, since the 1990s, with changes in the Chinese economy and society as well as in the international landscape, the strategic nature and significance of China-Africa relations are also slowly changing.

On one hand, after the end of the Cold War, the West had changed its attitudes towards Africa and has made the promotion of parliamentary and multi-party systems and of its values as a priority in its Africa policies. The West has also linked its aid to Africa with the promotion of a transition to multi-party systems in African countries. In the early 1990s, a number of African countries switched to the multi-party system from either military rule or one-party systems. Over the course of this process, some of these countries saw the occurrence of political upheaval. At the same time, the majority of African countries also faced criticisms and pressure from the West on the subject of human rights. African countries facing economic difficulties were forced to make concessions in the areas of domestic affairs and foreign relations in order to obtain Western aid. However, the privatization reforms undertaken at the behest of the World Bank or the International Monetary Fund, as well as the implementation of a multi-party system, parliamentary elections and human rights policies made in line with Western values did not bring political stability or economic growth to Africa. In the 1990s, the majority of African countries were plunged into economic recession and political turmoil only because they could not find better ways to solve their problems. Africa was further marginalized in the eyes of the world and its development prospects appeared to have dimmed further.

However, this change in the international landscape provided another opening for the development of China-Africa relations. This was because just as African countries were descending into political and economic difficulties, China was also facing significant political pressures and ideological challenges from the West. Since 1990, each year, Western countries with the United States at the head proposed that the United Nations condemn China and that the United Nations Conference on Human Rights review China's human-rights record. Had these proposals been passed, China would face tremendous difficulties diplomatically. At the same time, since the 1990s, as calls for Taiwanese independence grew stronger and the risk of such a split became greater, just how to counter the power of the proponents of Taiwanese independence on the international stage, to prevent various activities that would split the nation, and to maintain the nation's unity also became a key part of China's foreign-relations efforts. In the face of Western sanctions and splittist activity in the case of Taiwan, China very much needed the support of African countries. The strategic place of Africa for China became even more salient.

Beginning 1990, China has managed to defeat the anti-China human rights proposals of the West at the United Nations for several consecutive years, and the support of African countries in this matter was significant and critical. For instance, in 1997, at the United Nations Conference on Human Rights, China tabled a "no action" motion in response to the anti-China human rights proposal once again made by the West. The matter was put to the vote, and 27 votes were cast in favor of China's motion and 17 votes against. China's motion was passed. Among the 27 votes cast in favor of China, 14 (or more than half of the total) were from African countries. The importance of African support for China is clear. On the other hand, the 17 opposing votes were mostly cast by Western countries. Thus, we see that the developed countries and developing countries are on opposite ends of the spectrum on the matter of human rights issues, which had in fact gradually become a way for Western countries to oppress China and other developing countries.

It is worth noting that in the 1990s the Chinese economy had quietly begun to rise with Africa's influence. In the 1990s, Western countries had reduced their investments in Africa due to the political turmoil and poor economic conditions on the continent. Africa became further marginalized in the global economy and in global politics, and the outlook on Africa internationally was generally a pessimistic one. However, China worked to maintain its existing friendships with African countries thanks to its economic and political aspirations shared with these countries, and also established and expanded increasingly frequent and diverse economic and trade relations with these countries through its reforms of its aid to Africa. We should say that the post-2000 large-scale entry into Africa by Chinese enterprises and concomitant swift development in China-Africa trade were not sudden phenomena but date back to China-Africa economic and technical partnerships in the 1990s.

In 1995, China accelerated its reforms of its Africa aid and further diversified the ways in which both parties engaged in economic and technical cooperation in order to further improve on the economic outcomes of aid projects. Following negotiations with certain African countries, the Chinese government divided its aid into two components: interest-free, preferential loans from the Chinese treasury (including grants or interest-free loans) and discounted loans provided by financial institutions. These loans were granted for designated projects in order to enhance aid outcomes and to strengthen the awareness of shared benefits and risk-sharing on the part of the recipient country. At the same time, certain discounted loans and grants provided to African countries were also transformed into import/export loans to be used by African countries for bilateral trade and investment projects following negotiation between China and African countries. These loans were to be used to import urgently-needed equipment, goods, and public and civilian facilities from China as well as grow China's exports. The Chinese government hoped to encourage bilateral trade and investment and to promote the development of African economies through this approach.

Since the mid-1990s, the Chinese government has worked actively to encourage Chinese enterprises to "make it out of China" and to engage in trade and investment in Africa. In the second half of the 1990s, China continued to establish eleven trade and investment centers as part of this strategy in various representative regions. These centers served the function of providing Chinese enterprises with assistance for their information, management, policy and financial needs with the aim of growing China-Africa trade and investment. The Chinese government adopted a number of measures to encourage Chinese enterprises to venture forth in Africa, and provided discounted and preferential loans to Chinese and African enterprises engaging in China-Africa trade. These loans were meant to be start-up capital to be used in the establishment of joint ventures or to purchase equipment. The Chinese government also provided Chinese enterprises and China-Africa joint ventures with preferential tax policies and also worked to improve the operating environment of these enterprises as well as the risk resilience of these enterprises. The Bank of China established financial institutions in Africa which would provide assistance relating to financial issues to companies engaging in China-Africa trade and investment in order to help these enterprises overcome issues such as significant financial risks and the lack of financial services in African countries.

These efforts led to positive effects, and in the 1990s major advances were made in Sino-Africa trade cooperation with total trade volume significantly increased. China-Africa trade volume grew from USD1.022 billion in value in 1988 to USD3.92 billion in value in 1995, and USD5.67 billion in value in 1997. In the following years,

1.5 China-Africa Relations in the 1990s, and Challenges to These Relations

China-Africa trade began to grow at an average of 25% a year, making it the fastest-growing part of Chinese foreign trade. By the year 2000, the value of China-Africa trade crossed the USD10 billion mark. During this period, Chinese enterprises had already begun to enter Africa in a more obvious manner. By 1999, nearly a thousand Chinese enterprises and companies were engaged in trade and investment activities in more than 40 countries, while nearly 400 trade and investment companies had been set up in Africa. By the late 1990s, more than 600 Chinese "complete foreign aid projects" had been completed in more than 40 African countries. These projects were in the areas of infrastructure, agriculture, urban and rural building, civilian and public facilities, etc., and played an important role in improving the basis for economic development and the livelihoods of the local people in these countries.

In the late 1990s, there were already large-scale projects with significant investment and long building periods and which involved a fair bit of technology within the ambit of China-Africa economic and technical cooperation. The export of large equipment and engineering projects were also raised to a whole new level. For instance, China began to export to African countries civilian-use aircraft to be used on regional routes. By the year 1999, over 300 aircraft in deals worth more than USD1 billion had been exported. Certain African countries began to regard highly China's development experience. The government of Egypt reached an agreement with China to establish the China-Egypt Cooperation Economic and Technological Special Zone along the Suez Canal. The two countries also signed off on two plans in the areas of high-technology cooperation (the "Spark Plan") and poverty-alleviation partnership (the "Dawn Plan"). At the end of the 1990s, China reached an agreement with the government of Algeria on the development of nuclear technologies for civilian purposes. In 1997, China reached an agreement with the government of the Sudan for the joint building of an oil pipeline by Chinese and Sudanese enterprises between Sudanese capital Khartoum and the Port of Sudan. The project was valued at USD215 million. This project laid the foundation for future cooperation between the Chinese and Sudanese governments in the areas of oil exploration and energy. In the same year, the Chinese government also signed an agreement with Egypt on a "complete equipment" project worth USD145 million with an annual production of 1.3 million tons and involving 600,000 tons of concrete. At the same time, the China Civil Engineering Construction Group won an international tender to repair and rebuild railways in Nigeria. The project was valued at USD529 million. All these projects were the larger projects with broader impact which Chinese enterprises had won overseas at that time and which mark the beginning of a new era for China-Africa economic and technical cooperation.

One of the highlights of China-Africa relations in the 1990s was the establishment of diplomatic relations between China and South Africa in December 1997, and the subsequent swift development of these relations. South Africa is the most advanced country on the continent in terms of its economy and technologies. China had not established diplomatic relations with South Africa for a long time due to its policy of apartheid and its long-term diplomatic relations with Taiwan. China had actively supported the black Africans in fighting apartheid and kept in close contact with the African National Congress and other black-African parties. South African leaders like Oliver Tambo, Nelson Mandela and Desmond Tutu have all visited China before. Since the 1990s, with the gradual dissolution of apartheid in South Africa, China first established economic relations with South Africa before embarking on contact in the areas of politics and foreign relations. In early 1992, China and South Africa established the "China South African Studies Center" and the "South Africa China Studies Center" respectively in their capital cities to serve as official points of contact for the establishing of diplomatic relations. In 1994, apartheid was abolished in South Africa, and China and South Africa began to make efforts on multiple fronts towards the establishment of diplomatic relations after the new South African government was installed. However, as South Africa had established close economic relations with Taiwan, during the mid-1990s when the new South Africa had just been established Taiwan's trade with the country had also peaked. In 1995, Taiwan-South Africa trade reached to a new historic high of USD1.87 billion in value, and Taiwan became South Africa's seventh-largest trading partner. In 1995, Taiwan invested a total of USD1.5 billion in South Africa, with around 300 Taiwanese companies and enterprises operating in the latter. At that time, China-South Africa trade was only valued at USD1.3 billion. The scale of economic benefits from Taiwan, together with the carrots dangled by the Taiwanese authorities, meant that domestic debate on whether to break South Africa's relations with Taiwan and to establish relations with the People's Republic of China raged for a number of years. However, as China became more powerful and its international status became significantly improved, and as its trade relations with South Africa became stronger, the value of China-South Africa trade reached USD1.8 billion by the year 1997, surpassing Taiwan-South Africa trade that had a value of USD1.78 billion. Furthermore, China-South Africa trade was growing swiftly and bore tremendous prospects.

As a country with ambitions of being a regional power, South Africa had no choice but to consider the importance of establishing normal relations with China. In November 1996, South Africa president Nelson Mandela said in an address on the country's China policy that to continue to give Taiwan diplomatic recognition was "not in line with South Africa's role in international affairs", and that South Africa would eventually break off ties with Taiwan and acknowledge the People's Republic of China. On 30 December 1997, China and South Africa signed a joint communiqué and announced that the two countries would establish full diplomatic relations based on the 'One China' principle. South Africa was the most advanced nation on the Africa continent and the value of its country production is greater than the total of all the other African countries combined. As such, South Africa would serve as a leader in the process of rejuvenating African economies and societies, as the establishing of ties between China and South Africa would have a significant role in promoting the development of China-Africa relations and the expansion and enhancement of China's political and economic partnerships on all fronts in the subsequent years.

However, in the 1990s China-Africa relations were not all smooth-sailing. Severe challenges also emerged during this period.

In the 1990s, the challenges faced by China's Africa policy came from many quarters, and were very much linked to the particular changes in the international environment at that time. First, in the early 1980s, a number of African countries switched over to the multi-party system with a change in governing party in most cases. Then, most countries also established systems of parliamentary elections. During this process, the first generation of national leaders post-independence retired from politics one after another. Although the majority of incoming leaders continued to maintain friendly relations with China, most of them did not have personal relationships with China the way the founding leaders did. Most of them had come to power by means of election victories and had a preference for the Western election system. Thus, China-Africa relations were sometimes easily affected by the West. When the Western countries sought to suppress China ideologically and politically in the early 1990s and used the issue of human rights as the reason for such suppression, a small number of African countries chose to cool their relations with China, or distance themselves from China, under pressure from the West. Opposition parties in certain African countries responded to Western countries' calls for sanctions against China, and criticized the incumbent governments during elections for their friendliness towards China. Relations with China became a tool for criticizing the government and for the winning of votes. These changes in the politics of African countries had affected China's relations with certain African countries in the early 1990s to a certain extent. However, in general African leaders tended to pursue their national interests from the perspective of African nationalism and thus their policy choices were not fully dictated by the ideological foreign relations that were dominated by the West. African countries also began to rethink the paths available for Africa and their foreign policies as the continent saw political turmoil—and in the whole of the 1990s, economic recession—due to the switch to multi-party political systems. A growing number of African leaders saw the special significance of developing relations with China with the sustained growth of the Chinese economy in the 1990s. Hence, in general in the 1990s China-Africa relations continue to advance despite hiccups along the way due to the switch to multi-party systems and the installation of second-generation national leaders.

Second, in the late 1970s and the early 1980s, Chinese aid to Africa decreased and changes were made to the way it provided aid as it was busy with domestic economic building. The majority of African countries responded positively to China's proposal that its aid approaches be changed from the granting of direct cash gifts or uncompensated assistance to bilateral economic and technical cooperation and methods with a strong focus on economic outcomes. These countries also worked actively to adapt to these changes. However, certain African countries could not cope with these changes and believe that China was only considering her own economic interests and had abandoned her traditional friendship with African countries. Beginning in the 1980s, a broad swathe of African countries plunged into economic difficulty. A number of countries also saw prolonged drought, and economic growth slowed with contractions in the economy in some cases. Various governments saw their incomes decline and became even more reliant on foreign aid. Thus, they were unhappy with the Chinese government's decision to reduce her aid or to change the ways in which aid was given. Certain African countries that had been plunged into economic difficulties began to expect more of China's economic aid, and the basis of bilateral relations was easily shaken at a time when China could not meet such expectations.

In addition, since the 1980s there has been the issue of trade imbalance in China-Africa trade relations. Through the whole of the 1980s, due to changes in China's Africa aid policy the overall amount of aid given was reduced and growth in China-Africa trade slowed compared to the 1970s. This was related to the relative neglect of Africa by the rest of the world at the time and also to do with changes in China's Africa policy. In the 1990s, although growth in China-Africa trade began to pick up, the growth in African exports to China slowed and the trade imbalance between China and Africa became more severe. Reduced export volume led to difficulties in rectifying the situation of low foreign-currency income and worsening balance of payments on the part of the African countries, which saw their foreign debts increase over time. This situation led some African countries to distance themselves from China.

Third: it was in precisely this context that China-Africa relations were at one point sabotaged by Taiwan's "silver-bullet diplomacy" or "economic-aid diplomacy" in the 1990s. Hence, opposing Taiwanese splittist activity and restraining Taiwan from undertaking "silver-bullet diplomacy" in Africa became a key part of China's Africa efforts in this period.

After Lee Teng-hui came to power in 1988, he started moving towards the splittist objective of Taiwanese independence. He also doubled efforts to seek support on the international stage, and certain economically-backward, small- and medium-sized African countries became the focus of Taiwan's lobbying. In 1988, Taiwan established the Overseas Economic Cooperation and Development Fund with a fund injection of USD1.1 billion. The Fund was to provide developing countries with loans, cash gifts and other forms of economic aid. This was when African economies were plunging into recession and when China had to reduce her aid to Africa due to the reforms of her economy. These provided Taiwan with an opening. With such lures put out by Taiwan, certain African countries decided to establish "official ties" with Taipei. Between 1988 and 1997, a total of ten African countries—Libya, Lesotho, Guinea-Bissau, the Central African Republic, the Niger, Burkina Faso, Gambia, Senegal, Chad, and São Tomé and Principe—established "official relations" with Taipei. In addition to South Africa, Malawi, and Swaziland which already had relations with Taiwan, this wave brought the total up to 13 at one point. As such, at one point, Taipei had established "official relations" with as many as more than 30 countries around the world. At that time, the Taiwanese authorities claimed that if they had managed to establish ties with 40 countries, which would account for around one in four United Nations seats. Thus, this would strongly enhance Taiwan's capital on the international stage against the Chinese mainland, and provide international political support for Lee Teng-hui's "theory of two countries". The "silver-bullet strategy" adopted by Taiwan authorities as part of a foreign-relations offensive created a significant impact on, and damage to, China's foreign relations and national interests.

It was also precisely during this process that Africa's special position in China's foreign-relations strategy and the strategic significance of China-Africa relations to the maintenance of China's national interests were again foregrounded and brought to the attention of China's leaders.

1.5 China-Africa Relations in the 1990s, and Challenges to These Relations

However, the aforementioned challenges and issues faced in the context of China-Africa relations never once undermined the foundation of China-Africa relations. In fact, beginning in the mid-1990s China began to strengthen its efforts towards Africa and increased its Africa aid. It also began to work actively to promote trade and investment in Africa by Chinese enterprises. National leaders also began to visit Africa on a more frequent basis, and at the same time also invited African leaders on visits to China. Thanks to the aforementioned efforts, countries like Lesotho, the Niger, South Africa, Guinea-Bissau, the Central African Republic, Senegal, and Liberia cut off relations with Taipei and restored official diplomatic relations with China. Further, the establishment of relations between China and South Africa in 1997 has also had a catalytic effect, and since the late 1990s China-Africa relations have improved in general. Moreover, over this course of constant adjustment and improvements, China has finally established a mature set of principles and policies with regard to Africa.

Chapter 2
The Establishment of Forum on China-Africa Cooperation and a New Chapter in China-Africa Cooperation

China-Africa relations present a unique picture of evolution in the history of contemporary human relations. When we look at how the world has developed over the last five decades or so, we see that globally that had been a number of conflicts, with peoples suffering from the ravages of war. Relations between countries have been uncertain, and shifting landscapes have made it difficult to determine if one is a friend or foe. However, in such chaotic times China-Africa relations have remained steady with no major changes or volte-face since the beginning of such relations in the 1950s. Although during this half-century both China and African countries also saw their politics and economies change in various ways, and although their respective national leadership has been changed a few times over, China-Africa relations have continued to advance steadily. The friendship and trust between China and African countries can be described as strong and lasting. In this sense, China-Africa relations can even been regarded as a model in the history of contemporary human relations with their particular set of value and significance.

On 4 November 2006, the heads of state and government of 43 African countries gathered in Beijing to attend the Forum on China-Africa Cooperation (FOCAC) Beijing Summit, where they engaged in discussion with the leaders of China on China-Africa cooperation. This "Little United Nations-like" summit and the plans and visions for China-Africa relations laid out at this summit are clear evidence of the tremendous advances achieved by China in its relations with African countries in the three decades since its 'opening-up' and attendant reforms. Further, the event also signals to a certain extent that China has matured to become a diplomatic power in its own right. Thus, the event is highly significant. Then-United Nations Secretary-General Kofi Annan said in a statement that such cooperation mechanisms established by China and African countries would bring historic opportunities for the development of Africa. A commentary in French newspaper *Libération* on 4

November read: "If we are to say that there is a continent that can turn the world upside-down under the influence of Chinese economic growth, that continent would be Africa."[1]

2.1 The Establishment of the FOCAC in 2000 and the Enhancement of China-Africa Relations on All Fronts

Contemporary China-Africa relations have evolved over the period of more than a century. In recent years, such relations have been swiftly enhanced in what is the inevitable outcome of historical logic and which also point to more complex and deep-rooted historical trajectories leading into the future.

The commencement of a new era of China-Africa cooperation is not a simple process but the outcome of a difficult process of exploration and adjustments which began between the late 1970s and the early 1980s.

In the late 1970s, after ten years of tumult due to the Cultural Revolution, the economy of China was in shambles. It was the eve of reforms, and there were pressures from several quarters to reform China-Africa relations. At that time, China's leaders had told friends visiting from Africa on multiple occasions that China highly valued her friendship with Africa and would try her best to provide aid to Africa. However, China was still very poor then, and needed to first develop herself so that it would be better able to assist African countries in the future. Thirty years later in October 2000, the Chinese government announced at the FOCAC ministerial-level meeting in Beijing that it would write off RMB10 billion worth of debt owed by the least developed African countries. At the FOCAC Beijing Summit held in November 2006, Chinese President Hu Jintao announced eight policies and measures regarding Chinese aid to Africa, and undertook to grow the scale of such aid by 100% by the year 2009.[2] Historically, China has always emphasized the place of good faith in its foreign and other policies *vis-à-vis* Africa. China has fulfilled her promise and grown the scale of her aid significantly,[3] and more importantly, it worked together with the people of Africa to raise China-Africa relations from the level of simple aid to a new level based on strategic partnerships and the joint pursuit of the historic rejuvenation of Asia and Africa.[4]

---

[1] See: Foreign Media Review FOCAC Beijing Summit Positively, *People's Daily*, 7 November 2000.

[2] Zheng, Kejun (2000). Changes made by China to her Africa policies in the early 1980s. In Peking University Center for African Studies (ed.), *China and Africa*. Beijing: Peking University Press, p. 91.

[3] See: Xinhua News. China and African countries announce the establishment of new relationship based on strategic partnerships. *FOCAC Beijing Summit web site*. 6 November 2006. http://www.focacsummit.org/zxbd/2006-11/05/content_5184.htm.

[4] Liu, Hongwu (2007). On the historic and global significance of the establishment of new relations between China and Africa based on strategic partnerships. *Foreign Affairs Review*, 2007 no. 1, p. 12.

In the twenty-first century, changes in China's foreign relations, including its partnerships with African countries, have been accelerated. In the year 2000, China became a member of the World Trade Organization (WTO). This was a major outcome of the changes in China's relations with the outside world and at the same time the beginning of even greater changes. It was also in November the same year that China established the FOCAC, an all-new platform for strategic cooperation, with African countries. Based on subsequent developments, the establishment of the FOCAC Beijing Summit has kicked off a new era in contemporary China-Africa partnerships. In the decade or so since then, the strategic significance of this new form of China-Africa partnerships has become increasingly clear. At the same time, the influence of China's developmental experience in Africa is also becoming clearer by the day. Both these factors have facilitated the swift development of China-Africa partnerships towards new areas of cooperation.

These new advances all have to do with the new autonomous changes that are occurring with Asian and African countries in the new century. Overall, the distinctive path of China-Africa partnerships over the last few decades and the rich trove of experiences and refreshing experiences gained from the promotion of development in both China and Africa thanks to this path, have already provided the fundamental conditions for new ground in theoretical studies and knowledge-building. As contemporary China-Africa partnerships continue to develop and for an even broader promotion of development in Asia and Africa, various new practical experiences different from those of the developmental experience of the West are moving forward in even more complex ways. The experiences, developmental pathways or even the developmental models of mankind are also being re-written. The traditional Western-dominated system of international relations which had been forged over the past few centuries is slowly being superseded, with various developmental pathways, models of cooperation and modes of international interaction opening up for mankind in the future.

One salient feature in the development of contemporary China-Africa relations is that such relations have moved from level to level over various stages of advancement. After half a century of evolution, post-2000 China-Africa relations entered a new era where the scope of relations were broadly expanded, and the level of relations swiftly enhanced. The influence of such relations was also dramatically amped up. China had eventually come to a mature and complete set of policies and principles *vis-à-vis* Africa.

In the twenty-first century, as the Chinese economy took off and its power, comprehensively enhanced, the desire of African countries to further develop their relations with China became increasingly apparent. Following suggestions by certain African states, the Chinese government made a formal proposal to establish the FOCAC in order to establish new China-Africa cooperation mechanisms on all fronts. The proposal was received positively by African countries. The FOCAC was established in October 2000, during which its inaugural ministerial-level meeting was also held in Beijing.

The first mechanism established at the FOCAC was the ministerial-level (foreign ministers and finance ministers) meeting mechanism. The meeting would be held once every three years with hosting to alternate between China and Africa. The second ministerial-level meeting was held in Ethiopia in 2003. As China-Africa relations developed swiftly, and given the positive outcomes generated by this mechanism, the third meeting in 2006 was elevated to the level of heads of state. The Beijing summit, which was attended by heads of state from 43 African countries was an unprecedented meeting, a showcase of the immense energy and prospects of China-Africa relations, and triggered sustained global attention to the phenomenon of China-Africa relations. The fourth ministerial-level meeting of the FOCAC was held in the Egyptian capital of Cairo in 2009.

The establishment of the FOCAC has created for China-Africa relations a new mechanism and platform that has the strategic significance of enhancing China-Africa relations on all fronts. This was made increasingly clear in the subsequent few years.

First of all, the establishment of the Forum provided an effective institutional platform for the long-term development of China-Africa relations in the new century. Since the 1990s, various regional organizations had developed swiftly around the world. Integration was a common trend in many areas within international relations. As early as in 1993 Japan established the Tokyo International Conference on African Development (TICAD) while other Western and African countries also engaged each other through various mechanisms and platforms. The establishment of the FOCAC was in line with the developmental needs of China-Africa relations. The heads-of-state summits, ministerial-level meetings, meetings of senior officials, and follow-up committees, etc., organized under the ambit of the Forum form a multi-level operational structure that allows China-Africa relations to retain its traditional amity while engaging in institutional innovation and building of long-lasting significance at the same time.

Second: from the very beginning, this cooperation mechanism has been supported by a complete set of developmental concepts, strategic plans, and policy propositions. At the inaugural ministerial-level meeting held in 2000, two key documents were passed by China and participating African countries: the *Beijing Declaration of the Forum on China-Africa Cooperation* and the *Programme for China-Africa Cooperation in Economic and Social Development*. These two programmatic documents provide a complete description of the aims, structure, function, policies and measures of the FOCAC. The *Forum on China-Africa Cooperation-Addis Ababa Action Plan* was passed at the second summit held in Addis Adaba in 2003 in what was a summary and closing of the developmental achievements made by the FOCAC in the preceding three years. The *Declaration of the Beijing Summit of the Forum on China-Africa Cooperation* and the *Forum on China-Africa Cooperation Beijing Action Plan 2007–2009* were then passed at the Beijing Summit held in November 2006. At this juncture, the basic outlines of the new 21st-century strategic partnership between China and Africa had been put in place.[5]

---

[5] See FOCAC web site: http://www.focac.org/chn/zyzl/hywj/t280368.htm.

2.1 The Establishment of the FOCAC in 2000 and the Enhancement ...

Third, China-Africa relations have become the most mature area in contemporary Chinese foreign relations. The FOCAC, which is open, transparent and non-exclusionist, was established in line with the basic principles of modern international relations. The existence of this mechanism indicates that the form of China-Africa relations is compatible with the developments of the times. On 16 January 2006, the Chinese government officially released its *China's African Policy* document, the first officially-issued foreign-policy document to be released in the history of the People's Republic of China. With the release of this document, China has openly stated the basic objectives, policies and measures of its Africa policy as well as the benefit to the China-Africa relationship brought by China's development and the means by which this would be achieved. That China has put out an official document stating its Africa policy is in itself a symbolic move for Chinese foreign relations as the move reflects the growing maturity of China's foreign relations as well the confidence and rationality displayed in China's world-power diplomacy.

China-Africa relations developed rapidly following the establishment of the FOCAC and political relations between both sides became even closer. Between 2000 and 2008, over 200 Chinese and African leaders and foreign ministers had made visits to each other, including more than 50 individuals from China. Chinese President Hu Jintao made visits to Africa in two consecutive years: in 2006 (Morocco, Nigeria, and Kenya) and in 2007 (Cameroon, Libya, the Sudan, Zambia, Namibia, South Africa, Mozambique, and the Seychelles). Other Chinese state leaders also made more visits to Africa subsequently.

Since 2000, China-Africa relations have been enhanced not just in political and foreign-relations terms. Cooperation in the area of trade and economy has become the core driving force in the development of China-Africa relations in the new century, and Sino-Africa economic and trade relations are gradually moving from the simple aid model to a more comprehensive model of cooperation and development.[6]

The swift development of China-Africa trade and economic relations in this new period can be seen in several areas.

First: trade volumes increased by leaps and bounds. In 2000, the value China-Africa trade crossed the USD10 billion mark, and reached USD29.462 billion in 2004, USD 39.747 billion in 2005, and USD55.5 billion in 2006. During this period, average growth in China-Africa trade per annum was around the 30% mark, which is significantly higher than growth in overall Chinese overseas trade in the same period. In 2006, China surpassed the United Kingdom to become one of Africa's top trading partners after the United States and France. It was forecast that by the year 2010 China-Africa trade would cross the USD100 billion mark and that China would become China's second-largest trading partner after the United States.

Second: China-Africa economic and technical cooperation has expanded in scope and has been raised to higher levels, with partnership models and avenues increasingly consistent with international standards. Steady advancements have been made in efforts to shift the bulk of cooperation from trade to investment. In recent

---

[6] Luo, J., and Liu, H. (2007). On the various stages of Chinese aid to Africa and the special significance of such aid. *West Asia and Africa*, 2007 no. 11.

years, in order to address the issue of trade imbalances in China-Africa trade the Chinese government has worked actively to support the efforts of Chinese enterprises investing in Africa. There has been significant development in terms of the areas invested in and the scale of investment by Chinese enterprises, and investment-led trade has become a new feature of China-Africa economic cooperation. As of the end of 2006, Chinese investments totaled USD11.7 billion, including USD6.64 billion in direct corporate investment. This was an over 14-fold increase over 1999 figures. According to initial estimates, Chinese concerns have invested in 49 African countries in many areas including energy and resource development, infrastructural building, trade, production and processing, transport and logistics, and agriculture and agricultural product development. In 2006, the Huawei Group achieved sales of USD2.08 million in Africa, with products and services sold in 40 African countries. Companies and entities like the Khartoum refinery in the Sudan, the Sino-Zambian Friendship Farm, the Tianli textiles plant in Mauritius, Hisense (South Africa) Co., Ltd., Xinda Seafood Company in Mozambique, the Tongmei pharmaceutical plant in Togo, the Zhonghua Paper Company in Tanzania, and the Chongqing Huali Holdings Co., Ltd., all of which have been funded with Chinese investment, have not only settled in Africa but have also begun implementing the corporate strategy of localization.

There are a few salient characteristics to the swift development in China-Africa partnership in recent years.

First, since the establishment of FOCAC in 2000, China-Africa relations have entered a period of swift development on all fronts, on multiple levels, and in several areas. The scope of China-Africa economic, trade and technical cooperation continues to grow as partnerships become more broad-based and in-depth at the same time. In addition to partnerships on the political, security and international-relations fronts, China-Africa trade cooperation is now already occurring in multiple areas including agriculture, telecommunications, energy, manufacturing and processing, infrastructure, and social welfare projects. Many projects have already produced significant economic and social benefits.

Second: there have been significant improvements made to institution-building and the environment in the area of China-Africa economic and technical cooperation. As of 2006, China had signed the Agreement on the Bilateral Promotion and Protection of Investment with 28 African nations, and the Agreement on the Avoidance of Double Taxation and the Prevention of Fiscal Evasion with eight African countries. These intergovernmental agreements have great significance for the development of China-Africa economic and technical cooperation over the long term.

Third, the development of China-Africa partnerships has been visibly sped up and expanded in scale. A greater array of investment and trading players are now in the game and investment by private enterprises in Africa has also grown significantly. In 2006, Africa became China's second-largest supplier of crude oil, its second-largest works contracting market, as well as its third-largest investment target. China's home-appliance, automobile, aircraft and satellite products are among the many that are also sold to African buyers. On the other, marble from Egypt, coffee from the Côte d'Ivoire, automobile parts from South Africa, electronic products from Tunisia, tobacco from Zimbabwe, peanut oil from Senegal, cotton from Mali, and sweet potato from Nigeria, etc., are also being imported by China in large quantities. By the end of 2006, there were more than 800 Chinese enterprises (including over 700 private enterprises) that have invested, or set up operations, in Africa.[7] In 2006, Chinese enterprises signed new contracting and labor contracts worth a total of USD28.97 billion, or 31% of the total value of foreign contracting projects won in the year. Between 2000 and 2007, Chinese enterprises built within the ambit of contracting projects over 6,000 km of road, more than 3,400 km of railway, eight medium- and large-sized power stations, and large numbers of infrastructural facilities for public and civilian use.

Fourth: over time, China-Africa economic and technical partnerships have taken on the following characteristics: a focus on large-scale projects, the enhancement of technical content, and the integration of technology, industry and trade. Between 2001 and 2006, in Africa Chinese concerns signed a total of 41 large-scale contracting projects worth USD100 billion or more. The Nigerian railway modernization project and the Algerian east–west highway project, both clinched in 2005, were worth USD8.3 billion and USD6.3 billion respectively. They are to date the two largest overseas projects contracted by Chinese enterprises. In recent years, China has also jointly developed economic development zones, investment and trade processing zones, and technology and innovation parks with certain African countries, like the Zambia-China Economic & Trade Cooperation Zone and the Lagos Free Trade Zone which have become the new driving forces behind the further enhancement of China-Africa economic and trade partnerships.[8] These changes, which have long-lasting implications, have made China-Africa economic and technical partnerships more similar to the global norm as well as a new trend in South-South cooperation.

- At the FOCAC Beijing Summit in November 2006, Chinese President Hu Jintao announced that the Chinese government would increase the scale of its Africa aid by 100% by the year 2009 through key policy measures in eight areas.[9] These measures include:

    The provision of USD3 billion worth of preferential loans and USD2 billion worth of preferential export buyer credit to African countries;
    The establishment of a China-Africa Development Fund with an investment of USD5 billion;
    The write-off of all Chinese government interest-free loans due as of the end of 2005 by heavily-indebted African countries and the least developed countries that have diplomatic relations with China;
    A further opening-up of the Chinese market to Africa, with zero tariffs applied to more than 440 types (up from the previous 190) of goods from the least developed countries that have diplomatic relations with China;

---

[7] Liu, H., and Wang, T. (2008). An analysis of the current state of, and trends in, investment by private Chinese enterprises in Africa. *Journal of Zhejiang Normal University*, 2008 no. 5, p. 6.

[8] Alden, Chris (2007). *China in Africa*. London: Gutenberg Press, p. 68.

[9] See: FOCAC web site, http://www.focac.org/chn/zyzl/hywj/.

The building of three to five economic and trading partnership zones in the following three years in order to train 15,000 African talents in various areas;
The dispatch of 100 senior agriculture experts to Africa;
The building of ten agricultural technology demonstration centers in Africa;
The provision of assistance to 30 African hospitals as well as the provision of RMB300 million in gift aid for the purpose of epidemic prevention in Africa, with the establishment of 30 epidemic prevention centers;
The dispatch of 300 young volunteers to Africa in aid of 100 village schools in Africa; The increase of the number of China Government Scholarship places for African students from 2,000 a year to 4,000 a year; and so forth.[10]

After the Beijing summit, the Chinese government also established follow-up action committees to ensure the swift implementation of the aforementioned measures. We should say that China-Africa cooperation today is no longer about declarations and proclamations but based on rational and practical action plans projects that are specific and highly operable. This indicates that China's Africa policies are increasingly closer to modern government policies in that they are becoming better managed and are more focused on outcomes.[11] In fact, China had already begun action with its African partners even as some Western commentators continue to speak of various empty principles through the lens of their biased ideologies.

The gradual implementation of these major and specific measures in the area of China-Africa economic and technical partnerships have produced positive effects in terms of social and economic development in various African countries, as well as in the form of improved livelihoods in these countries. In recent years, the Chinese market has had strong demand for products from Africa, and China has already become a key driver of economic growth in Africa.[12] On the other hand, the value-for-money goods imported from China are an affordable option even for the impoverished peoples who live in the most remote areas in Africa. In certain countries, Chinese investment has already become a key driver of economic development.[13] For example, thanks to Chinese investment and technical assistance the oil economy has taken off in the Sudan, which has become a net exporter of crude oil and seen related industries develop. In 2005, the Sudanese economy grew as much as 8%, and economic growth hit double digits in 2006 and 2007, making the Sudan one

---

[10] As of March 2008, China has worked together with various African countries to establish a total of 12 Confucius Institutes on the continent: two in Egypt, two in Nigeria, two in Kenya, one in Zimbabwe, one in Rwanda, one in Madagascar, one in South Africa, and one in Cameroon. See: The Confucian Institutes. *Office of the National Leading Group for the International Promotion of the Chinese Language web site*. http://www.hanban.org/cn_hanban/content.php?id=3258.

[11] Thompson, Drew (2005). China's Soft Power in Africa: From the 'Beijing Consensus' to Health Diplomacy. *China Brief*, Volume V, Issue 21.

[12] Alden, Chris (2007). *China in Africa*. London: Gutenberg Press, p. 38.

[13] Guerrero, D. and Manji, F. *ed*. China's New Role in Africa and the South: a search for a new perspective. *Fahamu*. http://www.fahamu.org/pzbook.php#chinabook_2.

of the fastest-growing economies in Africa in recent years.[14] Studies have shown that in recent years China-Africa economic partnerships made of a contribution of at least 5% to the growth in Africa's economy. At the same time, Africa is also seeing the complex consequences produced by the structural enhancement of Africa's economies and the unleashing of development potential in these countries brought on by Chinese investment and trade.[15]

2.2 The Core Mission and Global Significance of Contemporary China-Africa Relations

Fundamentally speaking, the swift development and elevation of China-Africa relations are really a necessary strategic choice for China and Africa as they seek to survive in the modern world system and to leap to a new level of modernization. This is a choice that has significantly enhanced the positions of both China and Africa in the international strategic landscape, which has fully embodied the special value of South-South cooperation, and which has benefited both China and Africa.

The global significance of contemporary China-Africa relations lies in how such relations have strongly facilitated development in both China and Africa. Any advance made by China, a developing country that is home to one-fifth of the global population, in beating poverty and in the area of development is a contribution to the world. If China is able to bring opportunity to Africa and lead to the rejuvenation of African economies on the basis of mutual benefit, this will be a key contribution made by the ancient country of China to the world in the twenty-first century even as it seeks its own rejuvenation. As some Western media outlets believe, "If we are to say that there is a continent that can turn the world upside-down under the influence of Chinese economic growth, that continent would be Africa."[16]

After all, China is an ancient civilizational power which its own history, culture, and civilizational structure. Hence, although China would certainly adhere to certain traditional principles of modernization along its path of modern rejuvenation and development, and see changes to its civilization in terms of the market economy and democratic politics, this is not a process that is fully in the Western mold. In fact, "China's development model has already challenged many mainstream Western viewpoints in the areas of poverty eradication and good governance."[17] African countries understand China's significance to Africa in their own ways. Of course,

---

[14] Liu, H., and Jiang, H. *ed.* (2008). *Chronicles of Nations: the Sudan.* Beijing: Social Sciences Academic Press, p. 319.

[15] Peluola, Adewale (2007). China: A new partner for Africa's development? *Pambazuka News*, 21 March 2007.

[16] The Influence of China, *Libération*, 4 November 2006. See: Foreign Opinions Positive on FOCAC Beijing Summit, *People's Daily*, 7 November 2006.

[17] The Charm of the China Model, *International Herald Tribune*, 2 November 2006. Excerpted from *Reference News*, 6 November 2006.

Africa will not simply transplant China's experiences; however, they seek to benefit from China's development experience at the same time.

Asian and African countries in contemporary times are transitioning from traditional social structures to a modern structure. This process of modernization is one that is even more complex and difficult than what the Western countries have previously gone through. No outside power can replace the independent efforts of Asian and African countries to control this process and its trajectory. Africa today needs governments that are committed to development and which are able to implement and advance such development policies. This is a more attractive aspect of the China model for Africa. More importantly, the honest conversations and equal treatment accorded by China, which does not attach any political conditions to its interactions are attractive on the emotional level for African countries which have been humiliated in the past and which are today still poor and weak.[18] "The China model is not perfect. However, it has already enriched the world's political enquiry and knowledge about how to eradicate poverty and has provided countries all over the world with more choices and policies. As long as the American model cannot produce the desired outcomes the China model will only become more attractive for the poor countries of the world."[19]

China does not push for the implementation of its development model but is an advocate for learning and exchange between civilizations. At the Beijing Summit, China proposed that China and Africa conduct exchanges in the areas of governance and development experience and work on the building of their respective national strengths. This proposal is itself an expression of the fact that China-Africa cooperation had entered a more innovative period with more specific and practical plans in place. We should say that for a long time the relative weakness of, and poor government performance in, certain African countries have been structural factors that limited the development of Africa. On the other hand, China's strengths and the government's determination to develop the economy are important reasons for the swift development of contemporary China and an issue that African countries are paying a great deal of attention to. In addition, the Chinese have also developed much political wisdom with matters such as the handling of the complex relations between various peoples, the handling of religious relations, and the development of border regions. Such experiences may also be significant for young African countries that have long been mired in civil conflict. On the other side of the equation, in recent years China has also found opportunities for it to enter the global market and to enhance its abilities to adapt to the international environment in the course of trading with and investing in Africa. The promotion of mutual development and prosperity hand-in-hand on the part of both China and Africa has in fact become a

---

[18] A hundred years ago, a multitude of problems, including poverty and weakness, had brought China to her knees. At that time, Sun Yat-sen had told his countrymen that all countries that treated China as an equal and with sincerity were friends and brothers of the Chinese people who could be trusted.

[19] The Charm of the China Model, *International Herald Tribune*, 2 November 2006. Excerpted from *Reference News*, 6 November 2006.

vivid illustration of how the peaceful rise of China is definitely an opportunity for the world rather than a threat.[20]

The strategic meaning of China-Africa relations to Africa has already been expressed. In recent years, as China-Africa relations developed swiftly, Africa has moved from what was a marginalized position in contemporary global relations. The world now sees that Africa is not an insignificant player that only requires aid but a player that can bring wealth and opportunity to the world. Globally, a number of global powers like the US, the UK, France, Germany, Japan and India have 'made returns to Africa' by means of establishing various cooperation forum and holding summits involving heads of state with African countries. It is worth noting that while the major countries were in conflict with each other in Africa during the Cold War, this time round they are returning to Africa with a focus on investment, trade and market development. As long as the principles of mutual respect and trust are upheld, China is also willing to engage and work with the West and establish new points of intersection upon the joint promotion of economic development in Africa and thereby create more space for Sino-European multilateral cooperation.[21]

2.3 The Impact of the Swift Development of China-Africa Relations on the Relationship Between China and Western Nations

China-Africa relations are highly significant in the historical advance of China's foreign relations. One reason is that such relations had had an impact that was far broader than the scope of China-Africa relations at the very beginning. For China, in the last few decades China-Africa relations have often served as a 'fulcrum' upon which the structure of China's relations with the outside world had changed and as a platform upon which China has been able to walk out to the world outside with dignity. Since the 1960s, China's growing influence in Africa has, on multiple occasions, forced the West to look back and to think about what China and Africa mean to the West.[22]

The Chinese civilization of the East and the tropical civilizations of Africa are two fundamental forms in the body of global civilizations. Historically, China and Africa had always overcome various obstacles to achieve mutual understanding and engagement, and such relations were swiftly strengthened and enhanced in the second half of the twentieth century and have already led to profound and long-lasting influence on the overall state of human relations as well as on the approaches used in such

---

[20] Liu, Hongwu (2007). On the historic and global significance of the establishment of new relations between China and Africa based on strategic partnerships. *Foreign Affairs Review*, 2007, no. 1, p. 32.

[21] See: Liu, Hongwu (15 January 2007). China-Africa relations: an opportunity for Africa and the world. *People's Daily*, p. 7.

[22] Larkin, Bruce D. (1971). *China and Africa, 1949–1970: the foreign Policy of the People's Republic of China.* University of California Press, p. 83.

relations. We can say that from the perspective of inter-civilizational exchanges and equal dialogues the establishment of mutually-beneficial and respectful modern relationships between China and Africa after centuries of Western domination of global relations has special symbolic meaning. This is because on one hand the establishment of such relations reflects how basic outlines of global inter-civilizational exchanges and international relations are shifting from the "unidirectional" to the "multi-directional", and from the pattern of "center-periphery relations" to an "equal, web-like structure" where diverse civilizations engage each other on an equal footing and where individual civilizations have their respective independent voice. This is an indication that a new chapter of global history has already quietly come upon us.[23]

However, this transformation in the global structure will certainly be one that would take a long time to complete and one that would be filled with contradictions along the way. Various forces and interest structures in the existing world order will need to go through a long-term process to adapt to this transformation. In recent years, some Western political commentators and media outlets have already recognized the special impact that the development of China-Africa relations may bring to the global landscape in the future. However, the response of these parties has been crude and simplistic. They have arbitrarily accused China of practicing "neocolonialism" and "neo-imperialism" in Africa, and have claimed that China-Africa partnerships will "give rise to a structure where China colludes with the privileged class in Africa to extract interest and which may not benefit the local people."[24] These commentators and media outlets have claimed that Chinese aid to Africa has bred corruption in the politics of African countries and helped to strengthened the hand of authoritarian regimes in certain countries, etc.[25] Such bizarre, politicized distortions on normal international trade are actually a reflection of a deep-rooted sense of moral superiority on the part of certain Westerners.

For a few centuries, Africa has been the 'courtyard' or 'back garden' of Europe, where the wealthy of Europe would holiday or hunt. It is also a place for Europe to showcase its sense of superiority. There is in fact a certain "European-style Rashomonism" hidden in the minds of certain Europeans. Africa, previously colonialized by the Europeans, has always been dominated and influenced by Europe. This situation has not fundamentally changed even with the independence of African countries. In the eyes of certain Westerners, the swift development of China-Africa relations may lead Africa to 'deviate' from Europe's established framework and thus undermine Europe's traditional position in Africa. In fact, "the new trade and investment channels that have opened up between developing countries is a depressing

---

[23] Liu, Hongwu (2007). China-Africa relations: the significance of the history of civilizations. *West Asia and Africa*, 2007 (1).

[24] Fukushima, Kaori (5 November 2006). Europe and America Become More Wary of China's Foreign Relations with Africa. *Sankei Shimbun*.

[25] Kurlantzick, Joshua (2006). *Beijing's Safari: China Move into Africa and Its Implications for Aid, Development, and Governance*. Carnegie Endowment for International Peace, p. 1.

2.3 The Impact of the Swift Development of China-Africa ...

sight for the traditional powers."[26] Because of such anxieties and worries, they have shown an obvious bias and arrogance towards China's development and China-Africa relations from the very start. Very often, they practice double standards. In their view, the basis for Western trade and investment in Africa is in the free market and equality, etc., while Chinese trade and investment in Africa are described as the plundering of resources and the destruction of the environment.[27]

These individuals who have criticized China-Africa relations willy-nilly have not recognized that the development of China-Africa relations has, in some areas, already exceeded the scope of the traditional system that the West has completed dominated since the advent of modern times. A new global structure is gradually, but steadily emerging, and this new world cannot be fully comprehended using traditional knowledge and concepts.[28] Although Europe-Africa relations have existed for a few centuries already, and such relations do not appear to have brought any development to Africa. Objectively speaking, this has led to Africa looking towards other sources of developmental space and possibilities. China's rapid development in the last three decades and the pathways and policies it has chosen to realize this development have inspired African countries, which had begun to think on their own terms about the possible significance of China's experiences to Africa.[29] The West should slow down and reflect upon its traditional relations with Africa in response to Africa's need for this sort of change.

Dialogue on an equal footing and partnerships rooted in sincerity as well as the lack of conditions pertaining to domestic matters attached to aid have been the basic spirit and principles of China-Africa relations in the past few decades and the reasons for the long-lasting nature of such relations. Moeletsi Mbeki, the younger brother of South African president Thabo Mbeki told the *New York Times*: "China is not the first foreign power to arrive in Africa. However, the Chinese may have been the first power not to have self-righteously sponsored, guided, or conquered others. China and Africa resonate with each other on this point."[30] At a press conference at the 2006 FOCAC Beijing Summit, a reporter asked if there was a problem with Chinese colonialism in Africa. Ahmed Aboul-Gheit, foreign minister of Egypt (host for the next summit) answered forcefully: "There is no such thing as Chinese colonialism in Africa. In the next 50 years, and even in the 500 years, we will maintain this peaceful and friendly relationship. This is definitely not a colonial relationship."[31]

---

[26] Nel Walsh (29 October 2006). China the New Colonial Power in Africa? *The Guardian Online*.

[27] Kurlantzick, Joshua (2006). *Beijing's Safari: China Move into Africa and Its Implications for Aid, Development, and Governance*. Carnegie Endowment for International Peace, p. 3.

[28] Akin, C., and Kose, M.A. (2007). *Changing Nature of North–South Linkages: stylized facts and explanations*. International Monetary Fund.

[29] Kabukuru, W. (2006). Kenya: Look East My Son. *New African*, Jul 2006.

[30] http://www.focac.org/chn/wjjh/zyjh/default.htm.

[31] See: FOCAC web site, http://www.focac.org/chn/zyzl/hywj/.

2.4 Sino-Africa Development Relations Beneficial to Efforts to Resolve Global Developmental Issues Once and for All

What are the fundamental issues that mankind is facing? What are the true "universal ideals" of mankind? In our opinion, the complete resolution of all the developmental issues that developing nations are facing and the "reasonable delivery and acceptance outcome" in modern human development that such resolution would indicate as well as the building of a wealthy and harmonious modern world are the fundamental issues that confront contemporary man and also the "true universalist ideals" of the contemporary world. Thus, we say that history has not yet ended, and will continue to advance with the modern development of the nations of Asia and Africa.[32]

Overall, since the advent of modern times the rise of Western Europe and its entry into modern development ahead of the rest of the world did not resolve the world's developmental issues once and for all. From the perspective of world history, until the 1980s only the Western countries—that made up 20% of the world in terms of its population—had resolved the issue of wealth and modernization while 80% of the world outside of the West had remained impoverished and left behind. This is a global problem and also the root of various conflicts between men. However, it cannot be possible for Western countries to enjoy peace in a world where only they are wealthy. Wealth and peace should be shared by the world. Only when development has spread to all regions around the world and benefited all peoples can the world's problems be truly resolved. This is truly where hope for mankind lies.

This is precisely the significance of China-Africa cooperation and China-Africa development for the world. Although China's development has not been perfect and a number of issues remain, China is the world's largest developing nation while Africa is home to the largest number of developing countries. Hence, the development of China and African countries is a fundamental path for the future of mankind and thus bears global significance.

In the last ten years, developing economies have gradually become the most energetic parts of the global economy. According to the 2008 World Bank Development Report released by the World Bank on 11 April 2008, developing economies were on the rise, and developing nations' share of the global economy had grown from 36% in 2000 to 41% in 2008. In the past 30 years (1978–2007), the value of China-Africa trade grew a 100-fold from over USD700 million to USD73 billion. Between 2000 and 2007, exports to Asia as a proportion of total African exports rose from 14 to 28%. Asia-Africa trade ties were swiftly growing and being enhanced, and trade and investment with China, India, and Southeast Asia were swiftly becoming engines of growth for Africa. This was a "new dawn" for the African economy.[33]

---

[32] Liu, Hongwu (15 January 2007). China-Africa relations: an opportunity for Africa and the world. *People's Daily*.

[33] Akomolafe, Femi (2006). No One Is Laughing at the Asians Anymore. *New African*, No. 452, June 2006, pp. 48–50.

Perhaps all these are indications that a structural transformation is about to happen to global history, a transformation that will surely lead to profound changes in the global landscape and the characteristics of international relations in general. This is where the hope of Asian and African countries seeking to rise up lies, as well as Asia's and Africa's contribution to the world through their development. This is in fact what the advance of history looks like: countries and peoples rise and fall in their development, one after another. Historically, the nations of the East or Asian and African countries were also once at the forefront of history. That these countries have fallen behind in modern times does not mean that the possibility of another rise is forever lost.

In recent years, the idea of the "renaissance of the East" or the "renaissance of Asia and Africa" has already become a subject of serious discussion, and certain noteworthy concepts have also emerged. They include the BRIC countries (China, India, Russia and Brazil), the VISTA countries (Vietnam, Indonesia, South Africa, Turkey and Argentina), and the N11 countries (Egypt, Indonesia, the Philippines, Mexico, Vietnam, Turkey, Pakistan, South Korea, Bangladesh, Nigeria and Iran).[34] These, together with the original Five Dragons of East Asia, indicate that in the past 20 years developing economies had already begun what is a slow but long-term rise, a process that has accelerated in recent years. Sustained economic growth has even been seen on the African continent. In 2007, the African economy south of the Sahara grew as much as 6.1%. The truth is, although Africa is backward, it is also full of business opportunity. A study by the US Department of Commerce shows that since 1990 average rates of return for US multinational companies stood at 14% in Asia, 12% in Latin America, and as high as 33% in Africa.[35] High risk and high returns are the distinctive characteristics of the African economic environment and also what make this environment so enticing.

In January 2007, Harry G. Broadman, World Bank economic consultant for Africa, proposed in his book *Africa's Silk Road: China and India's New Economic Frontier* that a "new economic frontier" in history was emerging where Africa, India, and China are connected. In his opinion, the middle class in China and India was continuing to grow, and their purchasing power was also getting stronger. As such, their demand for products from Africa was also growing. And "this new Silk Road provides an excellent opportunity for Africa south of the Sahara to integrate into the global economy and to develop economically at a quicker pace. It is a rarely opportunity".

This "new economic frontier" is not limited to the traditional areas of trade and investment but in a more complex way it also involves a growth in power that would in turn lead to major structural changes in the world economy. Various statistics show that "the economic activity of China, India and Africa is opening up a new path for the African continent south of the Sahara. Africa has already become a

---

[34] Wang, Yusheng (2008). The swift rise of developing nations and the impact of such a rise. *Asia and Africa Review*, 2008 (2), 30.

[35] See U. S. Commerce Service: *Business Opportunity Events: Sub-Saharan Africa Trade Mission*, U. S. Department of Commerce, December 2007.

processor for primary products and a competitive provider of labor-intensive products and services for China and India. Compared to the economic relationship between Africa and Europe, which has remained unchanged over a long period, this is a major advance forward for Africa". "The prospects are bright for this South-South economic relationship. Both parties must resolve the issue of imbalance by means of reforms and overcome obstacles to continued development. This is in line with the interests of economic development in Africa as well as with the economic interests of China and India."[36]

We should say that in general currently Asian and African countries still lag significantly behind Western countries, and the renaissance of these countries is still a long way away. However, all great historical changes take place over a long time. In fact, in the last 20 years profound changes have been occurring with China, India, East Asia, Africa, and the entire Asian, African and Eastern world, which are gradually entering a new phase of developing and are rising up. Although these countries have developed to various extents and their rise appears to be still some time away, this process will eventually move forward. A report from US consultancy A.T. Kearney states that growth in capital flows, investment and trade is creating a market that spans the Indian Ocean and which involves multiple continents. The report dubs this market "Chimea", which comprises three parts: the technology, capital and demand for resources on the part of China and India ("Chi"), the resources and oil of the Middle East ("me"), and raw materials and opportunities of Africa ("a").[37] A 2007 by the International Monetary Fund also states that emerging developing countries like Brazil, China, India and South Africa have already begun to separate themselves from traditional developing countries and are growing quickly. The driving force behind their development is increasingly dependent on the strengthening relations between these nations and not on developed countries. According to Akin and Kose, this situation provides a reasonable economic explanation for the phenomenon that is the continued strengthening and enhancing of partnerships between emerging nations of the East like Africa and China.[38] Although currently the development and rate of development varies among Asian and African countries, and although a future rise appears far away and may even involve backslides and setbacks along the way, from the long-term perspective this is another "third wave" in the history of the modernization of the world. It is a "global wave" in the truly sense of the wave, one that moves our hearts. As this process advances, the structure and face of the world will certainly undergo fundamental changes. The swift development and enhancement of China-Africa relations in recent years can be thusly explained. From the perspective of an even long-term, strategic perspective: the historical advancement of this new model of China-Africa relations has but just begun, and the new characteristics of

---

[36] See Broadman, Harry G. (2006). *Africa's Silk Road: China and India's New Economic Frontier*. World Bank.

[37] Wessel, David (3 January 2008). The Rise Of South-South Trade. *The Wall Street Journal*.

[38] Akin, C., and Kose, M.A. (2007). *Changing Nature of North–South Linkages: stylized facts and explanations*. International Monetary Fund.

such relations may produce complex effects on both parties in the present and in the future. Currently, we can only see the tip of the iceberg, and when the growth wave that has already hit the developing nations in the twenty-first century finally reach Africa the picture will become even clearer.

Chapter 3
The Global Impact and Future Trajectory of China-Africa Partnerships

From the perspective of the progression of international relations globally, the development of contemporary relations between China and Asian and African countries will necessarily exceed the scope of the traditional system of international relations which has been dominated by the West in modern times in various key areas. In particular, a new type of world view and international relations will inevitably emerge. Conceptually and in principle, this sort of relations will reflect the history and culture inherent to the developing country as well as developmental needs and pathway choices that are both universal in modern development and distinct to the circumstances of the respective country or region. Of course, from the perspective of a long-term process, the establishment of this kind of new global relations requires both efforts from the developing nations of Asia and Africa as well as understanding and respect from developed countries. Only this way can we see global relations that are compatible with the changes that are happening today and in the true meaning of the term emerge.

In fact, behind the three decades of swift development in Sino-Asian and China-Africa relations is a complex story of the gradual acceleration of the Asian and African renaissance process and the impending structural and fundamental change in international relations worldwide.[1] History has not ended. It continues to move forward, and thus the tools with which we seek to explain history must keep up with the times.

---

[1] See: Liu, Hongwu (2008). Contemporary China-Africa relations and the wave of renaissance in Asian and African civilizations: questions on the special characteristics and significance of contemporary China-Africa relations. *World Economics and Politics*, 2008 (9), 29.

© Social Sciences Academic Press and Springer Nature Singapore Pte Ltd. 2021
H. Liu and J. Luo, *Sino-African Development Cooperation*, Research Series on the Chinese Dream and China's Development Path,
https://doi.org/10.1007/978-981-16-5481-7_3

3.1 "Out of Africa" or "Into Africa We Go"?

The significance of China-Africa relations for the contemporary system of global relations, is that impending structural change that will become clearer over time. Such a developmental process is precisely what has been neglected by those in Western-centric ways of thinking. This neglect exposes the blind spots in the Western world's knowledge of the contemporary development of Asian and African countries.

The characteristics of the impending new era, hidden in contemporary China-Africa relations, will not only be revealed to the world over time but also emerge further due to the frequent arrogance and interference shown by the Western world towards Asian and African countries. In the late 1980s and early 1990s, following the end of the Cold War, it was generally believed in the West that the course of history had ended at the best possible state for the West. The West even believed that the non-Western world had lost the possibility of making history and that what it was capable of doing was to reshape itself in the image of the West. Led by this belief, the Western world ignored Asia and Africa in general, and did not seek to think about, or look for, any autonomous potential for development or space for innovation that Asian and African countries might have. It was in this context that the Western world's blind spots *vis-à-vis* the Asian and African world accumulated over time. In the eyes of the West, the 1990s were the "lost decade" for the African continent. Sheer disregard and pessimism were the fundamental attitudes of the West towards Africa in the 1990s.

However, it was precisely in this environment of neglect by the West that a rare opportunity emerged for the strategic strengthening of China-Africa relations in the 1990s. China's influence in African grew over time.

First of all, China in the 1990s had expectations of Africa which were very different from those of the West, due to its specific strategic needs, emotional ties with Africa, and different cultural background and world view. China's understanding of Africa's future development prospects was imbued with a "judgment and confidence rooted in history". On the other hand, in the first part of the 1990s, Chinese diplomacy was at one time severely challenged and objectively speaking the country had to turn its focus to Africa as a result. Thus, the strategic value and significance of China-Africa relations in helping China improve its international situation and enhance its international position were accentuated. Just as Africa was gradually being marginalized by the Western world, China had turned its attention to Africa due to its specific and strategic needs. Beginning 1990, Chinese foreign ministers would make their first foreign visit of the year to an African country. The strategic significance of China-Africa relations is hence clear.

Second: as developing countries that are lagging behind in both economic and political terms, China and various African countries would naturally face certain economic and political issues, as well as problems with reform. However, with the West's arbitrary criticism of Asian and African countries on the matters of human rights and democracy, etc., as well as the West's obvious utilitarianism and double standards are but "curses" placed on developing countries, Asian and African countries have come to regard the West's invocation of universal principles like "human rights" and "democracy" as a "curse" upon developing countries by a discursively-dominant actor. Such behavior by Western countries underlines the opposing positions of developed countries and developing countries, and has also strengthened the basis for China-Africa strategic relations. We can say that the arrogance of Western countries has served to underline the strategic and historic value of China-Africa relations, which operate on the principles of equal standing and mutual respect.

Third: just as Western countries were regarding Africa's prospects with pessimism and swarmed to reduce their investments in Africa, China looked upon the development of Africa with a more positive and long-term outlook due to the strategic importance of African countries to China and thus its need to maintain its existing friendships with African countries. Since the mid-1990s, China has reformed its Africa aid policies and approaches using the "blood transfusion and hemopoiesis" (i.e., "teaching the man how to fish") it has developed with the impoverished peoples of its border regions. Aid was combined with trade and investment in ways appropriate to local conditions to form what is a new kind of development relationship between China and Africa, one that is "equal, mutually-beneficial, rational, and practical". China-Africa trade partnerships became enhanced over time as a result of this new impetus. By 1999, there were already over 800 Chinese enterprises and companies that were engaged in works contracting and trade and investment in more than 40 African countries. There were also nearly 400 trade and investment companies that had set up operations in Africa.[2] In the decade between 1997 and 2006, the value of China-Africa trade grew from less than RMB6 billion to RMB73 billion China-Africa. It is estimated that this figure will cross the RMB100 billion mark by 2010, making China Africa's second-largest trading partner after the US, and ahead of all the countries of Europe.[3]

Fourth, it is worth noting that with China and African countries all being developing countries, Chinese enterprises had entered Africa first in the 1990s by means of lower-level endeavors such as works contracting, labor service provision, and the transformation of the aid model. However, this process has special significance. This is because over the course of this process Chinese enterprises and companies were able to familiarize themselves with the economic and investment conditions of various African countries ahead of their competitors from other countries. They were thus able to win large shares of the infrastructural and engineering works markets in Africa, more than the Western countries, and earned themselves markets and strong reputations in Africa. For many Chinese multinational companies that had gained international success many years down the road, Africa was their entryway into the world market and where they learned to adapt to the fierce competition of the global economy. We are seeing from this process the expansive space and growth potential available within the scope of South-South cooperation.

---

[2] Ji, Peiding *ed*. (2000). *Fifty Years of Friendly Cooperation Between China and Africa*. World Knowledge Publishing House, p. 99.

[3] Thompson, Drew (2005). China's Soft Power in Africa: From the 'Beijing Consensus' to Health Diplomacy. *China Brief*, Vol. 5, No. 21.

Fifth: It was precisely in this period that characteristics distinctive to the era in China-Africa relations emerged. Such relations transcended the ideological binds of the Cold War era and advanced towards practical objectives of economic development and the betterment of the people's livelihoods. China-Africa relations became increasingly practical, rational, and forward-looking. In fact, when certain Western political commentators and media outlet discuss various empty principles through the distorted lens of their ideological world and arbitrarily accuse China of "neo-colonialism" in Africa in line with outdated attitudes, China was already acting with African countries on new shared ideals and visions. A willingness to move away from outdated ideological principles, a forward-looking orientation, and a focus on the practical are key reasons for the vitality and continued advancement of contemporary China-Africa relations. They are also the cumulative result of experiences from the advance of contemporary China-Africa relations, experiences that we should continue to learn from.

3.2 Resolving Developmental Issues and Universal Human Values

In the past 30 years, as China-Africa relations developed, much experience in multiple areas has been accrued. Such relations also bear lessons on many fronts for the structural transformation of the existing global system.

Overall, the West has had relations with Africa for a few centuries. This, as well as the time such relations could be considered as "modern", date back longer than the relations established between contemporary China and Africa. However, the West did not appear to have brought much development to Africa in the modern sense of the world, from the brutal exploitation of colonial times to the "benevolent" aid that was granted to African countries following decolonialization. However, China's rapid development over the last 30 years and the development pathways and policies that it had chosen together with the changes and outstanding effects brought by Chinese aid to Africa have inspired African countries. The intelligentsia and political leaders of Africa began to think about the possible significance of China's experiences to Africa in their very own ways.[4] The West should, in response to Africa's needs for such change, look back and reflect on its existing relations with Africa, including the possibility of breaking out of the so-called Western-centric "corset of Westphalia" and think on historical terms in order to truly understand and deal with the changes that are occurring with the contemporary global system as well as the innovations and contributions made by developing countries over the course of this change. However, generally speaking, to date the world of Western theory has not responded in a perceptive and strong manner.

The structural transformation in relations between developed countries and developing countries is a process that is full of contradictions. Developed countries would

---

[4] Kabukuru, Wanjohi (2006). Kenya: Look East My Son. *New African*, July 2006, p. 26.

require a long period to time to adjust to such a change, and if they were to cling on to their antiquated beliefs then they would find it even more challenging to adapt to this change. For a long time, the Western world's neglect of the history of, and contemporary changes occurring in, Asian and African countries or even the Eastern world has caused the Western world to accumulate many "blind spots" or even "blind zones" in its knowledge. Some Westerners are still completely ignorant of the changes that have occurred in the Asian and African world in the last few decades. Arrogance and bias have caused them to lack even an iota of sensitivity to strengthening China-Africa relations and the rejuvenation of Asia and Africa. Hence, Western countries were shocked when China-Africa relations finally reached a stage of swift development and enhancement following a long time of engagement, and when China's influence in Africa naturally presented itself, and they did not know how to respond. Some members of the Western media started using 'fashionable' headlines such as "China Appears Out of the Blue in Europe" and "China Takes Sudden Interest in Africa's Oil and Other Resources" to express the Western perspective on China-Africa relations and to define such relations. Of course, in the eyes of some Westerners the swift development of China-Africa relations may lead Africa to 'deviate' from the framework and structure established by the West and thus has an impact on Europe's traditional position in Africa. Because of such worries and anxieties, Westerners have shown a clear bias against China's development and against China-Africa relations.[5] This indicates that the a lack of knowledge about modern developments in the Asian and African world is a prevalent problem among Western intelligentsia, and that there is an entrenched sense of moral superiority within the Western body of knowledge, in the area of history.

History is a process of continuous evolution and change; the tides of history roll forward unceasingly. To paraphrase Tang-Dynasty poet Du Fu, "even as we look across time, across a thousand autumns, the sense of melancholy remains the same". Any understanding of history must be an open one that is empathetic, even "synesthetic" to the experiences of the period under study.[6] The individual makes but a brief appearance in the massive unfolding scroll that is history, and thus is in no position to make overreaching claims of "the end of history". Furthermore, the civilizations of Asia and Africa go back a long time and are highly complex. To understand the structure and nature of these civilizations is not an easy task, and at the same time the modern renaissance and development of these civilizations will also be a highly complex and diverse affair. Certainly, we will not see a single model of development, and neither will nations be able to simply transplant an existing developmental model from elsewhere. Over the course of self-molding and history-shaping in Asian and African countries, there will necessarily be breakthroughs in a number of key areas as well as developments that will not fit within the limits of the traditional system of international relations dominated by the West in recent history.

---

[5] Kurlantzick, Joshua (2006). *Beijing's Safari: China Move into Africa and Its Implications for Aid, Development, and Governance*. Carnegie Endowment for International Peace, p. 1.

[6] Please refer to: Liu, Hongwu (2006). Academic interest and ideological factors in the discipline of international relations. *World Economics and Politics*, 2006 (7).

New worldviews and models of international relations rooted in Asian and African civilizations and historical evolution will necessarily emerge. These new types of relationships and principles will reflect the historical and cultural characteristics of Asian and African countries, and also developmental needs and pathway choices that are both universal in modern development and specific to the needs of Asian and African civilizations.

What are the fundamental issues that mankind is facing? What are the true "universal ideals" of mankind? In our opinion, the complete resolution of all the developmental issues that developing countries are facing and the "reasonable delivery and acceptance outcome" in modern human development that such resolution would indicate the building of a wealthy and harmonious modern world are the fundamental issues that confront contemporary man and also the "true universalist ideals" of the contemporary world. Thus, we say that history has not yet ended, and will continue to advance with the modern development of the countries of Asia and Africa.

Overall, since the advent of modern times the rise of Western Europe and its entry into modern development ahead of the rest of the world did not resolve the world's developmental issues once and for all. From the perspective of world history, until the 1980s only the Western countries—that made up 20% of the world in terms of its population—had resolved the issue of wealth and modernization while 80% of the world outside of the West had remained impoverished and left behind. This is a global problem and also the root of various conflicts between men. However, it cannot be possible for Western countries to enjoy peace in a world where only they are wealthy. Wealth and peace should be shared by the world. Only when development has spread to all regions around the world and benefited all peoples can the world's problems be truly resolved. This is truly where hope for mankind lies.

As the global status of Asian and African countries rises, the transformation of global history will also accelerate. Economic relations between Asia and Africa are swiftly strengthening and growing, and trade with, and investment by, China, India and Southeast Asia are becoming the 'engine' of economic development in Africa. This is a "new dawn" for the African economy.[7] Although currently the development and rate of development varies among Asian and African countries, and although a future rise appears far away and may even involve backslides and setbacks along the way, from the long-term perspective this is another "third wave" in the history of the modernization of the world. It is a "global wave" in the truly sense of the wave, one that moves our hearts. As this process advances, the structure and face of the world will certainly undergo fundamental changes. The swift development and enhancement of China-Africa relations in recent years can be thusly explained.

In truth, as China-Africa relations swiftly develop Africa's marginalized position in the contemporary global system is also being improved. The world now sees that Africa is not an insignificant player that only requires aid but a player that can bring wealth and opportunity to the world. Globally, a number of global powers like the EU nations, South Korea, Japan, the US, and Russia have 'made returns to Africa' by

---

[7] Akomolafe, Femi (2006). No One Is Laughing at the Asians Anymore. *New African*, No. 452, June 2006, pp. 48–50.

means of establishing various cooperation fora and holding summits involving heads of state with African countries. Africa's position in the world is being elevated, and this is exactly what the African countries look forward to. This will bring to Africa, as well as the world, a new opportunity. At the same time, we should also see that while the major nations were in conflict with each other in Africa during the Cold War, this time round they are returning to Africa with a focus on investment, trade and market development and by means of multilateral economic partnerships and interactions. Hence, China and the West may establish a new intersection in interests in the joint promotion of economic development in Africa. There is also the possibility of new multilateral, win–win mechanisms between China, Africa, and Western countries.[8]

We should say that any advance made by China, a developing country that is home to one-fifth of the global population, in beating poverty and in the area of development is a contribution to the world. The development of the African economy is precisely an opportunity for China. Thus, in this sense if contemporary economic development in China can bring opportunity to Africa on the basis of mutual benefit, and if contemporary economic development in China can stimulate, or lead to the rejuvenation of African economies, and if the Chinese economy can provide African countries with the possibility of, and opportunities for, development in a mutually-beneficial manner, then the idea of the "China threat" as trumpeted by Western media will collapse upon itself, and Western accusations of China practicing neo-colonialism in Africa will become baseless. It will be a major contribution made by the ancient country of China to the world in the twenty-first century on its path to self-rejuvenation. After all, China is an ancient civilizational power with its own history, culture, and civilizational structure. Hence, although China would certainly adhere to certain traditional principles of modernization along its path of modern rejuvenation and development, and see changes to its civilization in terms of the market economy and democratic politics, this is not a process that is fully in the Western mold. In terms of the state of development of various countries around the world, the developed countries in the West are ahead of Asian and African countries in many respects. This is naturally an indubitable truth. However, when we consider the tremendous gaps in development around the world and the complexity of issues that various countries are facing we see that the Western model may not be the most suitable model for African countries in their current stage of development.

Asian and African countries in contemporary times are transitioning from traditional social structures to a modern structure. This process of modernization is one that is even more complex and difficult than what the Western countries have previously gone through. No outside power can replace the independent efforts of Asian and African countries to control this process and its trajectory. Even if Western countries are advocating for their systems and institutions out of good intentions they should understand the principle of not forcing choices upon others. Making demands of others, the use of sanctions or boycotts, or even the use of military force often bring about catastrophic conflicts and enmity that have long-lasting negative

---

[8] See: Liu, Hongwu (15 January 2007). China-Africa relations: an opportunity for Africa and the world. *People's Daily*, p. 7.

effects. On the other hand, the reasonableness of the "China experience" or "China pathway" lies in that it is gradual process of reform that aims to enhance the people's basic quality of life and to alleviate poverty. It is not a swift demolition of the existing system but a step-by-step reform of the system. Such reform takes place over stages, with the simpler tasks tackled ahead of the more complex ones. Change is implemented from the periphery to the core. This way, the foundation for reform is broadened, and costs, reduced. The way forward becomes smoother.

Africa today needs governments that are committed to development and which are able to implement and advance such development policies. This is a more attractive aspect of the China model for Africa. More importantly, the honest dialogues and equal treatment accorded by China, which does not attach any political conditions [to its interactions] are attractive on the emotional level for African countries which have been humiliated in the past and which are today still poor and weak.[9] In this regard, some Western media outlets believe that "the China model is not perfect. However, it has already enriched the world's political enquiry and knowledge about how to eradicate poverty and has provided countries all over the world with more choices and policies. As long as the American model cannot produce the desired outcomes the China model will only become more attractive for the poor nations of the world."[10]

African countries understand China's significance to Africa in their own ways. Of course, Africa will not simply transplant China's "model" or "pathway"; however, they seek to benefit from China's development experience at the same time. At the FOCAC Beijing Summit, it was proposed that China and Africa conduct exchanges in the areas of governance and development experience and work on the building of their respective national strengths. This proposal is itself an expression of the fact that China-Africa cooperation had entered a more innovative period with more specific and practical plans in place.

For a long time the relative weakness of, and poor government performance in, certain African countries have been structural factors that limited the development of Africa. On the other hand, China's strengths and the government's determination to develop the economy are important reasons for the swift development of contemporary China and an issue that African countries are paying a great deal of attention to. We can say that the so-called "China experience" or "China pathway" has drawn much attention. In addition, the Chinese have also developed much political wisdom with matters such as the handling of the complex relations between various peoples, the handling of religious relations, and the development of border regions. Such experiences may also be significant for young African countries that have long been mired in civil conflict. In fact, in recent years China has also found the opportunities to enter the global market and enhance its ability to adapt to this market in the process

---

[9] A hundred years ago, a multitude of problems, including poverty and weakness, had brought China to her knees. At that time, Sun Yat-sen had told his countrymen that all countries that treated China as an equal and with sincerity were friends and brothers of the Chinese people who could be trusted.

[10] The Charm of the China Model, *International Herald Tribune*, 2 November 2006. Excerpted from *Reference News*, 6 November 2006.

partnering Africa in the areas of trade and investment. Through China-Africa relations, a growing number of people are recognizing that the innovative developmental partnerships between China and African countries, which have brought beneficial development and shared prosperity to both sides, have already become vivid testaments to the fact that China's peaceful development is an opportunity for the world, and not a threat.

3.3 A Re-acquaintance with the Historic Civilizations of Asia and Africa

To tackle the global changes that are happening today, man will have to transcend certain biases and attitudes that have been formed over the course of decades of East–West conflicts and North–South differences, as well as make full use of the ways of thinking, wisdom and knowledge available to man and seek to understand the future development of man from a new long-term perspective.

In fact, since the advent of modern times, certain Western thinkers have sought to transcend the limited knowledge and experiences of Western society to better understand Eastern society, including classic thinkers in the Marxist/Engels tradition. In the course of formulating his full theoretical account of the various stages of economic development in human society, Karl Marx had already sensed that societies of the East, like China and India, could not be accounted for fully using theory rooted in the social and historical context of the West. Hence, at one point he considered the option of proposing a theory of economic structure or production for the "Asiatic" model in addition to his descriptions of production in primitive, slave, feudalistic, and capitalist societies.[11] Marx attempted to use the "Asiatic" concept to express the results of his reflections on the characteristics of the ancient nations and civilizations of the East. Although subsequently interpretations of what the "Asiatic" form is have differed, nevertheless we can sense that Marx had seen many differences between Eastern and Western societies, and that more theories and tools would be needed to explain different histories and civilizations. In his later years, Marx also recognized the significance of this issue. He spent quite a bit of time on studying various works in anthropology and ethnology, and made quite a bit of ethnographical notes in the hopes of gaining greater understanding on the issue of the peoples and society of the backward peoples of Asia and Africa. As such, Marx has always been respected by later generations for his spirit of scientific endeavor.[12]

---

[11] Marx, Karl (1972). *Anthology of the Writings of Karl Marx*. Beijing: People's Publishing House, p. 38.

[12] Krader, Lawrence, *ed*. *Marx's Ethnographical Notebooks*. See He, S. (2007). *Introduction to Social and Cultural Anthropology*. Kunming: Yunnan University Press, Chapter One.

We should say that in the Western world of knowledge efforts to study and understand the East and the African continent have been a sustained cultural phenomenon. This is a reflection of the spirit and tradition of openness in Western ways of thinking, and this is a tradition that the Western world of knowledge should further propagate.

However, due to cultural differences and the fact that the West had developed ahead of the rest of the world, since the advent of modern times the Western world's knowledge of the history, culture, and current circumstances of the East or of Asian and African countries have been somewhat lacking and erroneous in areas. This, together with a sense of moral superiority and self-centeredness that is sometimes covert and sometimes more overt, has further affected the West's understanding of the Asian and African world. The studies of Asia and Africa and of Eastern societies undertaken by those thinkers and academics, and the results of such studies, did not become part of the mainstream of Western knowledge and ways of thinking. The influence of these studies has always remained comparatively limited. In particular, since the end of the Cold War, it became increasingly clear that the dominant position of the West consisted of a closed-off system of theories and beliefs based on solely the historical experience of the West. During this period, in general, both so-called liberal and conservative theories, or theories that have been prefixed with the terms "neo-" or "post-" to indicate changes to existing theories, were the products of ways of thinking rooted in the experiences and discourse of the West. In recent years, as the non-Western world developed, the blind spots in the West's knowledge of the Asian and African world have also been broadening due to the arrogance of those possessing a sense of moral superiority, the historical bias against the nations of the East., and a kind of self-aggrandizing "myth" of "Western-style democracy". They have applied highly simplistic labels—like curse symbols—onto a diverse array of world civilizations and systems, such as "democratic nation", "totalitarian nation", and "rogue state", and have made use of these labels and their discursive dominance to arbitrarily categorize, rule over, and sentence others. Thus, the great diversity in various matters around the world has been simplistically categorized into a poor-fitting ideological frame.

In the face of growing diversity in the development of mankind and civilizational creation, it would appear that the West has lost the reason, tolerance and spirit of reform that have allowed it to be at the forefront of history once upon a time. From the perspective of a bystander, such a fall of the times and degradation rooted in arrogance is such an unfortunate process. We must recognize that history in itself will not "end" simply because a pronouncement of such by some. However, the outstanding tradition of understanding the outside world through rationality in the Western world of knowledge and the growth and development of Western wisdom due to what was once an open embrace of the outside world may "end" because of this arrogance and bias towards, and neglect of the outside world. Now, as reform continues apace in the Asian and African world, the Western world should also think deeply about change in the West, because only this way can the West be better able to adapt to this changing world.

3.4 The East's View of History, and the Future Trajectory of China

Today, major changes are happening in the world. China's relations with the world are also undergoing major adjustments. The arrival of this era of significant change demands that man adopt a strategic, open and historically-minded mindset towards history and reality. Man's understanding of China-Africa relations cannot be divorced from China's historical traditions and realistic needs. Generally speaking, China's choice of the strategy of peaceful development will be a long-term national policy. This is not due to pressure from the outside world but a proactive choice by China. It is also a natural extension of Chinese history. If the Western world can better understand the characteristics of Chinese civilization it will be better able to get along with the growing power that is China?

In recent years, as China continues to develop, the West has displayed much anxiety about, and voiced much criticism of, China-Africa relations. In fact, these criticisms are a reflection of the blind spots and misconceptions that the West has with regard to China's historical traditions and reality, and show that the West lacks what Barry Buzan calls an open understanding of world history.

China has actually been a power for thousands of years, and has consistently maintained the experiences and wisdom of a power. China's traditional wisdom believes that an adherence to the strategy of peaceful development and foreign relations will be of greater help to the existence of a power.

Over the long course of history, the Chinese have recognized that a higher economic social cost is needed to maintain the existence of a power compared to a smaller nation. As such, in the eyes of the Chinese people the rational adherence to the 'good neighbor' strategy within the established international system is a better approach than expansion and hegemony in terms of maintaining and developing the historical existence of a power. It is the way of the legitimate king (benevolent rule) and not the way of the tyrant (conquest) that aids the power in continued existence and in interactions with the rest of the world.

Second: before the advent of modernity, for a long time in East Asia there had been an international system centered on China. This system had accumulated the world historical experience in how countries big and small and different peoples can get along harmoniously and maintain inter-state stability and relations. Today, the policy of autonomous rule for China's minority peoples, its political system where different peoples live together harmoniously, and its long-standing foreign policy of good neighborliness, peaceful development and non-interference in the domestic affairs of another country are all the culmination of its historic experiences in this long-standing international system in East Asia. Such a heritage and political experiences continue to be highly vital in the globalized world of today.

Today, the international environment of developing countries is becoming increasingly intertwined with the matter of their domestic development. Developmental partnerships between developing countries, emerging economies, and developed countries are becoming increasingly important, and at the same time will also become increasingly complex. We would need to use the perspectives and methods of academic study to move towards practical developmental experiences in Asia and Africa, and away from the existing situation that is dominated by Western theories. We will have to formulate new theories from the changes we are seeing in Chinese society and the swift development of China-Africa relations, and more importantly, we will have to distill wisdom from the characteristics of Chinese history and civilization. These will be China's new contributions to the world.

In the early twentieth century, on the subject of Chinese history and development Liang Qichao stated that China was "China's China" before the country was unified by the Qin Dynasty over two thousand years ago, and that in the more than two thousand years up till the Opium Wars, China was "an Asian China". China post-Opium Wars, he said, was "a global China". Although this comment was not made in direct reference to China's foreign policy, it summarizes succinctly what China's external and foreign-relations environment was like in the span of over three millennia.

In fact, the examination changes in various countries and in the global system from the perspective of world history to gain a deeper understanding of the necessity of the fundamental nature of international relations is a must for the East and the right choice for Western countries. Just as former UK Prime Minister Tony Blair commented: "Now we will have to come to terms with a world in which the power is shared with the Far East. I wonder if we quite understand what that means, we whose culture (not just our politics and economies) has dominated for so long. It will be a rather strange, possibly unnerving experience."[13]

In this respect, and from the historical perspective, China's efforts in opening up to the rest of the world and its efforts in joining international society over the last thirty years are exactly the process by which an ancient Chinese society in East Asia has joined international society today under modern historical conditions. This process is an integral part of the development of world history, a development that cannot be reversed, both in terms of social transformation and social development. No matter it be before or since the beginning of reform and opening up, and no matter if the path taken is a winding, difficult one or one that will eventually open up to a broad and smooth highway, China's efforts are fundamentally in order to realize the call of the era for China to become a "global China".

Insofar as 'Chinese characteristics' are concerned, such a call and efforts are fundamentally pacifist in nature. The strategic concept of peaceful development advocated by Deng Xiaoping and the corresponding theories of international relations are thus also fundamentally imbued with the ways of thinking and theories characteristic of Chinese history and the times. If we are to borrow the international-relations concepts of realism and constructivism, we can also say that China's strategy of peaceful development represents the realism and constructivism of China's international relations on the philosophical level.

---

[13] Blair, Tony (28 Aug 2008). Helping China embrace the future through dialogue and cooperation. *The Wall Street Journal*.

The process of China's development and entry into international society must necessarily be a peaceful one. Practical foreign-relations experience over the span of thirty years and in the course of China's peaceful development has yielded the outlines of a body of international relations theories and theories of world history with distinctly Chinese characteristics. During this period, China has discarded step-by-step the ignorance and narrow-mindedness that had previously marked its understanding of itself and the world, and worked towards a shift from "an Asian China" to "a global China". At the same time, China has remained committed to upholding the excellent heritage that has been created and accumulated through inter-state interactions between ancient China and other Asian societies. This heritage, added to the international system of today, is a part of the modern Chinese and Asian nations as well as of the international system. Over the course of this process, China's politicians, diplomats and scholars are creating theories of international relations for a new era in Chinese history through international relations and learning, and by means of the re-evaluation of historical experiences and efforts of the times.

We have reason to believe that no matter it be academic exchanges or the creation of development, in terms of the ways of thinking on peaceful development the China of today can stand to learn even more from global society. Conversely, global society can also learn more about, and better understand, China through this process. We are optimistic and confident about this process.

Generally speaking, the developmental issues remain unresolved in the world today. However, development is already a global development and the political and economic conflicts between the countries of the global North and South caused by development and unbalanced development are also gradually becoming new global foci of conflict. The truth is, today, with active reforms underway, the international environment of developing countries is becoming increasingly intertwined with the matter of their domestic development. Developmental partnerships between developing countries, emerging economies, and developed countries are becoming increasingly important, and at the same time will also become increasingly complex. In the fact of such challenges, Asian and African countries have no choice but to continue with their reforms and to move forward. However, more importantly, they need new theories and wisdom, which of course includes Western experiences and the correct principles found in existing Western theories but more critically new theories based on the experiences and realistic needs of Asian and African countries undergoing the process of national rejuvenation.

China-Africa partnerships and developments in China-Africa relations over the last 30 years have already brought to the modern development of mankind powerful experiences and sentiments of the new century. The real-life basis for theoretical innovation has already appeared. In terms of Chinese theories of international relations and development, as well as even more fundamental theories of world history and global economics, Chinese scholars will also need to organize their ways of thinkings and theories based on the experiences and sentiments accrued from the practice of contemporary China-Africa relations. In order to do that, first of all we must shift our study methods and approaches, perspectives, and points of focus from what is a discourse dominated by Western theories towards a way of seeing that is rooted in the developmental experiences of Asia and Africa and which takes into account the global changes that are happening. With this shift, we will be able to pay greater attention to the changes that are currently occurring within Chinese society and to real-life trends in the rapidly-developing relations between China and other Asian and African countries. Only this way will we be able to provide ways of thinking, wisdom, and knowledge tools with stronger explanatory power and which are more forward-looking with respect to China's foreign-relations experience in contemporary times.

Chapter 4
Chinese Aid to African Countries: Evolution, Motives, and Outcomes

Chinese aid to African countries has always had an important and special place in contemporary Chinese policies towards Africa.[1] We should say that mutual aid based on sincerity, equal standing and mutual trust have always been at the core of China-Africa strategic cooperation. This sort of sincere mutual assistance and support is precisely what has helped China-Africa relations to continually develop over more than 50 years. It is an important link that has kept China-Africa relations going. Due to developmental differences between China and various African countries, both sides have had different expectations of each other in different periods. Furthermore, the types of aid provided, the aid approaches, and aid foci have also changed over time. In terms of Chinese aid to Africa, in the past 50 years we have seen clear changes over different stages. These changes are due to complex demands of the time and objective needs. They have also been measures that were necessary to enhance aid outcomes and the strategic significance of Chinese aid to Africa. In our opinion, if we are to closely examine the changes in Chinese aid to Africa over the last 50 years as well as the motivations, conditions, and outcomes of these changes, we will be able to establish aid policies that better can better meet Africa's needs. Doing so will have special and critical significance for the new China-Africa strategic partnership of the twenty-first century.[2]

---

[1] Here, we are referring broadly to aid to foreign parties, including economic aid, humanitarian aid, and aid in areas such as talent cultivation and security and public order.

[2] See Luo, Jianbo (2007). Changes in Chinese aid to Africa over various stages, and the significance of such aid. *West Asia and Africa*, 2007 (11).

4.1 Changes in Developmental Concerns over Time, and Changes in Chinese Aid to Africa over Various Stages

Some things in China-Africa relations have changed over the last 50 years, while others have remained unchanged. Among the things that have remained unchanged include mutual empathy, mutual respect, and mutually-beneficial arrangements rooted in sincerity. As for the things that have changed, they include the policy choices for mutual assistance, implementation approaches, and matters of focus. These changes, however, have been implemented in tandem with the times and are themselves subject to constant adjustments. This sort of adjustments and changes is actually part of a multi-stage evolution of China-Africa relations over 50 years, itself an adaptation to the course of cultural rejuvenation in China and Africa. In terms of Chinese aid to Africa, prior to the 1980s the emphasis was placed on aiding the liberation of the African peoples. Starting from 1980s, the emphasis shifted to social and economic development in Africa.

Africa had entered the diplomatic radar of the newly-minted People's Republic of China as a political ally. Between the 1950s and 1970s, China had faced a very tough and dangerous international environment. First, it was the subject of blockades and sieges by a Western camp led by the US; then, it became engaged with severe conflicts with the Soviet Union. At one point, China was facing two enemies at once. During the same period, Africa was seeing the peak of its people's liberation movements. Colonialists old and new attempted to prolong their rule in Africa through political, economic, and even military means. As such, the struggle and contestation between colonialism and African nationalism was a key part of African politics in this period. With its shared historical experiences and keen empathy with Africa, the People's Republic of China focused its diplomatic efforts on supporting national independence movements in Africa. Together with the African countries, China sought to resist imperialism, colonialism, tyranny and racism on the international stage. For China, Africa was a key ally in the "united international front". "Africa was regarded by China as the global forward position in the struggle against capitalism and imperialism, and was also regarded as a key middle ground between China and the Soviet Union in the 1960s and 1970s".[3] At the peak of the independence wave in Africa in the 1960s, Chairman Mao Zedong met with a stream of friends and organization heads from Asia, Africa and Latin America as a sign of the Chinese people's "full empathy with, and support for, the African peoples' courageous fight against imperialism and colonialism".[4] On 28 November 1964, Chairman Mao Zedong even took the effort to issue the *Declaration of Support for the People of Congo against the American Invasion*. The People's Republic of China and African countries came together because of their shared historical experiences and mission.

---

[3] Moumoni, Guillaume (2006). Domestic transformations and changes in China-Africa relations. *International Politics Quarterly*, 2006 (4), 44.

[4] Xie, Yixian ed. (1988). *A History of China's Foreign Relations (The People's Republic of China, 1949–1979)*. Henan People Publishing House, pp. 306–307.

4.1 Changes in Developmental Concerns over Time, and Changes in Chinese …

China had provided Asian and African countries with economic aid against this backdrop.[5] During his visit to Africa between December 1963 and February 1964, Premier Zhou Enlai proposed in succession the "Five Principles" of relationship development between China and Africa/Arabic countries and the "Eight Principles" of economic and technical aid to external parties. The formulation and statement of these principles signaled that China's policy on aid to Africa had been formally established. The "Five Principles" are:

1. Support for the efforts on the part of various African peoples against imperialism and colonialism both old and new, and for their fight for, and maintenance of, national independence;
2. Support for the efforts of various African governments in the policy of neutrality and non-alliance;
3. Support for the efforts on the part of various African peoples to realize their hopes for national unity in the way of their choosing;
4. Support for the peaceful resolution of conflicts between African countries by means of negotiation; and
5. Advocacy for respect for the sovereignty of African countries by all countries and opposition to invasion and interference by any party.

The Eight Principles of foreign aid are:

1. The Chinese government shall provide African countries with aid in adherence to the principles of equality and mutual benefit, and does not regard such aid as benevolent, one-way grants;
2. Aid from China does not come with any conditions. China strictly respects the national sovereignty of the aid recipient;
3. The Chinese government seeks to extend loan terms when necessary to minimize burden on the aid recipient;
4. Aid from the Chinese government is meant to help the aid recipient to move towards economic independence and independent development;
5. Projects for which the Chinese government is providing aid should require small investments and show results quickly so that the aid-receiving country would be able to grow its income;
6. The Chinese government shall provide the best equipment and material resources that it produces;

---

[5] On 21 June 1956, the Chinese and Cambodian governments announced the signing of a joint communiqué on the matter of economic aid. This marked the beginning of China's efforts in providing generous financial aid to nationalist countries. On 28 June the same year, Zhou Enlai said at the National People's Congress: "China is a newly-liberated country. Our economy is still very backward, and economically speaking we are not yet fully independent. Hence, we have very limited economic strength. We conduct economic cooperation with other nations mainly by means of trade. However, as we recognize the critical role economic independence plays in reinforcing political independence, while engaging in economic building we are also willing to contribute however little we can to aid the economic development of other nations." See: Xie, Yixian *ed.* (1988). *A History of China's Foreign Relations (The People's Republic of China, 1949–1979)*. Henan People Publishing House, pp. 239–240.

7. The Chinese government would guarantee that personnel of the aid-receiving country will be able to master all technologies provided as part of technical aid; and
8. Experts sent to the aid-receiving country from China may only enjoy benefits that are provided to local experts and are not eligible for any special treatment.

The "Five Principles" and the "Eight Principles" were major foreign-policy declarations by the People's Republic of China which clearly expressed China's determination to stand together with the African and Asian countries as well as its diplomatic stand and political determination for national liberation in the Third World.

Despite difficulties in its own economic situation, China still provided significant amounts of aid selflessly to African countries. Between 1956 and 1977, China provided African countries with aid totaling more than USD2.476 billion in value, or 58% of China's foreign aid.[6] These aid programs were in the areas of agriculture, agricultural product processing, utilities, transport and logistics, culture and education, and health, etc. The most classic example of such aid given by China to Africa would be the 1860-km-long Tanzam Railway that took six years to build. The building of the railway provided strong support to the independence and liberation efforts of the African people in southern Africa and at the same time demonstrated China's sincere determination in, and ability to, help the nations of Africa. The building of the railway expanded China's influence in Africa and enhanced China's reputation among Third World nations and even globally. As a symbol, the Tanzam Railway is the "Road of Friendship" between China and Africa, which has "closely linked China and Africa, a country and region respectively, both seeking their own independent position on the international stage".[7] Chinese aid to Africa proved that China fulfilled its promises to the people of Africa, and helped China to establish itself as a country that is sincere in its wishes to help Africa, and which shares both weal and woe with the continent. The positive impact of such aid has facilitated the development of China-Africa relations to the present day.

By the 1980s, China and Africa were facing significant different international environments and historical development scenarios. With the gradual easing of Cold War tensions between the US and the Soviet Union and the eventual end of the Cold War, the Asian and African countries were no longer confined to making a choice between two major camps. Their diplomatic space and space on the international stage were greatly broadened. With the threat of another world war dimmed, peace and development became the hallmark characteristics of the period. Countries around the world shifted their attention to competing with each other in terms of overall national strength rooted in economic and technological capabilities. In line with the dramatic changes in the international environment, China made timely changes to the national development strategy, and opened itself up to the outside world while strengthening domestic reforms. In addition, it also took proactive steps

---

[6] Li, Anshan (2006). On changes and transformations in China's policies towards Africa. *West Asia and Africa*, 2006 (8), 11–20.

[7] Stith, Charles (2006). China-Africa relations: a brief evaluation from the American perspective. *International Politics Quarterly*, 2006 (4), 21–31.

to make use of the international environment to further its reforms and development. In Africa, as Namibia became independent in 1990 and a new South Africa emerged in 1994, the people of Africa finally saw the end of a chapter marked by the historical and political mission of realizing national liberation. The fight against imperialism, colonialism, and racism became a thing of the past. These already-independent countries began to prioritize economic and social development in order to jumpstart their backward and stagnant economies and to mitigate what was their growing marginalization in the course economic globalization. It was against such a background that African countries hoped to strengthen their mutually-beneficial partnerships with China and to obtain from China the capital, technologies, and developmental experience needed for economic and social development. Hence, with historic changes as well as changes in the respective circumstances of China and Africa, the strategic basis for China-Africa cooperation gradually shifted from the struggle against imperialism, colonialism and tyranny (for which mutual support was given) to a shared pursuit of peace and development and the joint maintenance of the developmental rights of developing nations. Practicality and mutual benefit became characteristics of China-Africa relations.[8]

Chinese aid to Africa has been a key component of Chinese diplomacy towards Africa, and the historical mission and requirements of such aid have undergone changes. The focus has shifted from the provision of support for African peoples seeking liberation prior to the 1980s to peace and development in Africa. In 1982, the Chinese premier announced during a visit to Africa China's "Four Principles" for China-Africa technical cooperation: mutual benefit and equality, a focus on the practical outcome, the use of a diverse array of means, and joint development. The Four Principles became the basic principles underlying China-Africa trade cooperation, especially Chinese aid to Africa, in this period. In early 2006, the Chinese government released its China's Africa Policy, stating "China supports African countries' endeavor for economic development and nation building" and "supporting African countries' efforts to enhance capacity building, China will work together with Africa in the exploration of the road of sustainable development". The Chinese government also stated that "proceeding from the fundamental interests of both the Chinese and African peoples", it would work hard to "establish and develop a new type of strategic partnership with Africa, featuring political equality and mutual trust, economic win–win cooperation and cultural exchange".[9] The FOCAC Beijing Summit held in November the same year turned the "new China-Africa strategic partnership" into a key strategic understanding between China and African countries. Once again, China clearly stated its undertaking to support Africa's efforts in seeking peaceful development and to the realization of joint prosperity and development between China and Africa. Currently, Chinese aid to Africa has already become an important part of the

---

[8] Luo, Jianbo (2006). *The Integration of Africa and China-Africa Relations.* Beijing: Social Sciences Academic Press, pp. 276–287.

[9] *People's Daily* (13 January 2006). China's Africa Policy. p. 3.

new China-Africa strategic partnership and an important expression of joint efforts by China and African countries to realize mutually-beneficial cooperation and joint development in this new period.

4.2 New Models of Chinese Aid to Africa in the New Period, and Outcomes

As the historical mission in Africa aid changed, Chinese aid to Africa has taken on a more diverse array of forms. Aid methods have been revamped, with aid relations taking on an increasing number of forms, in an increasing number of areas, and on an increasing number of levels.

1. A more diverse array of forms in Chinese aid to Africa

Debt relief for African countries has become a new form of assistance. The African continent experienced an economic recession beginning in the 1980s, and which lasted more than ten years. By the late 1990s, Africa's debt had grown to USD270 billion.[10] This heavy debt burden was a grave hindrance to the economic and social development of African countries, and severely undermined the risk resistance of African countries within the international economic and financial systems. In recent years, China has called at multilateral forum for developed countries to either forgive the debts of African countries or to reorganize the debts of such nations. Furthermore, China—a developing nation—has also taken the initiative to forgive the debt of African countries. In the more than six years since the first FOCAC ministerial meeting in 2006, China forgave a total of RMB10.9 billion of debt owed to its by African countries. In line with the undertaking made at the 2006 FOCAC Beijing Summit, as of early 2009 China has made plans to forgive 168 debts owed by 33 African countries up to the end of 2005, and has signed debt-forgiveness agreements for 150 debts with 32 countries.[11] These debt measures are strong proof of China's desire and determination to help African countries realize joint development.

Events for exchanging experience concerning China-Africa cooperation in human resource development have been organized. The African countries lack technical and management expertise, and this has been a limiting factor in Africa's pursuit of sustainable economic development. In recent years, China has consistently sent experts in the fields of education, health, and agriculture to Africa. At the same time, China has also sought out new ways of aid in terms of human resource development. First, since 1998 China has held short-term training programs of many types within China. These programs are generally implemented by the Ministry of Commerce, the Ministry of Education, and the Ministry of Health, etc. As of April 2006, China

---

[10] African Development Bank (2005). *Enhancing Africa's Trade: From Marginalization to an Export-led Approach to Development*. (Economic Research Working Paper Series No.77, August 2005), p. 1.

[11] *People's Daily* (21 January 2009). Growing scale, expanded scope, enhanced levels, p. 9.

has trained around 14,600 African citizens in the areas of economics and management, health and healthcare, network communications, agricultural technologies, and environmental protection, etc. For the period 2006–2009, China has planned to train 15,000 African talents of various types in the period and to send 100 senior agri-tech experts to Africa. China has also planned to build 10 distinctive agri-tech demonstration centers and aid 100 African schools during this period.[12] Second, China has worked actively to develop means of experience-sharing in the area of development. China's swift economic development and sustained political stability, particularly its dramatic achievements in poverty alleviation, has established a positive model for the nations of Africa and stimulated their enthusiasm for learning from China. To help African countries seek out development pathways that are suitable for them, the Chinese government has held multiple events of various kinds to share its experiences in the areas of development and poverty alleviation. For instance, on 8 July 2009, the 2nd China-Africa High-Level Developmental Experience Sharing Seminar jointly held by China's Ministry of Commerce, Ministry of Finance and the State Council Leading Group Office of Poverty Alleviation kicked off in Beijing. The event was attended by over 100 individuals, including senior officials and ambassadors from 21 African countries, Chinese government officials from the corresponding ministries and committees, and domestic and foreign experts and scholars. At the seminar, topics such as "Countering challenges to development: China's experiences in countering crises"; "Agricultural reform, rural development and poverty alleviation"; "Strategies and funding for infrastructural development"; "Special economic zones, foreign direct investment and trade development"; and "China's cooperation with Africa" were discussed. The challenges faced by China over the course of its reform and development, measures taken, and achievements made were described. Comparisons and contrasts with the various economic, historic and cultural contexts of African countries were also made. All these were made to facilitate mutual learning in the areas of development experiences and models. Third, in 2005 China kicked off "volunteer services" to Africa to help the African people in their learning and to enhance their knowledge and skills in the areas of well-digging, computing, and agricultural development, etc. These new aid approaches embody the new approach of "teaching how to fish", which is more suitable to the needs of African countries seeking long-term development.

China has enhanced the scale of humanitarian aid. Historically, for a long time China has sent medical teams to African countries, as well as provided medicines and other healthcare resources, to help these nations establish and improve their healthcare facilities. In the course of 50 years, China has sent 16,000 medical personnel to 43 countries and helped 24,000 patients. According to the China's Africa Policy released in 2006, China would work actively to respond to urgent humanitarian requests from African countries, and that China encouraged and supported non-governmental organizations like the Chinese Red Cross in undertaking exchange and partnerships with the relevant organizations in Africa. The document also stated that

---

[12] See: Hu, Jintao (5 November 2006). Speech at the Forum on China-Africa Cooperation Beijing Summit. *People's Daily*, p. 2.

China would strengthen its exchanges and partnerships with African countries in the areas of HIV/AIDS and epidemic prevention and treatment, research on traditional medicines and their applications, and public health emergency response measures, etc. At the 2006 FOCAC Beijing Summit, China made an undertaking to aid 30 African hospitals and to provide RMB300 million in funding to aid in the form of anti-malaria drugs and the establishment of 30 epidemic prevention centers. In recent years, China has also put in more resources into humanitarian aid to help those suffering from natural disasters and civil strife in Africa. Following the 2004 Indian Ocean tsunami, the Chinese government immediately dispatched aid funds and material aid to Somali, Kenya and the Seychelles. China has also continued to pay attention to the situation in Darfur, Sudan. In July and September 2004 alone, China sent RMB5 million of material aid and RMB5 million of cash assistance to the Sudan.[13] Currently, China has already become one of the key providers of humanitarian aid to Africa.

Support for the self-strengthening and integration of African countries in unity. Africa is the continent with the highest concentration of developing countries. It is also the region with the most salient peace and developmental issues today. Given that self-strengthening in unity is one of the main developing pathways of African countries today, China has worked actively to support economic integration and regional security management in Africa. In the area of economic development, China joined the African Development Bank in 1985, and has subsequently been a strong supporter of the Bank's work. China has also been positive about capital injections for the Bank, as well as about its operations. In April 1996, China signed a partnership agreement with the African Development Bank and its subsidiary, the African Development Fund. Under the terms of the agreement, China would provide a cash gift of USD2 million to the latter to be used for research, consultancy, and other technical aid activities undertaken by Chinese companies and consultants at the Bank and in member states in Africa. In May 2007, China hosted the African Development Bank Board of Directors annual meeting. Key issues discussed at the meeting include: infrastructural development in Africa, capacity-building for African enterprises, debt management and poverty eradication. The groundbreaking ceremony for the African Union Conference Center and Office Complex that China undertook in 2006 to build as part of its aid to Africa was held in May 2007. Work was officially commenced in December 2008, and the project is expected to be completed and delivered in 2011.[14] In the area of security, China has provided support to African countries via various channels to aid regional peace and stability. Not only has China played an important role in encouraging and supporting the AU and other secondary regional organizations in maintaining peace in Africa, it has also dispatched personnel and peacekeeping troops to participate in United Nations peacekeeping missions in Africa. In

---

[13] Department of Foreign Assistance, Ministry of Commerce of the People's Republic of China. Once again, China provides humanitarian aid to Sudan. http://yws.mofcom.gov.cn/aarticle/b/x/200409/20040900273971.html.

[14] *People's Daily* (9 February 2009). Expanding China-Africa cooperation, enhancing aid outcomes, p. 3.

the "Peace and Security" section of the China's Africa Policy released in 2006, it is stated that "China supports the positive efforts by the AU and other African regional organizations and African countries concerned to settle regional conflicts and will provide assistance within our own capacity. It will urge the UN Security Council to pay attention to and help resolve regional conflicts in Africa. It will continue its support to and participation in UN peacekeeping operations in Africa." As of June 2009, China is participating in a total of six peacekeeping operations in Africa: the AU/United Nations Hybrid operation in Darfur, the United Nations Mission in Sudan, the United Nations Operation in Côte d'Ivoire, the United Nations Support Mission in Libya, the Mission of the United Nations in the Democratic Republic of the Congo, and the United Nations Mission for the Referendum in Western Sahara.[15]

2. Major reforms in aid approaches

China has introduced reform in ways of providing aid for Africa. Before the 1980s, China mainly provided aid to Africa by providing cash gifts or interest-free loans for turnkey projects. Since the beginning of the reform and opening-up, changes were made to the ways in which China provided its foreign aid. Greater attention was paid to the use of foreign aid to promote the mutual interests of China and various aid recipients. Enterprises with independent legal actor status began to participate more in foreign aid projects. Since 1995, greater reforms have been made to the ways in which China provided economic and technical aid, mainly through a diversification of aid approaches as well as of aid funding. Interest-free loans were reduced to the minimum, with strong encouragement of preferential loans and jointly-funded projects. At the core of such reform is the enhancement of aid project outcomes, and the objective of the reform is to help recipient countries to establish production projects in locations with the right resources and markets and to help domestic enterprises with the right resources and conditions to develop new markets in developing countries. Such an approach integrates aid with works contracting, trade, and investment, etc.[16] There are three key features to this reform: the provision of preferential loans, the development of production projects, and the joint funding of aid projects. The preferential loans provided are jointly provided by the government and banks. The broadening of funding sources has allowed a number of high-value projects to get off the ground. Under the South-South cooperation framework, China has provided aid in various forms to 53 African countries with nearly 900 turnkey projects in the areas of agriculture, industry, telecommunications, utilities, culture and education, and health completed.[17] The focus on production projects that bring economic benefits or infrastructural projects required by economic development as well as on the joint funding of aid projects is helpful in aiding domestic enterprises with the

---

[15] See: page on United Nations web site, "United Nations peacekeeping missions", http://www.un.org/chinese/peace/peacekeeping/currentops.shtml#africa.

[16] Wei, Hong (1999). China's experiences in reforming foreign aid approaches, and issues encountered. *International Economic Cooperation*, 1999 (5), 408.

[17] *People's Daily* (9 February 2009). Expanding China-Africa cooperation, enhancing aid outcomes, p. 3.

right resources and conditions to develop the investment or labor services markets of Africa and has thus greatly promoted the 'going global' of Chinese enterprises. Renowned brands like Hisense, Huawei, ZTE, and Haier have already successfully made inroads into Africa, while groups like PetroChina and the China Road And Bridge Corporation have also made significant achievements in Africa. Promoting investment in Africa, trade and technical cooperation through foreign aid is in line with the deployment and implementation of the state's "Big Trade" strategy.

China has enhanced the management and supervision of aid projects in Africa. To enhance the quality and competitiveness of foreign aid projects, in 1995 the Ministry of Commerce began to implement a tender system for foreign aid projects, and gradually included items such as survey and design, project works, and supervision into the aid project. In 2004 the Ministry of Commerce released its Interim Provisions for the Strengthening of the Management of Bidding for Foreign Aid Projects, and emphasized that the tender system must be strictly implemented for foreign aid projects, and in no way should attempts be made to avoid the tender process. The same year, the Ministry of Commerce also released the Enterprise Qualification Standards for foreign aid Projects Works and Task Implementation. The qualification was made open to enterprises that meet the relevant criteria in the areas of technical and business management capabilities, and which qualify in terms of past business performance. As of the end of 2006, a total of 196 enterprises have been rated as qualified, a 90% increase from 2003. Enhancing quality supervision for foreign aid projects involving the provision of material aid. On 1 September 2006, the Ministry of Commerce implemented the Interim Measures for the Administration of Foreign Aid Material, clearly stipulating that the Ministry is responsible for supervising and managing the implementation of foreign aid projects involving the provision of material aid and the use of funds relating to these projects. The Ministry of Commerce is also responsible for inter-governmental agency matters relating to such projects. Over the course of project implementation, enterprises implementing such aid projects should organize and file the corresponding documents and information and submit regular reports on project status to the Ministry of Commerce. Enterprises are also expected to submit the project completion report and the corresponding documents and information within 20 working days of project completion. Upon receipt of the project completion report from the enterprise, the Ministry of Commerce would then be responsible for the inter-governmental handover of the aid materials provided together with the government of the recipient country.[18] To enhance the supervision and management of production safety for turnkey foreign aid projects, on 1 October 2006 the Ministry of Commerce implemented the Measures for Safe Production in Turnkey foreign aid Projects (Trial Implementation). The Measures provided a detailed description of the survey and design enterprise's safety responsibilities, the safety responsibilities of the design management enterprise, the safety responsibilities of the works enterprise, the

---

[18] Department of Treaty and Law, Ministry of Commerce of the People's Republic of China. Measures for Safe Production in Turnkey foreign aid Projects (Trial Implementation). Refer to Ministry of Commerce official web site: http://www.mofcom.gov.cn/aarticle/b/bf/200607/20060702671822.html.

safety responsibilities of the works supervision and management enterprise, and the specific job responsibilities of, and matters of note for, safety production supervisory inspectors. The Measures document also stipulated the legal responsibilities that would be borne by units found to have contravened the Measures or which has caused a major incident.[19] The Ministry of Commerce also expanded pre-departure training for management personnel heading overseas to manage turnkey foreign aid projects. As of end-2006, a total of 48 training courses have been provided for 2,063 personnel involved in 229 turnkey foreign aid projects. In 2007, the Ministry of Commerce also established the Filing and Registration System for Management Personnel Involved in Turnkey foreign aid Projects to further enhance the long-term effectiveness of training provided and to enhance dynamic management.

China has provided development aid to Africa by means of multilateral cooperation mechanisms. This has been expressed mainly in two ways. First: through its support for the integration measures of regional organizations like the AU, China has helped to promote peace and development on the African continent. Second, China has made use of the FOCAC meetings to make overall plans for Africa aid projects to further ensure that limited aid funds are used effectively. At the 2006 FOCAC Beijing Summit, China announced its "Eight Measures" for Africa aid, which was a key action in its attempts to promote Africa aid and investment in Africa through multilateral channels. This approach has strongly enhanced the political effect of aid to Africa, and significantly promoted the development of China-Africa relations. The experiences gained, as well as the value of such an approach, are worth learning from and promoting.

4.3 The Basic Spirit and Characteristics of China Aid to Africa over 50 Years

For over half a century, China has consistently adhered to the diplomatic tradition of respect for the sovereignty of African countries and treating others as equals. In recent years, new developments in China's policies for Africa aid have also shown China's close attention to the changes in the development agendas of China and African countries. Hence, there are both changes and unchanging elements in Chinese aid to Africa.

1. Respect for the sovereignty of African countries

In contrast to aid provided to Africa by Western countries, the greatest feature of Chinese aid to Africa is that there are no political conditions attached to Chinese aid. China believes that the internal affairs of African countries should be mainly resolved through autonomous negotiation between African governments and their

---

[19] Department of Treaty and Law, Ministry of Commerce of the People's Republic of China. Refer to Ministry of Commerce official web site: http://www.mofcom.gov.cn/aarticle/b/bf/200608/20060802970939.html.

peoples. External development aid for Africa is a key condition for the realization of rejuvenation by African countries. However, such aid should be given with respect for the sovereignty and domestic governance of African countries and should be beneficial to these countries' efforts to realize national stability and development. China's principle of non-interference in the domestic affairs of African countries does not mean that China is not concerned with the peace and development of recipient nations. It is primarily an independent choice made out of respect for African countries, and is a demonstration of China's hope to provide sincere support for the independence and development of African countries. On the other hand, Western countries tend to attach harsh political and economic conditions to their Africa aid, or tend to provide aid in support of their narrow diplomatic interests. In these cases, the aid-providing countries demand additional political and/or economic privileges or hope to implement so-called democratic reform in African countries by such means and eventually bring African countries into the strategic path dominated by Western countries. For instance, the United has provided African countries with aid through its Millennium Challenge Account (MCA) program established in January 2004. The "carrot" here, which is of significant value, is designed to encourage African governments to practice good governance. The MCA is managed by the Millennium Challenge Corporation (MCC), a state-owned US company. The General Manager of the company is appointed by the US President and approved on Capitol Hill. The Chairman of the company is appointed by the US Secretary of State. Criteria for qualifying for MCA aid include the candidate nation's governance record, the levels of political freedom enjoyed by its citizens, the degree of economic freedom, and the levels of social and health development in the country, etc. As of August 2007, the MCA has selected 16 focus developing countries around the world for aid, including seven African countries.[20] In February 2008, then-President George Bush visited Benin, Tanzania, Rwanda, Ghana and Libya. One of the objectives of this trip was to promote values such as human rights, democracy, and good governance. Of the five countries selected, Benin and Ghana have been regarded as exemplars of good governance by the US Tanzania and Rwanda have also been praised by the US in recent years while Libya has been seeking to improve its governance and rule of law since the cessation of its civil war.

2. Adherence to diplomatic tradition of treating counterparts as equals

Although since the establishment of the Westphalian system in national sovereignty and the equality of nations has become one of the basic principles of international relations. However, for a long time, the equality of nations was only limited to Western countries, especially between the Western powers. From the perspective of the Western colonial powers, sovereignty was not a concept to be applied with the peoples and countries of Asia and Africa, let alone the equality of the countries.

---

[20] Economic and Commercial Counselor's Office of the People's Republic of China's Embassy to Ghana. *Millennium Challenge Account Executive Agency to Sign Agreement With Bank of Ghana.* http://gh.mofcom.gov.cn/aarticle/jmxw/200708/20070804965109.html.

Hence, since the advent of modern times the main objective of China's and African countries' struggles is to break the shackles of Western colonialism and to obtain independence and sovereignty. Because of such a historical experience, China and African countries have treated each other with respect and as equals since diplomatic relations have been established. At the 2006 FOCAC Beijing Summit, Hu Jintao emphasized that China-Africa relations have been strong and long-lasting because of those involved have treated each other as equals. He said: "This is an important guarantee of a continued growth in trust between China and African countries."[21] China's Africa aid policies are an expression of China's diplomatic approach of treating others as equals. The "Eight Principles" of foreign aid proposed by China in the 1960s clearly stipulate that "the Chinese foreign aid experts are required to enjoy the same material treatment as the local experts, without any special treatment." Mao Zedong once told friends from Africa: "Some of the people we send out to Africa may not be up to the task. We must check their work, and if we discover that someone has shown a poor attitude towards the foreign country we must rebuke him and order him to rectify his mistakes. If does not do so, then we recall him."[22] In 1982, China proposed its "Four Principles" of China-Africa economic and technical aid partnership which also places "equality and mutual benefit" as the top priority. Over the years, experts from China have worth the trust of the people of Africa with their sincere efforts and treatment of the locals as equals.

3. Giving priority to development needs of African countries

China's Africa aid policies are highly internationalist and humanitarian in nature. These policies are mainly centered on the actual revolutionary and nation-building needs of African countries, with many instances of aid fulfilling dire needs at critical moments. China's focus with the African liberation movement has been on providing support to anti-colonialism, anti-imperialism, and anti-racism struggles put up by African countries. In the current ear where African countries are pursuing peace and development, China has reinforced its Africa aid with the main aim of helping African countries realize political stability and economic rejuvenation. China's Africa aid became more closely aligned with the development agendas of the AU and New Partnership for Africa's Development (NEPAD), such as for infrastructure-building (roads and bridges, utilities), urgently-needed livelihood projects (drinking water, health and healthcare), processing enterprises (food processing, light textiles, etc.), and human-resource development based on school-building and technical training. The focus has also been on helping African countries realize political stability.

---

[21] See: Hu, Jintao (5 November 2006). Speech at the Forum on China-Africa Cooperation Beijing Summit. *People's Daily*, p. 2.

[22] Li, Jiasong ed. (2001). *A Diplomatic History of the People's Republic of China (Vol. II)*. Beijing: World Affairs Press, pp. 432–433.

African countries have praised China for its practical aid approaches and partnerships. For instance, then-Prime Minister of Ethiopia Meles Zenawi welcomed the "successful developmental experiences, technology transfers, trade development and investment" offered by China to Africa.[23]

4. Complementing changes in China's domestic development agenda

Foreign aid being an important part of diplomatic relations is also a policy tool that can service the interests of the nation. Following the founding of the People's Republic of China, particularly in the 1960s and 1970s, China needs desperately to win diplomatic support from other developing countries, including African countries to build a unified anti-imperialist and anti-war front in line with its domestic political as well as diplomatic needs. Its sincere aid to Africa as well as reputation won its the recognition and support of African countries and dramatically expanded its diplomatic space. Following the 'opening-up' of China, China has mainly conducted its diplomacy along the lines of economy-building. Its Africa-aid projects became increasing focused on issues such as economic impact and sustainability as well as on an appropriate consideration of the needs of China's economic development and the interests of its enterprises. Currently, in the twenty-first century, China's enhancing of its Africa aid is a form of contribution made by a rising China to world peace and development, and to the common prosperity of mankind. It is testament to China's image as a responsible power. We can say that China's Africa-aid program is of strategic importance and is closely related to China's rise.

4.4 A Few Ways of Thinkings on China's Future Strategy for Aid to Africa

For more than 50 years, China's Africa aid has effectively maintained China's national interests and promoted friendly relations between China and African countries. To a certain extent, its Africa aid has also promoted the development of African countries and enhanced the overall status of African countries in international society. In the new century, a strong focus on Africa aid and the further enhancement of the standards of aid rendered would be an important topic in Chinese diplomacy.

1. Enhancing the scale of Chinese aid to Africa at the right time, and at the right proportions

Determining the appropriate scale of aid is a key foundation of ensuring desirable aid outcomes and the realization of aid objectives. China, a developing country, is working actively to fulfill its international obligations and has borne the corresponding responsibilities in helping other developing countries realize development. However, we should also see that China's foreign aid still cannot compare to aid given

---

[23] See: Address by Ethiopian Prime Minister Meles Zenawi at the FOCAC Beijing Summit (translated) in *People's Daily*, 5 November 2006, p. 2.

by the likes of the US, Japan, and the European Union in terms of quantity. This is also rather incompatible with the swift growth in the Chinese economy in recent years. In this new era, as China's economy continues to develop and its international status continues to be improved, the expectations of China by African countries will also grow. These countries generally welcome various types of aid from China and hope that such aid can increase in tandem with China's strengthening economy and the continued development of China-Africa relations. An appropriate increase in Africa aid can also serve as a statement to the world that China is committed to the maintenance of world peace and to promoting common prosperity. It can also serve as a timely show of China's image as a responsible power. China's aid to Africa will show to the world that political bearing and global responsibility that a rising power of the East should have. Hence, to realize its overall diplomatic interests China needs to start from the principle of "as much as practicable" and ensure that its Africa-aid projects are of the appropriate scale.

2. Further enhancement of the quality and outcomes of Africa-aid projects

Historically, certain Chinese aid projects have performed poorly in terms of sustainability. With these projects, once Chinese experts have left the country continuing the project becomes challenging. As such, in terms of project planning China's Africa aid must be aligned with both China's long-term and overall strategic interests as well as with the objective of enhancing African countries' ability to develop autonomously. There should be an appropriate shift on the "image-burnishing projects" that were favored historically to production and livelihood projects that are closely related to the development of African countries with an appropriate increase in training and humanitarian aid. That is, the emphasis on both 'blood transfusion' and 'blood-making' should be balanced. China should provide African countries with projects that can aid in enhancing their ability to develop autonomously and focus on transferring China's technology and experiences in its foreign aid partnerships. For resource-rich countries in Africa, investment should be increased, and partnerships with African enterprises or training of local technical personnel undertaken to enhance their product development capabilities and to promote the diversification of these countries' exports. China has, in 2006, announced its intentions to establish three to five overseas economic and trade zones in African countries in what is a new model in China-Africa economic cooperation. In terms of project implementation methods, this would further promote joint ventures in foreign aid, and tie aid programs together with investments made by Chinese firms in Africa for greater sustainability of aid projects. To encourage Chinese firms to invest in Africa, and to support them in doing so, the Chinese government has established the China-Africa Development Fund with an initial investment of USD1 billion. As of the end of 2008, the Fund has already invested in 20 projects with almost USD400 million invested. These efforts have in turn encouraged Chinese enterprises to invest more than USD2 billion in Africa. With lessons drawn along the way, the Fund is expected to be funded to a total of USD5 billion eventually.[24] In terms of the tracking and management of aid programs, China should also place an

---

[24] *People's Daily* (21 January 2009). Growing scale, expanded scope, enhanced levels, p. 9.

emphasis on balancing political and economic outcomes and on the sustainability of the project. This is because in the case of many projects while the political objective is more or less accomplished with the completion and handover of the project, at this juncture other objectives and agendas such as the economic agenda have just come into play. Thus, just how to ensure the aid project's subsequent development should become a key part of foreign aid work.

3. Continued effort to diversify range of actors involved in foreign aid

As early as in the 1980s the Chinese government has begun to include non-governmental organizations in its humanitarian assistance. Such assistance has been mainly made through community groups like the Red Cross Society of China and the China Charity Federation. For a long time, there have been few players in China that are qualified to take on foreign aid work, with the majority of actors being state-owned enterprises. There have been far fewer private enterprises and non-governmental organizations that have played a role in China's foreign aid projects. Following the Indian Ocean tsunami in 2004, Chinese enterprises and non-governmental organizations began to offer international humanitarian aid. For example, the Huawei Group provided a large quantity of emergency supply of wireless communications equipment to Indonesia. In the future, more private enterprises and civil society organizations, especially those with adequate resources, strong capability and sound reputation, should be encouraged to get involved in China's foreign aid efforts. Doing so can (1) make more resources available for foreign aid, (2) achieve better results than simply donating money to governments can by allowing more parties to deliver more aid in more ways, and (3) help to depoliticize China's foreign aid and burnish the country's image as a champion of humanitarian values and commitments. Broad-based societal participation may be a useful new approach to increasing the overall effective of China's foreign aid.

4. The importance of publicizing China's foreign aid achievements and experience

In this globalized era where information transmission is highly advanced, the state needs to make an active move to publicize its development and policies in order to build confidence and dispel suspicions. The state's image needs to be actively 'shaped' rather than passively 'accepted' or even 'made up' by others. For a long time, China has adopted the bilateral agreement approach for its Africa aid projects, and these projects as well as project outcomes were little known to the world. Hence, while continuing its reforms of aid approaches China should do more to let the world know about what we have done for Africa. In addition to the Chinese government and aid agencies, enterprises, non-governmental organizations, scholars and individuals who have travelled to African countries can also help to get the word out. In particular, enterprises that are engaged in Africa aid or investment projects should publicize their social and charitable achievements in a timely manner. In recent years, many large Chinese enterprises have placed an emphasis on releasing annual reports of their corporate social responsibility (CSR) endeavors. For instance, in its *2008 Corporate Social Responsibility Report* the China National Petroleum Corporation described its

4.4 A Few Ways of Thinkings on China's Future Strategy for Aid to Africa

CSR efforts in the Sudan.[25] The publicity targets should include the governments and peoples of Africa and also more broadly, international society, particularly Western media and non-governmental organizations as criticisms of China's Africa policy has mainly come from Western countries. Publicity topics should be centered on engineering and livelihood projects with major impact in Africa, particularly projects that can significantly improve the lives of the local people and promote local economic and social development.

5. Considering working together with international society on aid in Africa

One way is to work together with foreign aid agencies from other countries. The majority of Western and developed countries have comparatively mature institutions and mechanisms for foreign aid, such as the UK Department for International Development (DFID) and the Australian Agency for International Development (AusAID). China's Ministry of Commerce, Ministry of Foreign Affairs, Ministry of Agriculture and Ministry of Finance, etc., have begun to place an emphasis on working together with the corresponding aid agencies from Western countries, such as by means of experience and information-sharing, to enhance the quality and effectiveness of foreign aid. At the same time, this also helps China to convey its aid philosophy and achievements to the rest of the world through diplomatic exchanges and thus build confidence and dispel suspicion. Another approach is to work with international or multilateral organizations in the realm of foreign aid. Currently, the most important multilateral aid organization is the United Nations system, mainly various professional institutions under the UN umbrella like the United Nations Development Programme (UNDP), the United Nations Children's Fund (UNICEF), the World Food Programme (WFP), the United Nations Population Fund (UNFPA), and the United Nations Environment Programme (UNEP). Also important are international economic institutions like the World Bank and the World Bank's International Development Association (IDA). Prior to 1971, China had only used the bilateral aid approach. After China's legal rights were restored at the 26th Session of the UN General Assembly in 1971, China began to participate in multilateral aid efforts through its donations to the UNDP. In 1980, China's legal position at the World Bank and the International Monetary Fund (IMF) was restored. Thereafter, the room for China to participate in multilateral aid efforts was expanded even more. The Chinese government began to work with UN agencies, and worked through both bilateral and multilateral means to provide certain developing nations with technical aid. For instance, in 1998, China and Ethiopia signed a three-way agreement with the Food and Agriculture Organization of the United Nations (FAO) through which China would send 38 technical experts in the area of agriculture to Ethiopia. Costs for the program were to be borne by Ethiopia and the UN. In 2005, the Chinese government provided (through multilateral UN-led efforts) USD20 million worth of aid to countries affected by the Indian Ocean tsunami. Since 2006, China has been designated a WFP donor country rather than a recipient country. However, generally

---

[25] China National Petroleum Corporation. *2008 Corporate Social Responsibility Report*. http://www.cnpc.com.cn/Resource/cn/other/pdf/团公司 2008 年企业社会责任报告(中文).pdf.

speaking, there is room for China to pay closer attention to multilateral aid channels. The amount of Chinese aid furnished through such channels is still comparatively little and China has yet to accrue sufficient experience in this area. In this new era, China should continue to focus on the strengthening of communication and relations with multilateral aid organizations for the following reasons: (1) Doing so can help win more aid for Africa from developed countries, and at the same time produce even better outcomes from aid funding through the coordination of aid actions by various countries. (2) The establishment of multilateral aid systems comprising key donor countries has already become common understanding in international society. In its *Economic Development in Africa Report 2006* released on 21 September, the United Nations Conference on Trade and Development (UNCTAD) has recommended that changes be made to the current emphasis on bilateral aid to African countries, as such efforts make for a chaotic situation with energies and resources dispersed. It was recommended that UN-managed multilateral aid mechanisms be established in order to concentrate resources on areas urgently needed for the economic development of African countries.[26] (3) Multilateral aid systems have an important role to play in international aid. Participating in such mechanisms and making China's voice heard can help to enhance China's position in international society.

---

[26] Economic & Commercial Counselor's Office of the Chinese Embassy in Kenya. United Nations Conference on Trade and Development Recommends Changes to Africa Aid Approaches. *Ministry of Commerce web site*, http://www.mofcom.gov.cn/aarticle/i/jyjl/k/200609/20060903238390.html.

Chapter 5
Changes in the Geopolitics of Africa, and Issues Pertaining to Three-Way Cooperation Among China, Africa and the West

Since the advent of the twenty-first century, China and Africa have, at the same time, embarked on the process of national rejuvenation, and have strengthened their partnerships in the course of this process. This is a major event in world politics in the new century. The West-centric global order is already finding it hard to adapt to the new changes that are occurring in the African periphery, and the topic of the establishment of multilateral partnerships pertaining to the peaceful development of Africa has swiftly made its way to the agendas of various parties. In the opinion of the authors, there are differences between China and the West in terms of historical experiences, diplomatic philosophies and diplomatic principles. However, both parties also share broad understanding and interests in Africa. Both parties should, logically, transcend their mutual suspicions and differences when it comes to Africa issues and establish more open and cooperative ways of cooperation and communication that would create mutual benefit. Both parties should seek to realize a situation that serves the interests of various parties as Africa's development is being promoted.[1]

5.1 High Levels of Attention Paid to China-Africa Relations by the West in Recent Years

Historically, China has built strong friendships with African countries in their joint struggles against imperialism, colonialism, and tyranny. In the twenty-first century, China-Africa relations have been enhanced on all fronts on this strong foundation. In October 2000, the first-ever FOCAC Summit was held in Beijing. This marked

---

[1] Refer to the following articles by Jianbo Luo: The Africa diplomacy of China and Western countries: seeking common understanding and cooperation within differences. *World Economics and Politics*, 2009 (4); and the process of Asian and African rejuvenation and changes in global geopolitics. *West Asia and Africa*, 2009 (5).

the start to the establishment of a stream of multilateral mechanisms for negotiations between China and African countries. In early 2006, the Chinese government released for the first time a policy document targeted at an entire continent, the Policy Document on China's Africa Policy. In November the same year, the FOCAC Beijing Summit was held, with heads of state, heads of government, and senior officials from 48 countries attending the event. China-Africa relations were elevated to the level of "new-type strategic partnership" based on "mutual political trust, win–win economics, and mutual cultural understanding". China-Africa trade grew swiftly from USD10.59 billion in value in 2000 to USD106.84 billion in 2008. The objective of realizing trade worth more than USD100 billion was fulfilled two years ahead of the planned 2010.[2] China-Africa relations reached their peak in more than 50 years.

Looking back on history, we see that Africa has always been the bedrock of China's foreign relations strategy and an important stage on which China has been able to show off its value and significance to the world. Currently, in the early part of the twenty-first century, Africa is a strategic partner of China's that allows China to further enhance its economic strength and its soft power, as well as to show off its image as responsible power. Continued promotion of China-Africa strategic cooperation and thus promoting China's peaceful development and the joint development and prosperity of the developing world is an important part of China's current global strategy.

The opinions of international society about positive developments in China's Africa policy and China-Africa relations have been mixed. There are those in the West who are able to correctly evaluate the value of China-Africa relations and objectively understand the significance of China to African development. Kenneth King, former head of the University of Edinburgh Centre for African Studies, has positively rated China-Africa relations. In his opinion, in contrast to the West, China's Africa policy emphasizes reciprocity, common economic interests, and exchanges as partners.[3] In the opinion of Uwe Wissenbach, member of the European Commission, China-Africa trade cooperation has brought to Africa opportunities for development and prosperity, and this development is also in line with Europe's interests.[4]

However, at the same time, many in the West lack full understanding of the history and current state of China-Africa relations, or are biased, misled, or even suspicious about China's Africa policy due to outdated ideological biases and narrow strategic considerations. In February 2006, British Foreign & Commonwealth Secretary Jack

---

[2] General Administration of Customs of the People's Republic of China. China's import and export trade with Africa continues to grow quickly in 2008, with trade value exceeding USD100 billion in value for the year. http://www.customs.gov.cn/publish/portal0/tab1/info158375.htm.

[3] King, Kenneth (2006). The partnership between China and Africa. *The Journal of International Studies*, 2006 (4), 10–20.

[4] Wissenbach, Uwe (2008). The revival or end of geopolitics?: trilateral cooperation in Africa. *International Issue Forum*, 2008 summer issue, pp. 111–123; Berger, B. & Wissenbach, W. (2007). E.U.-China-Africa trilateral development cooperation: common challenges and new directions. Discussion Pater, Bonn 2007, http://www.ec-an.eu/files/bergerweissenbach_0.pdf.

Straw was the first to criticize China's actions in Africa, accusing its in engaging in "neo-colonialism". Straw named China alongside poverty, regional conflict and terrorism, etc., as one of the top ten challenges that Africa was facing.[5] This technical term that was originally used to designate the ways in which Western colonialist powers had continued to exploit their ex-colonies by means of political intervention and economic control post-World War II[6] has been used by the West instead on China in its criticisms of China engaging in undisguised exploitation and blackmail of developing countries. Some Western scholars are of the opinion that the close attention that China has paid to Africa is motivated by the desire to obtain the strategic resources needed for the further development of the Chinese economy, and that China's utilitarian trade and economic policies have harmed the interests of Western countries and undermined fairness and transparency in international trade.[7] Certain Western media trade outlets have maligned China, accusing its of "undisguised transactions" that are part of a new "economic imperialism".[8] Some Western organizations and individuals have also politicized China's Africa policies. The US Council on Foreign Relations has criticized China's Africa policies as having presented challenges to America. It stated: "Chinese policies are endangering US goals by supporting African dictatorships, hindering economic development, and exacerbating conflicts and human rights abuses in troubled countries such as Sudan and Zimbabwe."[9] Joshua Eisenman, American Foreign Policy Council researcher for Asia and Joshua Kurlantzick of the Carnegie Endowment for International Peace have provided a 'kind reminder' that China's Africa policy would "make the building of democracy and good governance in Africa become even more complex, thus undermining China's efforts in becoming a responsible global power."[10] The statement above exaggerates the issues that exist

---

[5] Adelakun, Tunde. Is the influence of China growing in Nigeria. http://www.helium.com/items/439062-is-the-influence-of-china-growing-in-nigeria.

[6] Former Prime Minister of Ghana Kwame Nkrumah wrote in *Neo-Colonialism: the last stage of imperialism*: "The essence of neo-colonialism is that the State which is subject to it is, in theory, independent and has all the outward trappings of international sovereignty. In reality its economic system and thus its political policy is directed from outside.... More often, however, neo-colonialist control is exercised through economic or monetary means.... Control over government policy in the neo-colonial State may be secured by payments towards the cost of running the State, by the provision of civil servants in positions where they can dictate policy, and by monetary control over foreign exchange through the imposition of a banking system controlled by the imperial power." Nkrumah, Kwame (1966). *Neo-Colonialism: the last stage of imperialism*. Beijing: World Knowledge Press, p. 1.

[7] Klare, M., and Volman, D. (2006). America, China & the scramble for Africa's oil. *Review of African Political Economy*, No. 108, 2006, pp. 297–309; Tull, Dennis M. (2006). China's Engagement in Africa: scope, significance and consequences. *The Journal of Modern African Studies*, Vol. 44, 2006 (3), 459–479.

[8] Games, Dianna (21 February 2005). Chinese the New Economic Imperialists in Africa. *Business Day*; Hilsum, Lindsey (2006). China's Offer to Africa: pure capitalism. *New Statesman*, 3 July 2006, 23–24.

[9] Stith, Charles (2006). China-Africa relations: a brief evaluation from the U.S. perspective. *The Journal of International Studies*, 2006 (4), 21–31.

[10] Eisenman, J., and Kurlantzick, J. (2006). China's Africa strategy. *Current History*, May 2006, 219–224.

between China and Africa, and even distorts China's strategic intentions in Africa and makes the job of building China's soft power even more difficult with the negative impact on China's image.

In recent years, Western countries have, on the governmental level, paid closer attention to China-Africa relations.[11] Europe has looked upon China-Africa relations from the perspective of its global strategy from the very beginning. In October 2006, the European Union released a new policy document titled *EU-China: closer partners, growing responsibility*. In the document, the EU asked that China should urge African countries to realize "good governance" and work more closely with the EU in terms of its Africa policy. Javier Solana, senior EU representative responsible for foreign-relations and security issues, held that cooperation in Africa was a key element in the overall EU-China strategic partnership.[12] On 17 October 2008, the European Commission officially launched a policy document titled *EU, Africa and China: towards trilateral dialogue and cooperation*. In this document, the EC proposed its concept of trilateral cooperation mechanisms between China, the EU and Africa, as well as made policy recommendations.[13] Similarly, the US has paid close attention to China-Africa relations and US-China cooperation in Africa. On 4 June 2008, US Assistant Secretary of State Thomas J. Christensen (who was responsible for East Asia and the Pacific) and Assistant Secretary of State James Swan (responsible for Africa) jointly observed that China's influence in Africa continues to grow and call for greater contact between the two countries.[14] As China-EU and China-US relations transcend the scope of bilateral relations and become more global, dialogue on Africa issues will become a key part of China-EU and China-US relations.

Why is Western society suddenly paying attention to China-Africa relations? What are the issues and conflicts that exist between China and Western countries in the context of Africa? Can both sides achieve a win–win situation for everyone while promoting development in Africa? Deep reflection on these questions can help us to

---

[11] This is in contrast to the Cold War period. At that time, when the two superpowers that were the U.S. and the Soviet Union were locked in competition in Africa, older colonial powers like the UK and France had still retained some influence in their respective spheres. China's influence in Africa was, on the other hand, limited. The West did not pay much attention to China-Africa relations due to their realistic assessment of China's diplomatic influence and a Western-centric perspective that had long neglected the 'East'. In particular, "there are very few works, next to nothing, that have truly placed China-Africa relations within the context of changes in world history and at the same time placed together the histories and realities of China and Africa for close examination." See: Liu, Haifang (2008). Transcending Differences: studies on China-Africa relations within the ambit of the open social sciences. *World Economics and Politics*, 2008 (9), 45–51.

[12] Solana, Javier (24 January 2007). E.U. looks forward to working with China on Africa issues. *China Youth Daily*.

[13] Commission of the European Communities. The E.U., Africa and China: towards trilateral dialogue and cooperation. http://ec.europa.eu/development/icenter/repository/COMM_PDF_COM_2008_0654_F_COMMUNICATION_en.pdf.

[14] Christensen, T., and Swan, J. China in Africa: implications for U.S. policy. http://foreign.senate.gov/hearings/2008/hrg080604a.html.

better understand the relationship between Africa issues and the relationship between major powers, as well as promote more coordinated development in China-Africa relations and relations between China and the West.

5.2 Why Western Countries Are Paying Close Attention to China-Africa Relations

In recent years, the Western world has paid close attention to China-Africa relations for two main reasons:

First, in recent years Africa's position in the global strategic landscape has improved. Between the 1970s and the early 1990s, conflicts were commonplace on the African continent, and economic development slowed. This period has been described as the "lost decade" for Africa. Poverty, war, disease: these are all labels that have been commonly associated with Africa. However, since the late twentieth century we have seen positive developments in Africa. Africa's economies began to recover, with economic growth at an average of above 5% in the last ten years. In particular, the rise in the prices of energy and other resources has brought significant foreign-exchange income to countries more gifted with these resources and thus enhanced their status in international economic negotiations.[15] Along the arduous and painful road towards African democracy, a set of multi-party political systems appropriate to the history, culture and social structures of African countries has gradually emerged. To a certain extent, the emergence of these systems has led to the internal stability of African countries. The number of major armed conflicts in Africa has decreased from 11 a year between 1998 and 1999 to three between 2005 and 2006.[16] The continued development of African integration and of the AU has promoted economic development and political stability in Africa. The implementation of the New Partnership for Africa's Development and the establishment of the Peace and Security Council of the AU have been two landmark events in this regard. A number of multilateral cooperative mechanisms have been developed collectively with key countries and national groups around the world, with important platforms such as the US-Sub-Saharan Africa Trade and Economic Cooperation Forum, the EU-Africa Summit, the Tokyo International Conference on African Development,

---

[15] The World Bank estimates that the price index for primary agricultural products declined from 163 to 115 between 1970 and 2006, while the price index for oil rose from 19 to 254 in the same period. See: World Bank (2008). *2007 World Development Indicators*. Beijing: China Financial & Economic Publishing House, p. 330.

[16] Stockholm International Peace Research Institute *ed.* (2008). *SIPRI Yearbook 2007: armaments, disarmament and international security. Trans.* China Arms Control and Disarmament Association. Beijing: World Knowledge Publishing House, p. 100.

the India–Africa Forum Summit, and the Forum on China–Africa Cooperation. In a show of the power of its unity and integration, Africa is the only continent that has proposed to join the UN Security Council as a single entity.[17]

Western countries have begun to place more emphasis on Africa. In December 2005, the EU released a historic strategic document on Africa (its very first): *EU and Africa: towards a strategic partnership.* In recent years, each year the EU has provided around USD25 billion of aid to various multilateral and bilateral arrangements. This is almost 60% of all EU aid provided to developing countries.[18] The EU has also enhanced its military presence in Africa. In June 2003, it sent for the first time troops to the Democratic Republic of the Congo and established the African Peace Facility at the request of the AU In recent years, the US has also 'returned' to Africa, engaging in more partnerships with African countries in the areas of energy and anti-terrorism. In October 2007, the US approved the establishment of the United States Africa Command (US AFRICOM). Since the 2003 G8 Summit in Evian Les Bains of France, the Group of Eight countries have conducted a number of North–South dialogues on development issues in Africa. Although compared to Europe and Asia the African continent still has a relatively weak position on the international scene but as Africa continues to rejuvenate itself and as common foreign policy continues to be developed between African countries the continent's global influence will surely be enhanced. Once again, Africa is standing at a key point in history.

Second, with swift development in China, the enhancement of China-Africa relations on all fronts has created an unprecedented impact on the global order.[19] In the thirty years since the beginning of reform and opening-up, China has worked proactively towards peaceful development by seeking to integrate into the global system. It has realized the comprehensive enhancement of its national strength through win–win arrangements with other countries and has embarked on the process of national rejuvenation and the shift from regional power to world power. An important mark of China's global rise is the swift growth of its influence in Africa in recent years, as evidenced by the development of China-Africa partnerships on all fronts and consequently the 'Look East' trend in Africa.[20] To a significant extent the impact of Chinese development on the world order and the Western world is largely exerted through current China-Africa relations and the impact of such relations.

---

[17] Since 2005, the AU has called on several occasions for the reform of the United Nations along the principles of universality, equality and balance between regions, and for at least two veto-wielding seats and five non-permanent seats for Africa on the United Nations Security Council. Sirte Declaration on the Reform of the United Nations. http://www.africa-union.org/root/au/Doc uments/Decisions/hog/Decisions_Sirte_July_2005.pdf.

[18] Xing, Yuchun (2006). New developments in Western countries' African policies, and the impact of such developments. *Chinese International Studies*, 2006 (6), 26.

[19] For a discussion on the impact of China-Africa relations on the current world order, see Li, Anshan (2008). Righting China's Name: China's Africa strategy and national image. *World Economics and Politics*, 2008 (4), 6–15.

[20] Liu, Hongwu. China-Africa relations: a pivoting point for the three-way relationship between China, Africa and Europe. http://ias.zjnu.cn/index.asp.

5.2 Why Western Countries Are Paying Close Attention to China-Africa Relations

China's political influence has served to diversify Africa's foreign-relations landscape. Historically, China and Africa have been political allies, and Chinese aid to Africa has helped to promote the independence of Africa's peoples. Currently, China and Africa have found a new basis for cooperation in the process of maintaining their national sovereignty and the rights of their peoples, and are promoting the democratization and diverse development of the world. Development-related expectations of China held by African countries are growing greater. Not only do these African countries hope to harness China's swift development for the rejuvenation of Africa, they also hope that a rising China can play a bigger role on the world stage and help African countries to protect their political and economic rights. "Africa's leaders have made China out to be a 'trump card' to ensure their new global position and as an expression of a new-found confidence. Sometimes they would even use this trump card as a kind of revenge against Europe for its past oppression."[21] China has developed friendly relations with all African countries in accordance with principles such as the principle of non-interference. Not only does such behavior show that China respects its counterparts as equals and conducts its foreign affairs on the basis of mutual trust, it is also a stark contrast to the Western practice of imposing liberal values on African countries. China has shown consistent support for Africa in international settings, such as at the United Nations, helping Africa to become more independent, more proactive, and more confident in its dealings with the West. The FOCAC Beijing Summit was held to great success in November 2006. Heads of state, heads of government, and senior officials from 48 nations gathered in Beijing in what was a display of China's tremendous political influence and appeal in Africa.

China's economic influence has weakened the Western powers' domination of interests in Africa which had been built up over hundreds of years. China has already become Africa's third-largest trading partner after the US and the EU, and the value of China-Africa trade has, in 2007, already exceeded the value of trade between Africa and any one European country. Chinese investment in and aid to Africa has also seen rapid development. Mutually-beneficial partnerships on all fronts have also led to rapid economic development in Africa. Statistics from China's Ministry of Commerce show that currently China-Africa trade contributes around 20% to African economic growth.[22] Historically, Western economic activity in Africa tended to marginalize Africa. On the other hand, current China-Africa economic cooperation has instead helped to put Africa firmly on the road to globalization. Africa is integrating into the global system in a more independent manner and in a better position.

As Africa continues to rejuvenate and as China-Africa relations continue to improve and be enhanced, structural changes are occurring in Africa's geopolitics.[23] This change in global politics has had a great impact on the relationship between

---

[21] Wissenbach, Uwe (2008). The revival or end of geopolitics?: trilateral cooperation in Africa. *International Issue Forum*, 2008 summer issue, pp. 111–123.

[22] African Development Bank annual event in Shanghai uncovers points of mutual benefit. http://www.mofcom.gov.cn/aarticle/i/jyjl/k/200705/20070504702076.html.

[23] From the perspective of the history of Africa and even world history, since the advent of modern times Africa's geopolitics has undergone three major changes. In the first instance, in the four

China and the US/Europe. In the traditional sense, China and Europe are not in any direct geopolitical conflict anywhere around the world. However, in recent years both parties have been competing with each other in Africa in terms of values and economic interests in what is another kind of geopolitical contest. Compared to China–Europe relations, China-US relations have an even broader scope globally. Thus, China-US contestation and cooperation in Africa are of greater strategic importance in the world in a longterm. The Africa issue has become a key part of global China–Europe and China-US relations. China's relationships with the Western world have become more complex, diverse and also more challenging because of the Africa issue.

The objective truth is: the major power factor in China-Africa relations, or the Africa factor in relations between major powers, is becoming increasingly clear. Africa has once again become the center of focus for international society and a key factor in changes in the global landscape and in relations between major powers. The international power structure and hierarchy that have been dominated by the West are no longer adequate in dealing with the new changes that are occurring in Africa's geopolitical situation. The establishment of Sino-European-African and Sino-US-African, and even multilateral cooperation mechanisms with global significance between China, Europe and the US, have appeared on the historical agenda. The development of multilateral relations related to peaceful development in Africa is the ideal model for China and the US as they seem to deal more effectively with global challenges in the twenty-first century.

5.3 Differences in Opinion and Policy Regarding Africa Between China and Western Countries

It is normal for players on the international scene to seek commonalities and opportunities for cooperation amidst differences. A good understanding of each other's beliefs, policies and motivations is the foundation of effective communication and the building of mutual trust *vis-à-vis* Africa.

---

centuries beginning with the fifteenth century European colonizers established what were vertical colonial relations in Africa through the cruel slave trade and bloody colonial wars. Africa was forcibly brought into the global system dominated by the West. In the second instance, which happened throughout most of the twentieth century, the peoples of Africa broke free of the shackles of colonialism under the banner of pan-Africanism and won for themselves the political independence that they had desired for a long time. Africans began to step on the world stage as independent state actors. In the third instance, since the advent of the twenty-first century, Africa's strategic position in the world has been significantly enhanced with the rejuvenation of Africa and changes in its relationships with the rest of the world.

1. Different historical experiences: relationship of dependence or mutual benefits for equal partners?

In modern times, the relationship between Africa and the West began with European's expansionist and colonialist moves. After the Portuguese occupied Ceuta in Morocco in 1415, Western colonialists started to swarm to Africa, which was forcibly brought into the Western colonialist system. Although in modern times Europe had established the diplomatic principles of "nation" and "sovereign equality" earlier than the others, those in the West never treated the peoples of Africa has equals but as slaves and targets of oppression. Economically, the Western colonialists forced Africa to develop single-product economies and placed Africa at the lowest end of the Western capitalist and economic chain. Famed black scholar Walter Rodney noted that diversity is an African tradition, and the single-product economy was the invention of the colonizers.[24] The impact of such colonialist vestiges has been deep. Even today, the majority of African countries have yet to succeed in diversifying their economies. Politically, Western countries dictated what happened on the African continent. Africans never had the chance to participate in international politics or even in African affairs as equals. In terms of cultural relations, to dress the slave trade and colonial aggression in a cloak of legitimacy the Western colonialists took pains to come up with various racist theories. The shameless defamation and evil slander targeted at the blacks of Africa lasted for as long as four centuries. Such slander was made in order to turn fabricated claims of blacks being an inferior people into the truth.[25] This approach, which trampled on the character and dignity of the African peoples, dealt a severe blow to the dignity and self-confidence of the African people, who started believing that they were inferior to the whites in terms of culture, psychology and biology. The negative impact of these covert-yet-fatal mental shackles that were placed on the peoples of Africa has yet to be completely eradicated today. The modern history of Africa involved aggression and enslavement, and this is a key background to understand the modern history of Africa.

This sort of vertical relationship of dependency has had a direct impact on the relationship between post-colonial Africa and the Western world. Currently, European countries like France and the UK continue to maintain their special relationships with African countries through various political, economic and cultural ties. For instance, the franc is accepted for use in dozens of African countries; the location of the biennial Africa-France Summit alternates between France and Africa. France also maintains military bases in Africa and has the largest military presence in Africa among all Western countries. For France, Africa is within its traditional sphere of influence and is also a focal point for its diplomatic efforts. Unlike the European nations, America's position in Africa improved after World War II. The US established broad political influence in Africa through its contestation with the Soviet Union during the Cold War and its aggressive efforts to promote "democratization"

---

[24] Rodney, Walter. (1974). *How Europe underdeveloped Africa.* Washington, D.C.: Howard University Press, pp. 142–143.

[25] Esedebe P.O. (1994). *Pan-Africanism: the Idea and Movement, 1776–1991*, Washington, D.C.: Howard University Press, p.18.

after the Cold War. Even the EU, which now advocates a "Europe-Africa strategic partnership", has also valorized partnerships with Africa in the area of politics and security, and has attached a good number of strict conditions to its Africa aid.[26] We can see that the US and Europe have not completely given up on controlling Africa's development. These players have tried to dictate Africa's development based on their own social development standards, frame Africa's development in a certain manner, and strengthen the West's interests in Africa.

The development of contemporary China-Africa relations has seen varying historical developments and defining characteristics over time. In the 1950s to the 1970s, China and Africa were political allies along the same international front, and were jointly engaged in resistance to imperialism, colonialism, and tyranny. Since the 1980s and 1990s, both China and Africa have continued to develop their political partnerships while placing a stronger emphasis on mutual economic benefit in their partnerships in order to adapt to changes in the international landscape and to better meet the needs of their respective interests. China-Africa relations became increasingly focused on the practical, on mutual benefit, and on equal relations. There are three key features to China-Africa relations for the past half a century:

The first is the commitment to unity, no matter weal or woe. China has, once upon a time, selflessly provided large amounts of aid to Africa, to the best of its ability, in order to support the liberation efforts of the African peoples. Between 1956 and 1977, China provided over USD2.476 billion worth of aid to African countries. This amount was 58% of all aid provided by China to external parties.[27] In particular, China has helped to build the Tanzam Railway in Africa, thereby lending strong assistance to the independence and liberation movements of southern Africa. In terms of individual strength, China and Africa will have no chance if they were to come up against the Western countries and their allies. However, when the Third World—comprised mainly of Asian and African countries—comes together it is a power to behold. In fact, in the past, the Western world has to reckon with this power.

The second id the principle of treating each other as equals. "Equality" in the context of international politics has special significance for Asian and African countries that had once been bullied by the Western powers. Since the establishment of relations with African countries, China has stuck to the principles of sovereign equality and non-interference in domestic politics. As long as African countries recognize the "One China" principle China would establish friendly relations with these countries as equals regardless of how different their political beliefs, development models or state of development are.[28] On the other hand, the majority of Western

---

[26] The Africa-E.U. Joint Strategy was announced at the 2007 Africa-E.U. Summit. The Strategy comprises four objectives for the E.U.-Africa strategic partnership, which are: the strengthening of relations between Africa and the E.U.; promoting peace, security and sustainable development in Africa; the joint facilitation of the development of multilateralism and multilateral mechanisms; and the joint facilitation of the development of non-state actors.

[27] Li, Anshan (2006). On changes and transformations in China's policies towards Africa. *West Asia and Africa*, 2006 (8), 11–20.

[28] The China's African Policy released in 2006 stated: "the one China principle is the political foundation for the establishment and development of China's relations with African countries

countries have conducted their development relations with Africa selectively, or placed their focus on reinforcing relations with ex-colonies, or placed an emphasis on developing relations with African countries with significant resources or regional powers. Further, the strongest point about China's soft power is its respect and belief in equality evidenced in its foreign aid. Since the 1960s China has emphasized that its Africa aid would not come with any strings attached. This principle has remained in place today, and has become the greatest difference between aid provided by China and aid provided by the West. China's leaders have on many occasions emphasized in the international setting that China respects the autonomous choices made by African countries in terms of their social systems and development pathways in accordance with their specific national circumstances. China has also emphasized that development experience should be suitably referenced while autonomous development taking precedence, and that it opposes the West's insistence on imposing its values and social models on Africa without regard for the actual developmental circumstances involved. At the same time China has maintained the necessary calm attitude towards the so-called "Beijing Consensus" held by the international community, and showed its respect and regard for African countries as equal partners.

The third is the principle of "mutual benefit" in economic interactions. In 1982, the Chinese government announced its "Four Principles" of economic and technical partnership with Africa, which are equality and mutual benefit, a focus on efficiency, a diverse array of approaches, and common development. China began working actively to seek out new ways of aiding Africa, and encouraged Chinese enterprises to engage more in investment in, and technology transfer with, Africa. For more than 50 years, China has completed nearly 900 turnkey projects in Africa, trained 30,000 African talents in various fields, and sent a total of 17,000 healthcare personnel to 43 African countries.[29] China is already building overseas economic and trade partnership zones in Zambia, Mauritius, Botswana and Egypt, etc., to help these countries enhance their industrial development capabilities.

The fundamental difference between China and colonialism in the traditional sense of the word is that China does not have any political demands of Africa and does not seek to dominate or rule Africa in the political arena. The increase in Chinese investment in Africa and China's aid policies (which are different from those of the West) have given Africa more foreign-policy options and thus enhanced Africa's position in international affairs. As Tanzanian scholar Mwesiga Baregu put it, currently Africa is facing two windows of opportunity: the first window is the opportunity to promote regional and African integration, while the second window is the opportunity to accelerate the development of relations with swift-growing

---

and regional organizations. The Chinese Government appreciates the fact that the overwhelming majority of African countries abide by the one China principle, refuse to have official relations and contacts with Taiwan and support China's great cause of reunification. China stands ready to establish and develop state-to-state relations with countries that have not yet established diplomatic ties with China on the basis of the one China principle." Refer to the China's African Policy in the *People's Daily*, 13 January 2006, p. 3.

[29] *People's Daily* (9 February 2009). Expanding China-Africa cooperation, enhancing aid outcomes, p. 3.

economies like China and India.[30] Currently, China is conducting trade relations with African countries as equals. Although disagreements happen from time to time in the course of such relations, this is normal in international economic activity and any dispute can be resolved by means of equal negotiation. If China is accused of engaging in neo-colonialism because of lop-sided economic structures or even worse, if an economic issue is elevated to the level of political problem, one is perhaps over-analyzing China's influence on Africa.[31] This is why Chinese Premier Wen Jiabao has said on a visit to Africa that "neo-colonialist" is not a label that can be applied to China.[32]

2. Differences in foreign-relations attitudes: "Washington Consensus" versus "Beijing Consensus"?

Since the 1980s, the West has, in series, sought to make African countries implement "economic and structural reform", "democratization and political reform", and the building of "good governance". These moves were based in the liberal "Washington Consensus".[33] This so-called "consensus", which was really promoted by Western countries through coercive means, required various countries to liberalize

---

[30] Baregy, Mwesiga (2008). Africa-China–Europe Relations: a perspective from Africa. *International Issue Forum*, Summer 2008 issue, pp. 124–133.

[31] In recent years, the Chinese government has, on several occasions, responded to accusations of China practicing "neo-colonialism" in Africa. Generally, there are four lines of argument used. They are: (1) The majority or "mainstream" of China-Africa trade relations are positive, and the problems lie with the "non-mainstream". (2) China's diplomatic stance with regard to Africa is rooted in sincerity and friendliness, and that the negative behavior of individual Chinese firms does not represent China's foreign policy. (3) The majority of existing issues between China and Africa are economic in nature and can be brought under control and resolved. (4) The majority of African nations and those in the know have evaluated China-Africa trade partnerships positively. See Luo, Jianbo (2008). African non-governmental organizations and China-Africa relations. *Contemporary International Relations*, 2008 (4), 10–15.

[32] *People's Daily* (19 June 2006). Wen Jiabao holds press conference in Egypt, p. 5.

[33] The term "Washington Consensus" was proposed by World Bank economist John Williamson in 1989 to summarize the economic reforms and responses to the economic crisis advocated by the World Bank, the International Monetary Fund, and the U.S. government at that time. At the heart of the Washington Consensus are ten thrusts: (1) Low government borrowing. Avoidance of large fiscal deficits relative to GDP; (2) Redirection of public spending from subsidies ("especially indiscriminate subsidies") toward broad-based provision of key pro-growth, pro-poor services like primary education, primary health care and infrastructure investment; (3) Tax reform, broadening the tax base and adopting moderate marginal tax rates; (4) Interest rates that are market determined and positive (but moderate) in real terms; (5) Competitive exchange rates; (6) Trade liberalization: liberalization of imports, with particular emphasis on elimination of quantitative restrictions (licensing, etc.); any trade protection to be provided by low and relatively uniform tariffs; (7) Liberalization of inward foreign direct investment; (8) Privatization of state enterprises; (9) Deregulation: abolition of regulations that impede market entry or restrict competition, except for those justified on safety, environmental and consumer protection grounds, and prudential oversight of financial institutions; and (10) Legal security for property rights. See: Williamson, John (2005). A short history of the Washington Consensus in Huang, P., and Cui, Z., eds. (2005). China and Globalization: the Washington Consensus or the Beijing Consensus? Beijing: Social Sciences Academic Press, pp. 63–85.

their respective economies, implement the privatization of state-owned companies and relax government regulation. The central line of ways of thinking here is to minimize the role that government plays in the economy and allow the market to take the lead in economic life and economic development. Although theoretically speaking the Washington Consensus is exquisitely and comprehensively structured, it has led to a string of dismal performances in practice. Economic restructuring plans have caused Africa and Latin America to plunge in economic crisis, while at one point Russia was thrown into the abyss thanks to "shock therapy". Erroneous crisis responses had also exacerbated the Asian financial crises at one point.[34] Although the "post-Washington Consensus" has relooked the flaws in the Washington Consensus, such as an over-reliance on the market and the consequent neglect of the role of the government and social equilibrium, and has been bolstered with new content on governance, government controls and institution-building, etc., the West's neo-liberalist tendencies have remained at the core.[35]

Unlike the Washington Consensus, the "Beijing Consensus" represents another path to economic growth and even social development. This concept was first mooted by Goldman Sachs senior advisor Joshua Cooper Ramo in May 2004 in his summary of China's economic and social development models. According to Ramos, the success of the Beijing Consensus can be attributed to an emphasis on principles, proactive innovation, and bold experimentation.[36] In the three decades since the beginning of reform and opening-up, China has established a development pathway different from the West in an autonomous fashion and in accordance with its specific circumstances. China has refused to transplant the experiences of the West and has, instead, emphasized the need to cross the river by feeling the stones. Further, China has also refused to employ the extreme "shock therapy" method but rather gradual reforms. While China has learned from the market economy policies of other countries it has placed its focus on the maintenance and exercise of the government's macro-management and mobilization capabilities. At the same time, while encouraging reform and innovation China has also dealt correctly with the relationships between development, reform, and stability. The Chinese government prefers the term "developmental model" to "Beijing Consensus". This cautious attitude embodies the

---

[34] Zou, Dongtao (2006). The Washington Consensus, the Beijing Consensus, and China's distinctive development path in Yu, Keping et al., eds. (2006). *The China Model and the Beijing Consensus: transcending the Washington Consensus*. Beijing: Social Sciences Academic Press, pp. 409–434.

[35] For discussions on the "Washington Consensus", refer to: World Bank (1997). *World Development Report: the State in a Changing World*. New York: Oxford University Press, p. iii.; Stiglitz, Joseph E. The Post-Washington Consensus in Huang, P., and Cui, Z. (*ed.*), *China and Globalization: the Washington Consensus or the Beijing Consensus?*, pp. 86–102.

[36] Ramo, Joshua C. (2006). Appendix: The Beijing Consensus in Ramo, Joshua C., et al. (*ed.*). *China's Image: China in the eyes of foreign scholars*. Beijing: Social Sciences Academic Press, pp. 283–333.

Chinese government's consistent support for the independence of partner countries and consistently-held principle of non-interference in the domestic affairs of other countries.[37]

The Washington Consensus has not brought development and prosperity to Africa. Many countries have, in succession, witnessed political turmoil and economic stagnation while at the same time China was drawing the attention of the world with achievements rooted in its reform and opening-up, and modernization. Many African leaders who attend China-Africa summits are not only attracted by the aid and trade opportunities offered by China's developmental model. Thabo Mbeki, President of South Africa, later on wrote "At the Heavenly Gate in Beijing Hope is Born!", praising China-Africa cooperation for bringing Africa to a future full of hope.[38] The President of Senegal even wrote: "Not just Africa but the west itself has much to learn from China."[39] For many African countries that are still facing severe issues in the area of governance the need for an efficient and clean government indeed exists. What they need is a developmental model with local origins, and perhaps this is the greatest attraction about China's developmental model for Africa.

In the past, during the Cold War, the world was divided into two, the East and the West. Developing countries had to either follow the Western model or emulate the Soviet Union. After the Cold War, the Western world sought to push its political beliefs and developmental model to the developing world with the arrogance of "the one who has ended history". Currently, with China's rapid development, these developing countries that have already realized political independence and which have undergone some painful developmental experiences have begun to see the hope of realizing national rejuvenation in an independent manner. The "Look East" trend has emerged with African countries is actually an independent attempt by Africa to seek out its own developmental path. It has given Africa another possibility and opportunity to consider in its quest. The success of China's developmental model has shown its tremendous desirability, influence and external reach in a time where social, governance and development issues are becoming increasingly pressing, and have won for China more soft power and a greater voice on the international scene. As Ramo wrote: "China is marking a path for other nations around the world who are trying to figure out not simply how to develop their countries, but also how to fit into the international order in a way that allows them to be truly independent, to protect their way of life and political choices in a world with a single massively powerful centre of gravity", and "China is in the process of building the greatest asymmetric superpower the world has ever seen, a nation that relies less on traditional tools of power projection than any in history and leads instead by the electric

---

[37] Luo, J., and Zhang, X. (2009). China's Africa Policy and its Soft Power. *AntePodium*, Victoria University of Wellington (2009), www.victoria.ac.nz/atp.

[38] Mbeki, Thabo (10 November 2006). At the Heavenly Gate in Beijing Hope is Born! *ANC Today*; Mbeki, Thabo (2006). At the Heavenly Gate in Beijing hope is born!. http://www.chinese-embassy.org.za/eng/zfgx/zfhzlt/t279923.htm.

[39] Wade, Abdoulaye (24 January 2008). Time for the West to Practice what it Preaches. *Financial Times*.

power of its example and the bluff impact of size."[40] Some Western scholars have even described the Chinese government's ability to establish alternative political and economic models as "the biggest ideological threat the West has felt since the end of the Cold War".[41] Undoubtedly, African countries' decision to "look East" may lead African development down a path that deviates to a certain extent from the expectations of the West, and naturally this would lead the Western countries to be worried and suspicious.

3. Differences in diplomatic principles: intervention or non-intervention in the domestic affairs of another country?

Europe has, with the beliefs of political liberalism, tried to force-promote its human-rights, democratic and good-governance standards to African countries, typically through political conditions attached to economic aid. From the African slave trade and European colonization of Africa in the early days to the imposition of European political and economic control over independent African countries later on and then to the various "structural reform programs" and human-rights interventions made following the Cold War, we see that Western countries have tried to dominate historical choices in world development and steer nations along certain pathways in accordance with their preferences. In recent years, the US has also placed an emphasis on the promotion of good governance and the building of democratic institutions in Africa. In February 2008, then-President George Bush visited Benin, Tanzania, Rwanda, Ghana and Libya. One of the objectives of this trip was to promote values such as human rights, democracy, and good governance. Through the Millennium Challenge Account (MCA) established in January 2004, the US has rewarded these countries with aid, using massive 'carrots' as a means of encouraging African countries to embark on the path of good governance.

China has consistently adhered to the policy of non-interference in its Africa policy. This is a cornerstone of China's foreign relations and a key principle in the founding of the country. China's policy of non-interference comprises at least the following: first, such non-interference refers to non-interference where the political and economic sovereignty of African countries is concerned. China believes that African countries have the ability to choose their own developmental paths. However, this does not mean that China pays zero regard to peace and development issues in Africa. In fact, in the past few decades China has consistently supported Africa's anti-imperialism, anti-colonialism and anti-racism struggles, and has for a long time supported African countries in their economy-building efforts. In particular, China has helped Africa to realize self-reliance through the building of major infrastructural facilities through its Africa aid projects. To date, China has completed 519 infrastructural aid projects in Africa, including 375 social and public facilities, 144 economic

---

[40] Ramo, Joshua C. (2006). Appendix: The Beijing Consensus in Ramo, Joshua C., et al. (*ed.*). *China's Image: China in the eyes of foreign scholars*. Beijing: Social Sciences Academic Press, pp. 283–333.

[41] Gill, B. and Yan, Z. (2006). Sources and Limits of Chinese 'Soft Power'. *Survival*, Vol. 48, 2006 (2), 17–36.

facilities, 2,233 km of railway, 3.391 km of road and highway, ten bridges, and a total of 780,000 stadium seats.[42] In recent years, China has been paying close attention to peace and stability issues on the African continent and has participated in a number of UN peacekeeping nations in Africa. China has also provided support for the peacekeeping efforts of the AU For instance, China called for the UN Security Council to pass Resolution No. 1,769 on 31 July 2007 for the dispatch of around 26,000 AU and United Nations troops to Darfur for peacekeeping purposes. China was also the first, in the first half of October 2007, to send a 315-man engineering unit to Darfur in preparation for the arrival of the peacekeeping troops. Second: the principle of non-interference in the domestic affairs of another country also means that China-Africa relations have transcended ideological differences. As long as the African country concerned recognizes the "one China" principle no matter how different it is in terms cultural background, political system or diplomatic beliefs China is willing to establish diplomatic relations with it and treat it equally as it does with all other African countries. Third: the principle of non-interference in the domestic affairs of any country means that China-Africa relations are directed at any third party. Although both China and its African partners have emphasized on a number of occasions the importance of promoting democracy globally and of improving the global political and economic order, China and Africa have inadvertently created a competitor either real or potential. What the two oppose is merely the unilateral behavior often seen in international society and where the international order is being unreasonable, and not against any specific parties in particular.[43]

However, the Western countries are of the opinion that China's longstanding Africa policy of decoupling politics from economics is not only in conflict with the diplomatic principles practiced by Europe in the post-Cold War era but also a hindrance to the realization of good governance in various African countries.[44] Hence, they have requested that China participate in existing multilateral aid and investment arrangements in an attempt to include China in the existing international system and make China adhere to the existing rules of this system. Actually, China is also concerned with governance issues in Africa. However, China's concern with governance outcomes is fundamentally different from Europe's concern with so-called "good governance". "Good governance" as spoken of by Europe is based on value judgments and modeled on the political systems of the West. The aim is turn Africa in "white Africa". On the other hand, China's Africa policy emphasizes effective governance in what is a results-oriented approach. The focus is on effective government operations, orderly social management, political stability and the

---

[42] *People's Daily* (9 February 2009). Expanding China-Africa cooperation, enhancing aid outcomes, p. 3.

[43] Luo, Jianbo. How to promote China's multilateral relations. *Contemporary International Relations*, pp. 24–29.

[44] Games, Dianna (21 February 2005). Chinese the New Economic Imperialists in Africa. *Business Day*; Hilsum, Lindsey (2006). China's Offer to Africa: Pure Capitalism. *New Statesman*, 3 July 2006, pp. 23–24.

appropriate policies for economic development.[45] China will not accept the political values of the West, and it is not possible for individual African countries to define "good governance" entirely by the values of the West, either.

5.4 Cooperation Between China and the West in Promoting Development in Africa: In Search of Possibilities and Methods

The theory of constructivism in international politics holds that the structure of international society is a dynamic one with constant developments. Interactions and encounters between various parties can constantly build new knowledge, beliefs and identities, and thus lead to changes in the relationships between actors.[46] Hence, both China and the West should move past their mutual suspicion and differences on the Africa issue and seek to realize situations that benefit various parties. Only by seeking out commonalities amidst differences can there be harmony despite differences.

1. Changes in attitude and thinking that will be necessary

China and the Western countries should, while working to understand each other's foreign-relations strategies and Africa policies, seek to change the way they think as there are—on both sides—still emotional or even ideological tendencies on certain issues to various extents. Only this way can China and the West move from the ossified, the superficial, and even the Cold War-esque to a more open and cooperative way of thinking that will in turn enable win–win situations.

First of all, all parties need to recognize their intersecting interests and common strategic objectives in Africa. The greater coordination of policy between China and Europe with a focus on interests can help to avoid possible vicious competition. Joint efforts by China and the West to promote peace, stability and development in Africa and to enhance capacity-building in the continent are the best interest of all parties. As Guan Chengyuan, head of China's delegation to the EU and ambassador to Belgium said: "China and Europe… both advocate peace, stability and development of the African continent; both want to strengthen capacity building in Africa; both hope to see an Africa that is continuously growing; both are making efforts to practice what they advocate in Africa."[47] In a broader sense, Africa is the one region in the world with the most salient issues and is key to the resolution of existing North–South issues. The positions adopted by China and Western countries in response to peace and development issues in Africa will have an impact on whether the world can better

---

[45] Fang, Xiao (2008). Summary of the 'Sino-European Cooperation: opportunities and challenges' seminar. *International Issue Forum*, Summer 2008 issues, pp. 139–143.

[46] Wendt, Alexander (2006). *Social Theory of International Politics*. Shanghai: Shanghai Century Publishing Group, pp. 1–58.

[47] Guan, Chengyuan. China and her strategic partnerships with Africa and the European Union. How to balance the two? http://www.chinamission.be/chn/sgxx/t335118.htm.

realize harmonious and sustainable development. Developing multilateral relations concerned with African development is the ideal model for China and the West as they seek to deal more effectively with global challenges in this century.

Western countries should regard the development of China-Africa relations with a more rational and practical eye. It is critical that the following points are recognized: (1) Ideological color has been completely abandoned with China-Africa relations, and China-Africa strategic relations are not targeted at any third party and certainly not any Western country. China has no intention of changing the West's existing political and economic contacts in Africa, and in fact neither does it have the ability to do so in the near future. (2) China will make gradual changes to its foreign-relations policies in accordance with the corresponding UN resolutions and the actual needs of various African countries. For instance, on the Darfur issue, since 2006 China has, through various means, urged the government of the Sudan to work with the AU and the UN, and to a certain extent has facilitated the restarting of the political resolution process in the Sudan and the deployment of AU and UN peacekeeping troops in the region. China has slowly earned the recognition and praise of international society through this process.[48] (3) China-Africa trade cooperation is non-exclusive, and is becoming more open and transparent by the day. The Chinese economy is becoming increasingly integrated with the global economy and most Chinese enterprises are also playing by international rules when they conduct economic activity in Africa. Although China enjoys closer political relations with certain African countries, china has never relied on its political advantage to score projects in competitive tenders in Africa. Chinese enterprises have won out for their balance of price and service/product quality, and for the strong reputation they have forged as a result. (4) The scale of Chinese economic activity in Africa is still far smaller than what those in the West have made it out to be. Chinese companies produce far less oil in Africa compared to multinational companies from Europe and America. In 2006, Chinese companies produced on average 267,000 barrels of oil in Africa each day. This is one-third of the production volume of ExxonMobil, the largest foreign oil producer in Africa.[49] In April 2008, China's Ministry of Foreign Affairs issued the following rebuttal in response to the European Parliament's criticisms of China-Africa partnerships in the area of energy: "In terms of scale and quality, China's energy partnerships with Africa have a long way to go before it can catch up with the European nations and with the US 79% of oil produced in Africa is exported. 36% of exports go to Europe, and another 33% go to the US Only 8.7% of Africa's oil exports go to China. If we regard the 8.7% exported to China as the

---

[48] Although an article titled 'The Neo-Colonists' published in the 13 March 2008 issue of the *Economist* had once again mentioned China's "resource hunger", the magazine had at the same time also recognized positive changes in China's foreign policy, particularly its policy changes on the Darfur issue. *The Economist* print edition (13 March 2008). The New Colonialists. http://www.economist.com/opinion/displaystory.cfm?story_id=10853534.

[49] Downs, Erica S. (2007). The Fact and Fiction of China-Africa Energy Relations. *China Security*, Vol. 3, 2007 (3), 43–47.

'plundering of energy resources' as alleged, then what do we call the 36%?"[50] (5) China-Africa trade cooperation is already producing positive effects. China's low-priced products are a match for the consumption power of African consumers and have improved the quality of their lives. China's investments and aid have driven economic development in Africa, and made African markets more active. Objectively, these developments also benefit the Western countries. The UKDepartment for International Development had admitted that "China's trade with, investment in, and aid to Africa have had highly positive effects, making Africa's prospects of realizing the Millennium Development Goals greater."[51] (6) Chinese enterprises are still exploring and developing international markets. As such, their focus at this point is on capital accumulation. Furthermore, they also lack experience in international operations. Hence, certain enterprises can do better in terms of improving their image with regard to social responsibility. However, for the long term, Chinese enterprises will have to make adjustments to their trade and economic activity in accordance with prevailing international rules. As Fredrick Mutesa of the University of Zambia said, Chambishi Copper Mine, a member of the China Nonferrous Metal Mining Group, has already learned its lessons from a gas explosion in April 2005 and a workers' strike by Zambian workers in July 2006, and is working to improve working conditions and compensation for its workers.[52] Most importantly, the negative behavior of a number of Chinese enterprises cannot be equated with China's Africa policy. As Thomas J. Christensen and James Swan have reminded their peers: "we must distinguish between Chinese energy companies' pursuit of exploration agreements and the Chinese government's Africa policy.... There are often exaggerated charges that Chinese firms' activities or investment decisions are coordinated by the Chinese government... In reality, Chinese firms compete for profitable projects not only with more technologically and politically savvy international firms, but also with each other."[53]

China and African countries should on their part acknowledge that Western countries do have good intentions for African countries in their foreign policies. At least up till today, Western countries led by the EU and the US have had a positive effect in terms of promoting peaceful development in Africa. In fact, these countries have played a leading role in certain areas. Both China and African countries should also look upon the West's global role and changes in its Africa policies in recent years from the perspective of development and change. Due to conditioning by historical experiences and assessments of actual interests Western countries will certainly

---

[50] Ministry of Foreign Affairs of the People's Republic of China (2008). Daily Press Conference Hosted by Ministry of Foreign Affairs Spokesperson Jiang Yu on 24 April 2008. http://www.fmprc.gov.cn/chn/xwfw/fyrth/t428635.htm.

[51] Department for International Development, UK Realizing the Millennial Development goals in Africa in partnership with China. http://www.dfid.gov.uk/countries/asia/China/partners.asp.

[52] Mutesa, Fredrick. *China's footprints in Zambia.* Paper presented at the meeting of "China's Footprint in Development Countries Research Sharing Workshop", January 22–24, Hong Kong, YMCA International House.

[53] Christensen, T.J., and Swan, J. China in Africa: Implications for U.S. Policy. http://foreign.senate.gov/hearings/2008/hrg080604a.html.

continue to seek dominative power in Africa and try to guard against overly-rapid growing emerging forces on the continent. However, since the advent of the twenty-first century we have also seen some positive changes in the Africa policies of Western countries: first, these countries have begun to place an emphasis on developing equal relations with African countries. France has claimed that it seeks to break free of the post-colonial mindset and has emphasized its desire to develop "new partnerships" with African countries. To this end, in 1998 France has changed the name of the France-Africa Summit to the Africa-France Summit.[54] The *2006 National Security Strategy Report* released by the US has also defined US-Africa relations as a "friendly partnership" and not a "parent–child relationship of dependency".[55] The linear thinking that links colonial rule, the post-colonial world and Cold War politics is no longer tenable. Western countries can never go back to the old models of engaging with African countries. Second is an advocacy for multilateralism in African affairs. With the rapid growth in the influence of developing powers like China and India in Africa, the Western countries have cautiously welcomed the participation of developing powers like China and India in efforts for peace and development in Africa. Multilateral partnerships relating to Africa have precisely been made possible under such circumstances. The idea that one can establish monopolistic interests in Africa is an outdated one.

Cooperation between China and Western countries should be based on the developmental needs of Africa and on what has been articulated by African countries themselves. Further, there should be ample consideration given to Africa's interests and strengths in the course of multilateral cooperation. In cooperation between major powers relating to Africa, Africa is not a target for dictation but a partner and stakeholder equal in status to the major powers. In recent years, the AU has worked in unity to enhance the autonomy and initiative of African countries in the course of development. As such, the concept of autonomous development has been emphasized in the New Partnership for Africa's Development (NEPAD) program, which has a focus on new, equal relationships between developing nations and developing nations/multilateral institutions.[56] African countries should, with the AU as basis, and the development goals prioritized by the NEPAD, establish a clear and unified stand for the further development of relations with China and Western countries.

2. Areas of cooperation and pathway choices

It is advisable for all parties to employ practical and step-by-step approaches to their Africa partnerships. In the first stage, coordination and cooperation can be conducted on the project level and on specific issues. Areas of possible cooperation in this stage include: (1) environmental issues, including food crises, natural disasters, global

---

[54] Utley, Rachel (2002). 'Not to do less but to do better…': French military policy in Africa. *Internal Affairs*, Vol. 78, 2002 (1), 129–146.

[55] The White House. The National Security Strategy of the United States of America. http://www.whitehouse.gov/nsc/nss/2006/nss2006.pdf.

[56] The New Economic Partnership for Africa's Development. http://www.nepad.org/2005/files/documents/inbrief.pdf.

warming, and the use of water resources, etc. Not only can non-traditional security issues in the environmental arena undermine economic development in Africa, they can also lead to political conflicts. The direct spark to the Darfur crisis was in a conflict over water and land resources.[57] (2) energy resource issues. Various parties can work to ensure the proper development of energy resources and to prevent irrational rises (that deviate from the balance of supply of demand) in the price of energy resources globally. This will work to everyone's interests. (3) infrastructure building. As outdated infrastructure places constraints on economic development in Africa, it is also an area of focus for both the AU and the NEPAD program. Complementarity can be achieved with funding and project management experience from the Western countries as well as affordable and high-quality engineering from China. (4) peace and security. Emphasis should be placed on participating in UN-led peacekeeping operations in Africa and at the same time seek to develop Africa's independent peacekeeping capabilities. (5) education and public health. Chinese teams sent on aid missions to Africa have accrued a trove of experience, and various Western charities, religious missions and community organizations, etc., have consistently been working at the grassroots level in various African countries in the areas of primary education and public health. China and the Western countries can strengthen their cooperation in the areas of human resource development, the fight against epidemics, and the fights against HIV/AIDS and tuberculosis, etc.

Based on experience and mutual trust built up in the aforementioned areas, cooperation can then be extended to areas with stronger political overtones, such as governance in Africa, political beliefs and attitudes, and development models. Various parties can reduce mutual suspicion and animosity, as well as build mutual trust and understanding, through communication and coordination. However, the fundamental way out remains that Africa must seek out its very own developmental model and locate internal pathways to creative value, self-confidence, and dignity.

3. Cooperative mechanisms and main partners

Cooperative mechanisms between China and Western countries can be bilateral, such as how China and Europe have established a regular communication channel on Africa issues, a Sino-European strategic dialogue mechanism, and regular Asia-Europe meetings on Africa-related issues. Outside of the EU framework, the Chinese government has established mechanisms for building trust and communicating with various European powers, including the UK about such issues as international development pertaining to Africa. On the subject of aid to Africa, a key objective of China-UK cooperation is to promote the realization of self-development in Africa, particularly the objectives set out by the New Partnership for Africa's Development and the AU[58] In terms of Sino-US relations, Africa-related issues have also

---

[57] Luo, J., and Jiang, H. (2008). The process of resolving the Darfur crisis and the shaping of China's national image. *Foreign Affairs Review*, 2008 no. 3, pp. 44–50; Adam Al-Zein Mohamed and Al-Tayeb Ibrahim Weddai, *eds.* (1998). *Perspectives on tribal conflicts in Sudan*. University of Khartoum Institute of Afro-Asian Studies.

[58] Department for International Development, UKRealizing the Millennial Development goals in Africa in partnership with China. http://www.dfid.gov.uk/countries/asia/China/partners.asp.

been incorporated into the agendas of Sino-US strategic economic dialogue and other high-level meetings. China and the US have met three times on their respective activity in Africa. Cooperative mechanisms can also take the form of trilateral partnerships, such as China–Europe-Africa partnerships or China-US-Africa partnerships. In June 2007, the EU held a conference titled "Partners in Competition? The EU, Africa and China". Trilateral cooperation between China, Europe and African countries rapidly became a hot topic at the event. The European Commission released a policy document, *EU, Africa and China: towards trilateral dialogue and cooperation*, in October 2008. In this document, the E.C. proposed that long-term trilateral partnerships between China, the EU, and Africa be established at four levels: at continental level, at regional level, at country (Ambassador) level, and in EU/China bilateral dialogue.[59] On issues pertaining to Africa, actors can even consider even broader four-way partnerships between China, the EU, the US, and Africa.

Possible partners include regional organizations, governments, and the general public. China should continue to strengthen its bilateral partnerships with regional powers in Europe and Africa and use these partnerships to guide the China policy in the region concerned. At the same time, attention should be paid to strengthening interactions with the EU and the AU as the political, economic, and diplomatic powers of regional organizations grow in tandem with deeper integration. China should invest more towards developing diplomatic and other kinds of ties at the grassroots level with Europe and Africa.[60] The targets of such diplomatic work should be media outlets and non-governmental organizations with a certain degree of global political influence. As such, efforts will have to be made to mobilize people-to-people diplomacy resources in China to help build confidence and dispel skepticism. This is because people's voices tend to be more easily accepted by the outside world than information the government puts out through its own international publicity campaigns. Exchanges on the grassroots level have played an important role in opening up the diplomatic space for China. Thus, henceforth, China should also focus on the supplementary effect of such "second-rail diplomacy".

Overall, multilateral cooperation between China, African countries, and the West is a subject that requires further in-depth examination. Cooperation between the various parties in this issue is but in a preliminary stage, and multilateral cooperation mechanisms and the corresponding distribution of rights and interests with such mechanisms have yet to take shape. Active efforts to establish forward-looking and

---

[59] Commission of the European Communities. E.U., Africa and China: towards trilateral dialogue and cooperation. http://ec.europa.eu/development/icenter/repository/COMM_PDF_COM_2008_0 654_F_COMMUNICATION_en.pdf.

[60] A new phenomenon has that emerged in recent years is that certain African non-governmental organizations and civil-society players have begun to criticize China's trade activity in Africa as well as some of her Africa policies. Such negative assessment have had a significant impact on the African masses' understanding of, and attitudes towards, China. These 'native' voices have also often been exploited and amplified by Western media, bringing unwarranted uncertainty to China-Africa relations that have been otherwise developing positively. See Luo, Jianbo (2008). African non-governmental organizations and China-Africa relations. *Contemporary International Relations*, 2008 no. 4, pp. 10–15.

prescient mechanisms are in line with China's diplomatic interests. On the strategic level, China should work actively but cautiously to study this new topic. On one hand, China should welcome the attention paid by the West to Africa issues and China-Africa relations, and adopt a constructive stance to participate in, or even push for, coordination and cooperation between various parties on Africa issues. On the other hand, China should act cautiously and should not seek to rush matters. China is currently in a stage when its national strength is swiftly growing. Any arrangements regarding mechanisms should be made after due consideration of the fact that its political and economic interests are likely to grow over time, and should be made with room for further development for China. On the policy level, China should maintain a dynamic balance between multilateral diplomacy and bilateral diplomacy, and between official diplomacy and mass diplomacy. At the same time, China should place an emphasis on both developing coordination and cooperation with Western powers and regional African powers as well as on developing its relations with regional organizations like the EU and the AU.

Chapter 6
China's "Going to Africa" Policy in Post-crisis Era: Adjustments and Improvement

Since 2007, the global financial and economic crisis originating in the US has seriously worsened the international economic environment for China, and China's opening up and international economic cooperation is facing growing difficulties. Against such a background, different opinions emerged as to whether China should continue the "Go Global" strategy. We believe the financial crisis didn't make that strategy outdated, but in the long term, the implementation of it, including the path, approach and focus, needs substantial adjustments and requires more comprehensive policies and more flexible measures.

6.1 New Understanding of the Significance of "To Africa" Strategy After the Financial Crisis

After the People's Republic of China was founded, the Chinese economy was seriously introverted and isolated due to various domestic and foreign factors and was barely connected with the world economy. After it launched the reform and opening up, China began to embrace the outside world for development. When it came to the mid-1990s, it picked up speed in foreign cooperation, and overseas development became an inevitable trend. Against such a background, the central government put forth the strategy that the Chinese economy and Chinese enterprises should "go global". It was a strategy of national economic and social development for China to deal with the challenge of economic globalization, and it proved effective and fruitful after long years of implementation. Because of it, the Chinese economy became much more internationalized and foreign trade and investment was largely expanded. However, the global financial crisis that broke out in 2007 seriously squeezed the external space for China's economic development, and the economic development model that highly depended on export and the international market was facing mounting challenges. Therefore, some people began to doubt whether it was necessary and possible for China to continue the "Go Global" strategy. In our opinion, although the international economic situation has undergone tremendous changes because of the financial and economic crisis and the external space for China's economic development has been seriously squeezed, the impact caused by the crisis varies from one country to another because of their huge differences in the level of economic development. Asian and African countries, which are in the early stage of industrialization and modernization, still have vast space for international cooperation. In particular, the tens of African countries still have high expectations for China-Africa economic cooperation. Therefore, China needs to adjust the focus and perfect its policies according to the changed domestic and international environment and improve the quality and benefit of the "Go Global" strategy.

First, the international financial crisis hasn't changed the general trend of economic globalization, and China's "Go Global" strategy still has new opportunities and space if properly steered and timely adjusted. (1) When joining the WTO, China pledged to gradually open the domestic market to other WTO members, so even if Chinese enterprises don't want to go global, the fierce competition with foreign enterprises is unavoidable. (2) After China launched the reform and opening up 30 years ago, it has actually undertaken international industrial transfer through the "bringing in" campaign and become a large manufacturer. But in this process, overcapacity becomes increasingly prominent and most industrial products are in oversupply. The overcapacity can be exported to developing countries in Africa, achieving industrial transfer and the upgrade of industrial structure at the same time. (3) With the rapid economic growth in China, resource strain becomes increasingly serious, and China is in serious shortage of energies and resources. Therefore, it has to accelerate the exploitation and utilization of overseas resources and energies and build diverse and stable energy supply channels, so as to guarantee the security and sustainability of national economy.

Second, for provinces in eastern China, like Zhejiang, there is much room to explore in the economic and trade relation with Africa, and tapping the African market is of great importance for them to diversify the "Go Global" strategy. Zhejiang is a large province by foreign trade and investment with the export dependence of up to 52%. Owing to the international financial crisis, its export growth to Europe and America fell by 8.2 and 6.2 percentage points respectively from January to September 2008, but its export to Africa and Latin America increased against the general decline. In 2008, Zhejiang's total trade volume with Africa reached USD9.3 billion, including USD7.52 billion export, a year-on-year increase of 27.8%. Africa became an emerging key market for Zhejiang to "go global". At the end of 2008, Zhejiang had approved the establishment of 267 companies in Africa, with a total investment of USD365 million. In the latest three years, Zhejiang approved 85 companies to invest in Africa with the total investment of USD312 million, over 80% of the combined investment in previous years. In 2008 alone, it had 30 African investment projects with the total investment of USD123 million, indicating a high growth rate. According to statistics from Yiwu Foreign Economy and Trade Bureau, in the first 11 months of 2009, Yiwu's accumulative export to African countries exceeded USD240 million, a year-on-year increase of 29.07%, and African businessmen were a rising force of foreign purchasers in Yiwu.[1]

Third, Zhejiang's investment in Africa has displayed new characteristics with obvious advantages and huge potential. If steered properly, it will be beneficial for the long-term and healthy development of China-Africa relations. At present, Zhejiang's investment in Africa not only grows at a fast pace, but also displays the following characteristics. (1) The investment is mainly concentrated in industries such as textile processing, mechanical product processing and mineral resource exploitation, with obvious industrial advantages. (2) There are many physical projects, particularly large ones, indicating that investment is taking the place of trade step by step. (3) Investment increases rapidly with considerable late-comer's advantages. (4) Zhejiang's investment meets Africa's urgent need for capital and its demand for developing physical economy and increasing local employment, which is of positive significance for China-Africa relations. For example, private Zhejiang enterprises built two industrial parks in Africa—the textile industrial park in Nigeria and the Hengda textile industrial park in Botswana, with the investment of USD49.8 million and USD50 million respectively in phase one. The construction of the two industrial parks encouraged some enterprises to invest and build factories in Africa, and received close attention from the governments of both sides for their positive role in boosting economic growth and increasing employment.

Therefore, how to deal with the substantial changes in international economic structure after the financial crisis, follow the general trend, and seize the opportunity to expand the economic and trade relation with African countries and raise the level of cooperation is an important question for export-oriented provinces like Zhejiang.

6.2 Difficulties in Chinese Enterprises' "Go Global" Efforts After the Financial Crisis

But Chinese enterprises still face a lot of difficulties in "going to Africa" these days and there are many problems they need to deal with effectively.

First, when the state supports enterprises in "going global" as part of the business diplomacy, it focuses on large state-owned enterprises (SOE) and doesn't pay enough attention to private and medium and small enterprises (SMEs). Zhejiang investors are mostly private, but the government doesn't provide enough favorable and supportive policies for Chinese private enterprises in Africa. As a result, it's hard for them to obtain financing and loans and capital shortage has become the main obstacle to their expansion and upgrade in Africa. The Bank of China (BOC) has set up operations in several African countries, but when private enterprises apply for loan with the pledge of assets, BOC only recognizes their assets in China, not those in Africa. But many Zhejiang investors have worked in Africa for many years and most of their assets are

---

[1] http://www.gov.cn/jrzg/2010-01/13/content_1509485.htm.

based there, so they cannot obtain loan from BOC. Meanwhile, the financial market in Africa is backward and local banks set interest rates that are too high for Chinese investors. For instance, the bank loan interest rate in Zambia in 2008 was 18.2% and Tanzania 16.3%, which was unaffordable for Chinese businesses.

Second, the Chinese government needs to intensify the legal negotiations with African countries and improve bilateral agreements on trade, investment, taxation and finance. China hasn't signed the agreements on the avoidance of double taxation and on product import with certain African countries yet, so Chinese enterprises in Africa face the problem of double taxation and product import discrimination. Take medicine import in Zambia for example. As Chinese pharmacopoeia differs largely from the Zambian one, which follows the British system, Chinese medicine has to be registered when imported to Zambia, but the registration isn't a one-time deal. The same medicine has to be registered again and again every time it is imported. It takes about USD500 to get a medicine batch number, and this process has to be repeated over and over. If tens or even over 100 kinds of medicines are imported at the same time, the medicine registration alone will cost over 10,000 US dollars, which is too much for Chinese enterprises and clinics. If China and Zambia can sign a bilateral agreement on medicine import to provide a package solution to medicine taxation, it will facilitate the development of Chinese hospitals in Zambia.

Third, China's diplomatic and commercial activities are not well aligned in combining the nation's aid to Africa with its efforts to push Chinese enterprises to "go to Africa". Promoting the China-Africa economic and trade cooperation and driving Chinese enterprises to go to Africa through African aid programs has been an important content in China's African aid reform since 1996, and has yielded good results in the past ten-plus years, but some problems still exist. At present, a lot of capital or projects of China's African aid are still handed over to the government of African countries directly and then distributed by themselves. This has three shortcomings. (1) There is no project demonstration or evaluation, so the benefit of aid is limited. (2) Aid corruption is serious, which gives western media an excuse. (3) The aid is mostly of "blood transfusion" type and unsustainable.

Fourth, at present, Chinese enterprises in Africa, especially private ones, face many structural problems, and they need the state to improve its work, strengthen management and provide better services. (1) Compared with western multinationals in Africa, Chinese enterprises in Africa lag far behind in overall strength, talent, brand, core technology and sales network, the domestic and foreign markets are obviously disconnected, and they don't have competitive advantages. (2) Chinese enterprises in Africa lack the talents who are familiar with the local situation and economic environment, don't have sound internal governance, tend to make decisions blindly, and their capability of identifying and controlling operating risks and dealing with emergencies is weak, resulting in many mistakes. (3) More Chinese people are going to Africa nowadays, but schools and hospitals for Chinese children are lacking, and the Chinese community faces many difficulties in long-term development. (4) Chinese enterprises in Africa have poor operating order, tend to take short-term actions, and have serious disordered competition. Some of them are unaware of social responsibility. Zhejiang is the first Chinese province to tap the African market, and

Yiwu, Wenzhou and Taizhou have the largest number of enterprises and migrants there in the country at the moment. But from textile, clothing and toy in the early period to light industrial products in recent years such as household appliances, motorcycle and TV set and to communication, resource and project contracting in the latest two years, many industries and enterprises are engaged in blind development and vicious competition in Africa, not only harming their interests, but also smearing China's image in the region. (5) Compared with enterprises from the west, India and Pakistan, Chinese enterprises in Africa are often subject to discrimination and unfair treatment. Chinese Chamber of Commerce in African countries is quite backward with a weak sense of service and poor capability of coordination. (6) Some provincial and municipal governments in China don't fully recognize the importance of tapping the African market, government departments have a weak sense of coordination, relevant legal system isn't established, and a sound management system isn't in place yet. As a result, decisions are not targeted, regulation is absent and public service is poor. (7) Chinese enterprises that invest in Africa have a weak awareness and poor capability of risk prevention. The situation in Africa is getting more stable in general, but local turmoil and religious and ethnic conflicts break out incessantly, public security and order is bad in certain countries, and Chinese citizens are constantly attacked in Africa. Besides, the west is hyping up China's so-called new-colonialism and plundering of resources, and the "China threat" theory is gaining ground, causing adverse effects on the operation of Chinese enterprises in Africa.

6.3 Adjustment of Chinese Enterprises' "To Africa" Strategy After the Economic Crisis

To better promote the economic and trade cooperation between China and Africa and push Chinese enterprises to "go to Africa" faster, the central government, local governments and enterprises in China should make new efforts together to improve policies, adjust focuses and work out new strategy and policies.

First, further elevate the strategic significance of developing China-Africa economic and trade cooperation and tapping the African market, specify the focus of work, and actively push for institutional innovation and functional improvement. State diplomatic department, local foreign affairs authorities and embassies and consulates overseas should create more smooth and effective channels of communication with Chinese enterprises and chambers of commerce in Africa, and foster a relation of more effective service, cooperation and coordination with them. They should provide more policy support and non-discriminate services for both SOEs and private enterprises in Africa, in order for them to all play their best and enter Africa in all aspects.

Second, make active use of national diplomatic means and resources to maintain and promote China's interests in Africa. China should intensify the business consultation and negotiation with the government of African countries, solve relevant disputes and positively influence their policy toward Chinese enterprises, so as to create a better environment and provide better policy guidance and information service for them to "go to Africa".

Third, Chinese diplomatic department, especially embassies and consulates in Africa, should energetically promote the establishment and institutionalized and standardized development of Chinese chambers of commerce, friendship associations and industrial associations in Africa. The function of chamber of commerce should be brought into play to regulate the behaviors of enterprises, raise the quality of the general industry, create a benign internal punishment mechanism, and avoid vicious competition. Chamber of commerce can also be allowed to participate in the business diplomacy conducted by embassies, whereby its advantages such as being professional, widely connected and well informed can be exerted to serve Chinese enterprises in participating in international competition, improving industrial competitiveness and exploring the international market.

Fourth, we can make full use of local Chinese businesses when implementing China's African aid programs to improve their quality and benefit. Before implementing the aid program, we can consult with local Chinese because they've lived in Africa for a long time and are very familiar with the local situation, thus making the aid more targeted. The aid programs had better combine the local needs with the development demand of Chinese enterprises, thus becoming more effective. China has proposed to build 100 ordinary elementary schools in Africa, but this program hasn't yielded much effect so far. At the moment, China is exporting electromechanical products, cars and household appliances to Africa in large quantities, and has begun to build factories there, but local schools that cultivate repair mechanics are in serious shortage. In view of this, China can adjust the contents of educational aid to Africa and turn to focus on building vocational-technical schools and holding training programs. This can nurture a large group of mechanics for African countries and also create the source of mechanics for Chinese enterprises to boost their development. Surveys show that Chinese enterprises in Africa suggested the state "provide more technical aid than capital aid" to Africa because technical aid not only helps African countries cultivate technical talents, but also fosters pro-Chinese forces and is sustainable. They raised the example of India's Tata Motors. The Zambians generally accepted Tata cars thanks to the company's technical aid.

Fifth, China should actively help its enterprises to realize and protect their interests overseas, support them in lobbying the government of the host country to adjust relevant trade policies and dealing with the foreign government directly, and support Chinese industrial association to take a part in building fair competitive order. Chinese diplomatic department should use diplomatic resources to promote the products, brands and strength of Chinese enterprises, and the enterprises should closely communicate with the government and provide information. When carrying out aid programs and projects for Africa, China should purchase the products and services from local Chinese enterprises as much as possible.

Sixth, the diplomatic department should better the coordination and cooperation with other relevant departments such as the Ministry of Commerce, Ministry of

Finance and Ministry of Education and set up an effective national risk pre-warning mechanism for Chinese enterprises "going global". China has started this work in recent years, but more efforts are needed. Relevant departments should form a joint organization, invite experts, scholars and external organizations to participate, and build a smooth and timely information release network. There are some renowned country risk consulting service companies with great influence in the world, such as the PRS Group, Moody's Investors Service and Standard and Poor's Rating Group. We can selectively draw on their experience, encourage the professional development of country risk evaluation, foster a group of Chinese country risk consulting service groups, and improve the capability of risk prediction.

Seventh, China should accelerate the diplomatic negotiation with African countries, sign agreements on avoiding double taxation and bilateral investment protection, and step up the publicity of them. China has signed the agreements on bilateral investment protection and double taxation avoidance with some African countries, but Chinese enterprises seldom make use of those agreements and many don't even know about their existence. Therefore, Chinese diplomatic organizations should step up the publicity of those agreements and train and guide Chinese enterprises to make full use of them to protect their own interests.

Eighth, Chinese diplomatic department can help provincial and municipal governments to set up investment service centers in major cities of Africa. Chinese embassies and consulates in Africa, especially the commercial department, should visit local Chinese enterprises regularly, take the initiative to create direct connection with them, introduce the service functions and programs of business diplomacy, and intensify the coordination with industrial associations. This will raise Chinese enterprises' capability of removing non-tariff barriers and help them obtain larger market share.

Ninth, Chinese diplomatic department should strengthen the formulation and study of laws and systems of diplomatic protection, intensify domestic legislation and international judicial cooperation, and continuously perfect the consular protection system. China hasn't signed the consular mutual assistance agreement with some African countries yet, which isn't good for carrying out effective consular protection, so capability building in that respect should be strengthened. (1) Diplomatic personnel directly engaged in consular protection should keep studying to raise their competence. (2) China should further improve its capability of diplomatic coordination, open more channels of communication with the government, civil groups, enterprises and celebrities in the host country, and assist overseas Chinese in fitting into the local society and enhancing internal solidarity. (3) Take active steps to strengthen the instruction of people going abroad and urge them to study local laws and stay away from trouble as much as possible.

There is vast room and great prospects for China-Africa economic and trade cooperation, but western powers are also adjusting their Africa policies, and one of the key contents in the diplomatic adjustment of Obama administration is intensifying the business diplomacy with Africa. As western powers return to Africa, China is facing growing competitive pressure there, but as a socialist country that has deep traditional friendship and sound political foundation with Africa, China has abundant and immense advantages in diplomatic resources toward Africa. Today, as

China-Africa relation has come to the stage of comprehensive strategic partnership, China should fully tap, utilize and enhance those advantages explore vaster space, create a more favorable environment and provide more effective services for Chinese enterprises to "go to Africa".

Acknowledgements Acknowledgement to Dr. Xiaofeng Zhang and Dr. Hengkun Jiang for their help in writing this chapter.

Chapter 7
China-Africa Cooperation and Cultivating China's Soft Power

Hard power in the traditional sense mainly refers to coercive power represented by such traditional power resource as military threat and economic sanction, while soft power refers to assimilative power, the ability of swaying other nation's wishes and invisible power resources such as foreign policy, cultural tradition and development model, as well as international rules and systems. As an intangible force, soft power generates a kind of attraction that hard power can hardly achieve and can obtain the other party's understanding and recognition by affecting and changing its ideas and values, thus achieving the ideal situation of "influencing things unknowingly". American scholar Joseph Nye said, "A country may obtain the outcomes it wants in world politics because other countries—admiring its values, emulating its example, aspiring to its level of prosperity and openness—want to follow it."[1] For China, a sound national reputation, authority and image can push it to participate in international political, economic and security affairs in greater depth and breadth and help it obtain the various resources and favorable external environment needed for national development. A sound national reputation, authority and image can also cushion the impact on the existing international power structure because of China's fast-growing national strength and expanding external influence, and mitigate the international community's misperception and doubts about the strategic approach of China's rise and its behavioral tendency afterwards. Therefore, improving China's soft power diplomacy and demonstrating its image as a responsible power that pursues peace, cooperation and mutual benefit timely and fully is critical for achieving the goal of rise and for its being recognized and accepted by the international community to some extent.[2]

---

[1] *Soft Power: The Means to Success in World Politics*, translated by Wu Xiaohui, et al. (Taipei: The Eastern Publishing Co., Ltd., 2005), p. 5.

[2] Refer to the following articles by Jianbo Luo: "Optimizing Africa's Soft Power in Africa," (*China Diplomacy*, 2nd issue, 2008); "Shaping China's National Image in Diplomacy with Africa," (*Contemporary International Relations*, 7th issue, 2007); "Evaluation of China's Soft Power and

Enhancing China's soft power and reshaping its national image doesn't just mean gaining the trust of surrounding countries and western powers. In recent years, Africa has become an important stage for China to practice soft power diplomacy and build its national image, and the continuous development and world influence of China-Africa friendliness has become a key yardstick to measure how far Chinese soft power has developed in the new age. The essence and style of China's African policy is an important foundation for building its soft power in Africa, cultural influence is an important form to demonstrate it, the exemplary role of development model is a key element for expanding it, and the multilateral cooperation mechanism between China and Africa is an effective way to enhance it. Timely analysis of the form, achievements and problems of China's soft power in Africa is necessary for improving its African policy and pushing the China-Africa relation forward.

7.1 Essence and Style of Diplomatic Policy: Important Foundation for China's Soft Power in Africa

When talking about China-Africa relations, western and African scholars frequently ask the following question: how is China's Africa policy different from western countries'?[3] We believe that compared to western countries, China's Africa policy fully reflects the essence and style of its diplomacy—equality, respect, sincerity and mutual benefit. That's the most basic feature of China-Africa relations and the fundamental reason why the relations have remained firm and steadfast after so many years of wind and waves.

China sincerely pursues equality and respect in diplomatic relations. In history, both China and African countries suffered from the bully and oppression of western colonialists for a long time, so they attach special importance to equality and respect today, which is something the westerners, who exercised colonial rule in Asia, Africa and Latin America for hundreds of years, cannot understand. The Chinese government declared that all countries, big or small, strong or weak, rich or poor, are all equal, and it put this idea into practice. Ever since China formed diplomatic ties with African countries, it has adhered to the principle of "sovereign equality" and "non-interference in internal affairs", and always respected their right to choose a path suitable for their own development. In terms of etiquette, China has always treated friends from all countries equally, whether they are from the poorest countries in Africa or wealthy developed countries in the West. The Beijing Summit of the Forum on China-Africa Cooperation in 2006 put such diplomatic equality on full display. The summit brought together the leader of a large country and those

---

Development Path," (*International Issue Forum*, 5th issue, 2008); "China's African Policy and its Soft Power," (*AntePodium*, Victoria University of Wellington, 2009).

[3] Dot Keet, "The role and impact of Chinese economic operations in Africa", in Dorothy-Grace Guerrero & Firoze Manji (eds.), *China's New Role in Africa and the South*, Cape Town, Nairobi and Oxford: Fahamu-Networks for Social Justice, 2008, pp.78–86.

from a few dozen countries from the same continent, something without precedence in China's diplomatic history and a rare event even in world diplomatic history. China's aid policy to Africa reflected its diplomatic respect to and equal treatment of all African countries. Unlike western countries, which based their aid to Africa on harsh political and economic conditions, China provided aid to Africa with the aim of promoting the development of African countries and consolidating its friendly and cooperative relation with them, without any strings attached. As to the approach of aid provision, China never posed as an almsgiver, but emphasized solidarity, mutual assistance and common development in the process of China-Africa cooperation. Some foreign scholar noticed that in the book *China's African Policy*, there was no such expression as China helping African countries "mitigate poverty", but the phrase "common prosperity" appeared multiple times, highlighting the cooperation between the two sides in such fields as economy, education and health care.[4] Many people in Africa feel deeply about the biggest difference between China and western countries—China help them do what they want to do, but western countries impose their own objectives on them. Ding Xiaowen, China's ambassador to Botswana, wrote an article that was published on *Global Business & Finance*, in which he said that regarding issues African countries are concerned about, China always listens to their opinions first. If African countries have a common standpoint, China supports it; if they have different opinions, China urges them to reach a consensus through consultation; if a consensus cannot be reached, China stands by the majority of African countries. When it comes to internal affairs in some countries, China is very cautious in taking a stance, whereas certain western countries always interfere on the excuse of democracy and the lack of human rights. On hot-button issues such as the reform of the UN, Darfur of Sudan and the situation in Zimbabwe, African countries saw China's understanding and support, which reflected its respect for the continent.[5] While China is by no means the first foreign power to come to Africa, it is the first one that does not treat Africa paternalistically or condescendingly.

Sincere assistance and mutual benefit is the most prominent characteristic of the China-Africa economic cooperation in the past 50-plus years. In history, China helped African countries build nearly 900 projects when it was extremely poor itself, including the world-renowned Tan-Zam Railway. Today China is still helping African countries pursue their development goals even though it is not itself a wealthy country yet. It pledged to help build the Conference Center of African Union and 100 rural schools across Africa. Chen Deming, former Minister of Commerce, made the following remarks after visiting Africa: China will, as always, do its best to provide aid to African countries with no political conditions, with special focus on social development and public wellbeing. We will continue to help build a group of public facilities and infrastructure projects, especially social, cultural and public welfare projects such as hospitals, schools and stadiums, and help African countries further

---

[4] Kenneth King, "Partnership between China and Africa," *The Journal of International Studies* 2006 (4), 10–20.

[5] Xiaowen Ding, "Secret to China's African Policy: Help Africans Find Self-respect," published online at http://finance1.jrj.com.cn/news/2008-01-31/000003253855.html.

enhance their capability of disease prevention and treatment and improve their agricultural production level.[6] China not only sincerely helped others, but strived to achieve mutual benefits in foreign economic cooperation. Teaching one how to fish is better than giving them fish. China will not only teach African countries how to fish, but will provide "fishing rod", "fishing net" and "bait" to help other developing countries obtain "more fish" and achieve mutual benefits and win–win outcomes by "sharing the fish".

In the past half century, China and African countries established a friendship characterized by "sharing weal and woe" and "sincere help". China has won their recognition and support with sincerity and reputation, and they view China as an "all-weather" reliable friend and the China-Africa relation as the example for South-South cooperation. African countries also requited China for its political support and selfless assistance at critical moments, as evidenced by the following examples. In 1971, African countries used their votes to help China restore its legitimate position in the UN. Twenty-six of the 76 countries voting in favor were from Africa. Chairman Mao pointed out vividly that it was our African brethren that carried us into the UN.[7] After June 1989, African countries resolutely stood by China despite strong pressure from the west. Leaders of nine African countries visited China that year, playing a critical role in helping China break the sanction and isolation imposed by western countries. China also received strong support from African countries on the Taiwan question and human rights issues.[8]

Some people in the west are unhappy to see the historical solidarity and cooperation between China and Africa and the consequent friendship. They either turn a blind eye to China's sincere with to help African countries and describe China's recent outreach to the continent a kind of abrupt entry, or peddle a highly ideologically-charged or politicized interpretation of China-Africa cooperation throughout history in which China's involvement in African affairs is entirely driven by the country's geopolitical objectives. In particular, some western scholars or people in the strategic circle doubted, misunderstood and even distorted the rapid development of China-Africa relations in modern times, accusing China of the so-called "neo-colonial" plunder of Africa. They claimed that China's African diplomacy is a kind of "economic mercantilism" or "political realism" rather than "equal", "mutually beneficial" and "win–win" relationship claimed by China. As stated in *China's New Role*

---

[6] "Larger Scale, Wider Scope, Higher Level," *People's Daily*, January 21, 2009, p. 9.

[7] Miaogeng Lu, "Glorious History of China-Africa Friendliness," *China International Studies*. 2006 (6): 7–52.

[8] Soon after the Cold War ended, Taiwan, utilizing the drastic changes in Eastern Europe and the economic dilemma of some African countries, strongly promoted the "Silver Bullet Diplomacy". In 1997, eleven African countries had "state relations" with Taiwan, and it still has four so-called "diplomatic allies" in Africa today, namely Swaziland, Burkina Faso, Gambia and Sao Tome and Principe. Most African countries firmly support the "One China" policy and are an important force that China relies on in safeguarding national sovereignty. In history, African countries helped China foil Taiwan's attempt to return to the UN and join the WHO in improper capacity many times. In the new age, closely uniting with African countries to effectively preserve both sides' national security and sovereign interests remains an important content of the strategic cooperation between China and Africa.

in Africa and the South, "open any newspaper and you would get the impression that the African continent, and much of the rest of the world, is in the process of being 'devoured' by China. Phrases such as the 'new scramble for Africa', 'voracious', 'ravenous' or 'insatiable appetite for natural resources' are typical descriptors used to characterize China's engagement with Africa. In contrast, the operations of Western capital with the same ends are described with anodyne phrases such as 'development', 'investment', 'employment generation'."[9] The negative comments from the international community have put considerable external pressure on China's diplomacy and disrupted the normal development of China-Africa relations, and should be given close attention.

7.2 Cultural Influence: An Important Manifestation of China's Soft Power in Africa

"Culture" here refers to the concept of "big culture", which covers a wide range of topics, including culture and art, education, HR development and conceptual innovations. Cultural influence is an important component and reflection of soft power. If a big country wants to gain the respect of other countries, it must put a cultural premium on friendliness and kindness, and be able to influence, facilitate and contribute toward cultural development in other countries around the world. As China continues to pursue peaceful development, cultural soft power has direct implications for the overall preservation and overseas expansion of its national interests and to what extent the rising China will be accepted and recognized by the international community.[10] In recent years, the African continent has become an important stage on which China expands its international influence and establishes its image as a responsible power, and cultural exchanges with Africa is an effective tool to shape China's national image and enhance its soft power.[11]

When China and Africa started diplomatic relations in the 1950s, educational and cultural exchanges played the important role of a diplomatic "forerunner". At that time, 24 foreign students from Egypt, Cameroon, Kenya and other countries and regions came to study in China, and China assigned students and teachers specializing in language, literature, history and other humanities subjects to African countries such as Egypt and Morocco. China and certain African countries also assigned educational delegations to each other. In the 1960s, most African countries claimed independence successively, and China timely increased the number of African students it

---

[9] Dorothy-Grace Guerrero & Firoze Manji, "Introduction: China's new role in Africa and the south", in Dorothy-Grace Guerrero & Firoze Manji (eds.), *China's New Role in Africa and the South*, Cape Town, Nairobi and Oxford: Fahamu-Networks for Social Justice, 2008, pp. 1–6.

[10] Jianbo Luo, "Building Foreign Cultural Strategy for China's Rise," *Contemporary International Relations*. 2006 (3), 33–37.

[11] Jianbo Luo, "Shaping China's National Image in Diplomacy with Africa". *Contemporary International Relations*. 2007 (7): 48–54.

accepted. By the mid-1960s, 14 African countries assigned 164 students to China, and China assigned mathematics, physics, chemistry and Chinese language teachers to more African countries to help with the discipline construction in their colleges and middle schools.[12] However, the China-Africa cultural and educational exchange was of limited forms and small scale up to the 1970s. After China launched the reform and opening up, especially in the twenty-first century, China, with its growing national strength and progress on education and cultural development, considerably intensified the cooperation with African countries in such fields as culture, education and HR development. To date, it has conducted educational and cultural exchanges with 50 African countries, and such exchanges have evolved from the single form of assigning students to one another to educational communication and cooperation on multiple levels, in multiple fields and in multiple forms.

The number of African students in China has increased drastically. Since 1998, China has provided scholarship to more than 1,000 students from African countries each year.[13] In 2000, China set up the African Human Resources Development Fund under the framework of the Forum on China-Africa Cooperation (FOCAC), under which it has gradually increased enrollment of students from Africa. In November 2006, the Chinese government committed at the Beijing Summit of the Forum on China-Africa Cooperation that it will increase the annual number of scholarships to African students from 2,000 to 4,000 person-times in the next three years. In 2007 alone, more than 2,700 African students received the Chinese government scholarship, accounting for 26.9% of all the government scholarships China provided to foreign students that year.[14] According to the latest statistics from the Chinese Ministry of Education, by the end of September 2007, about 21,000 person-time students from 50 African countries came to China on the Chinese government scholarship, as well as about 8,000 African students who came here at their own expenses. In the past five years, the number of African students to China has increased rapidly at the average annual rate of around 20%.[15] Today China is one of the main destinations for African students and the Asian country that accepts the most African students.

China assigned teachers to Africa in more forms. It began to implement the cooperation program of higher education and scientific research with Africa in the late 1980s. The Chinese government provided the capital to support intercollegiate communication and cooperation between Chinese and African institutes of higher education, and helped African institutions to build specialized labs they were in urgent need of. China even assigned teachers and experts to provide guidance to

---

[12] China-Africa Education Cooperation and Compilation Group of the Ministry of Education, *Educational Cooperation and Exchange Between China and African Countries*. Beijing: Peking University Press, 2005, p. 2.

[13] China-Africa Education Cooperation and Compilation Group of the Ministry of Education, *Educational Cooperation and Exchange Between China and African Countries*. Beijing: Peking University Press, 2005, p. 16.

[14] "Remarkable Achievements in China-Africa Educational Cooperation and Exchange through Joint Efforts," *People's Daily*, February 8, 2009, p. 3.

[15] "More African Students Study in China, Love China," *People's Daily Overseas Edition*, January 3, 2008.

them and carry out joint research with them. This approach combined assigning teachers, providing material aid and helping HR development, conformed to China's reform of the foreign aid policy and the adjustment of talent cultivation model for Africa, and was helpful for raising the level of education and technological development in African countries. From 1956 to 2008, China assigned more than 500 professional teachers to 35 African countries, teaching courses of a dozen subjects covering physics, engineering, agriculture, culture and sports.[16]

The teaching of Chinese language made major headway in Africa. Starting from the 1950s, African countries such as Egypt, Tunisia, Algeria, Mauritania, Benin, Mauritius, Cameroon, Madagascar and South Africa began to develop the teaching of Chinese language. China provided strong support for this undertaking, not only supplying a large amount of teaching materials and linguistic equipment, but also dispatching teachers to those countries. In the twenty-first century, China has been setting up Confucius Institutes across many African countries. In December 2005, the first Confucius Institute in Africa was unveiled at the University of Nairobi in Kenya, and 21 Confucius Institutes or Confucius Classes have been opened in 14 African countries to date. In April 2006, the then Chinese President Hu Jintao met with teachers and students of the Confucius Institute at the University of Nairobi during his state visit to Kenya, and encouraged the students to study hard and contribute to China-Kenya friendship and development.

Exchanges of art troupes intensified. From 2001 to 2005, 34 Chinese art troupes performed in Africa, accounting for 30% of the number of all art troupes that have visited Africa in the last 50 years, and 33 art troupes from African countries came to perform in China in the same period, accounting for 41% of the total from the past 50 years. In 2004 particularly, China launched the Chinese Culture to Africa program, whereby it assigned four art troupes and three art exhibitions on a performing and exhibition tour across Africa. The tour fully demonstrated the sound image of Chinese culture that values harmony among ethnic groups, wellbeing for the people and prosperity and development of the nation, and largely boosted its attraction for Africa.[17] The Chinese government also initiated the "China-Africa Youth Gala" and "African Cultural Figures Visit Program" in succession to further deepen the mutual understanding and trust between Chinese and African people, especially the young generation.

Concept innovation is another important way to demonstrate the unique charm of Chinese culture. To enhance national soft power and foster a favorable national image, it is necessary to put forth values, ideas and political concepts that adapt to the trend of the time and utter one's own voice about the peace and development of the international community and the common interests of the human society. China is the main advocate, supporter and practitioner of the "Bandung Spirit". The principle of "seeking common ground while shelving differences and reaching consensus

---

[16] "Remarkable Achievements in China-Africa Educational Cooperation and Exchange through Joint Efforts," *People's Daily*, February 8, 2009, p. 3.

[17] Xie Fei, "Cultural Communication and Cooperation Between China and African Countries," *West Asia and Africa*. 2006 (6), p. 59.

through consultation" that was proposed by the Chinese government delegation was supported by the majority of African representatives. The propositions that China put forth, such as the Five Principles of Peaceful Coexistence, building a new international political and economic order, and promoting world multi-polarization, were also recognized and supported by African countries. At present, the best reflection of China's value and concept innovation is the idea of a "harmonious world". At the Asian-African Summit held in April 2005 in celebration of the 50th anniversary of Bandung Conference, former Chinese President Hu Jintao initiated the proposal of "building a harmonious world together", which soon received positive responses from many African countries.[18] The *Declaration of the Beijing Summit of the Forum on China-Africa Cooperation* and *Beijing Action Plan (2007–2009)*, two guiding documents adopted at the 2006 Beijing Summit of the Forum on China-Africa Cooperation, enriched and developed the concept and practice of building a "harmonious world". Chinese and African leaders agreed that the harmonious development of China-Africa relations was indispensable for the harmonious development of the world.

Due to scarce historical connections and vast geographical distances, people-to-people and cultural communication between China and Africa is still not as close as it ought to and can be, and western and Islamic civilizations are still more readily recognizable among the people of Africa than the Chinese civilization. This situation won't change fundamentally for a long time to come. Western media, especially CNN, BBC and various publications, are very popular in Africa, facilitating cultural infiltration and promoting western values, ideas and lifestyle. By contrast, China has limited cultural presence in Africa. Influenced by public opinion in European and the US, many people in Africa have an incorrect understanding of China and China's African policy. Just as important, many among the new generation of African leaders have been educated in the west. They identify strongly with such western values and ideas as democracy, human rights, freedom and good governance, and are very responsive both politically and emotionally, to mainstream western media, which will have potential negative impact on deepening the political mutual trust between China and Africa. To enhance China's soft power in Africa, we must strengthen educational and cultural diplomacy in Africa in order to help the people of Africa better understand and appreciate China and the Chinese civilization. Doing so requires great foresight, patience and endurance. This work plays an irreplaceable role in further deepening China-Africa friendship.

---

[18] "Fostering New Strategic Partnership Between Asia and Africa," *People's Daily*, April 23, 2005, p. 1.

7.3 Exemplary Effect of Development Model: A Key Element for Expanding China's Soft Power in Africa

After China started the reform and opening up, it entered a historical period that witnessed the fastest development, greatest progress and most profound changes. Its fast economic development and sustained political stability has doubtlessly set an example for other developing countries and stimulated African countries' enthusiasm to learn from and emulate China. In recent years, a trend of "Look East" and "Looking to China" appeared in Africa, and African countries generally hope to intensify the cooperation with China and learn from its development experience, so as to board the express train of its economic development. Many African leaders attending the China-Africa Summit weren't just attracted by aid and trade opportunities, but also by China's development model. *Revival of Africa,* a magazine published by the UN, printed an article titled *Progress in China-Africa Relations*, in which the Ethiopian President Meles was quoted as saying that "China is an inspiration for all of us, and for African businesspeople in particular. What China shows to Africa is that it is indeed possible to turn the corner on economic development." The World Bank admitted "these Chinese interventions bring direct economic opportunities for other developing countries. China's engagement also opens new opportunities for partner countries to tap China's extensive development knowledge and experience."[19]

The most attractive part of China's development experience for Africa is that China's reform is gradual and progressive from the easy to the difficult areas. Its biggest characteristic is "crossing the river by groping the stone". Instead of copying the development experience of the west blindly, China has selectively drawn on and utilized it based on its own situations. Its reform is based on a government dedicated to development and capable of promoting its development policy, and it stresses social stability and effective governance in the process of development. China's reform doesn't just concern economic growth, but is a systematic undertaking that also involves political reform, social harmony and cultural development. The China model is essentially a strategic choice made by this developing country to achieve modernization against the background of globalization. It is a whole set of developing strategies and governing models developed by China in the process of reform and opening up to deal with the challenges of globalization. China didn't pursue its own development completely independent of the world political and economic order, as claimed by the "dependency theory", nor did it adopt the radical "shock therapy" advocated by the "Washington Consensus", but chose to carry out progressive reform and opening up, thus ensuring sustained economic and social development and steady political reform. The useful experience that China has accumulated in economic development provides references and lessons for African countries. More

---

[19] International Bank for Reconstruction and Development/World Bank, *China and the World Bank: A Partnership for Innovation*, 2007, published online at http://siteresources.worldbank.org/EXTEAPCHINAINCHINESE/Resources/innovation_cn.pdf.

importantly, its path of independent development gives them a strong mental encouragement and makes them realize that all countries, including those in Africa, have the chance to achieve development and prosperity.

To intensify the bilateral cooperation in HR development and help African countries find the suitable path of development, China has hosted a series of seminars or training courses for managerial and technical personnel from African countries since 1998, usually undertaken by relevant departments such as the Ministry of Commerce, Ministry of Education and Ministry of Health. For example, from August 3 to September 28, 1998, the first "China-Africa Seminar for Officials of Economic Management" was held in Beijing, and officials from 22 African countries participated in it.[20] The African Human Resources Development Fund was set up under FOCAC in 2000, whereby China has cultivated nearly 20,000 technical and managerial talents for African countries so far, covering a wide range of fields including administrative management, economic management, health care, network communication, agricultural technology, consular protection and environmental protection. The Chinese government also organized international seminars where China and experts from Africa can share their experience in economic development, particularly poverty alleviation. To give the African officials a comprehensive understanding of China and deepen their feeling about China's current development, the seminars organized the participants to visit some economic development zones and specific poverty alleviation projects in China. At the annual meeting of the Governing Council of African Development Bank held in Shanghai in May 2007, for instance, the participants discussed such topics as Africa's infrastructure construction, corporate capability building, debt management and poverty elimination. It was another major step taken by China to boost the communication and cooperation with Africa in developing experience and state governance. It is stated in *China's African Policy* that "learning from each other and seeking common development. China and Africa will learn from and draw upon each other's experience in governance and development, strengthen exchange and cooperation in education, science, culture and health. Supporting African countries' efforts to enhance capacity building, China will work together with Africa in the exploration of the road of sustainable development."[21] Helping African countries to develop human resources embodies the spirit of "teaching one to fish" rather than "giving him fish", which is more suitable for them to pursue long-term development. This can also deepen the affection of African people, especially the elite class, toward China and enhance China's affinity, appeal and influence in Africa.

---

[20] "Deep Friendship, Ample Fruits," *People's Daily*, November 3, 2006, p. 7.
[21] "China's African Policy," *People's Daily*, January 13, 2006, p. 3.

7.4 Multilateral Cooperation Mechanism: Effective Way to Enhance China's Soft Power in Africa

For a very long time after the People's Republic of China was founded, China paid close attention to developing bilateral relations with other countries. Although it sent a delegation to the Geneva Convention in 1954 and the Asian-African conference in 1955 and played an important role on the two occasions, although it resumed its legitimate position in the UN in 1971 and assigned a resident delegation there, multilateral diplomacy as a diplomatic concept and approach was still new for China. After the reform and opening up began, however, China participated more actively in international economic organizations, and the admission of it into the WTO in 1999 made it realize more deeply the important value of multilateral international platforms for preserving national interests. Therefore, China began to participate in multilateral affairs more actively, both internationally and regionally.

Against such a background, China introduced multilateral diplomacy and institutional cooperation into the agenda of African diplomacy. It began to take the African Union and other integrated organizations as important objects in diplomatic work, not only coordinating with African Union on international occasions, but also providing appropriate support in Africa's economic integration and regional collective security governance. In the meantime, China and African countries created the new cooperation model of the Forum on China-Africa Cooperation. From October 2000 till now, four ministerial meetings have been held successfully under the forum, and the Beijing Summit was especially convened during the third FOCAC in 2006, attended by 48 senior African delegations including the heads of state of 35 countries and six prime ministers. Taking the forum as a platform, China and African countries held substantial dialogue and consultation on how to push the establishment of an equitable and rational new order of international politics and economy to protect the common interests of developing countries, and how to further boost the China-African cooperation in economy, trade, culture and education. As the first intergovernmental mechanism of multilateral consultation and collective dialogue set up between China and African countries, the FOCAC symbolized that China had successfully introduced multilateral diplomacy into its African work. Through this multilateral cooperation framework, China and African countries fixated in the form of law their consensuses concerning each other's major strategic interests. In this way, they could not only consolidate the existing cooperation achievements and lay a solid political foundation for conducting mutually beneficial cooperation, but also further enrich the connotations of South-South cooperation and largely raise the position and influence of China-Africa cooperation on the international political stage.

The rise of a big country is based on the increase of overall national strength. To become a major power, China needs to pursue not only the fast growth of economic aggregate and gradual buildup of military force, but also to pursue cultural prosperity and social harmony, improve national image and undertake global responsibilities. African countries are China's important allies and African continent is an important stage for China to fully embrace the world. The historical cooperation between China and African countries not only gave a strong impetus to the national liberation and economic development of the latter, raised the position of the African continent in the world system, but also helped China preserve its own value and dignity in the international community and showcased its due international standing and influence. The tremendous energy of South-South cooperation demonstrated in China-Africa cooperation notably boosted the revitalization of the Asian-African world and became an important factor that pushed the evolution of world system and the transformation of international landscape. Improving and enhancing China's soft power in Africa is of great importance for tightening the China-Africa relation in the new age, realizing China's peaceful rise smoothly and promoting the world's harmonious development.

Chapter 8
African NGOs and China's Public Diplomacy in Africa

In the new century, the China-Africa relationship has been comprehensively expanded in contents and levels. The content of bilateral exchange is no longer limited to the high-level political domain between countries, but has reached out to every aspect of people's lives; and the form of exchange has extended beyond the traditional official exchanges to the level of public diplomacy, including NGOs. A "big diplomacy" landscape is taking shape in China-Africa relations. African NGOs begin to pay close attention to China's African policy, which has a direct bearing on China's image in Africa and the world at large and the international public opinion environment it is in, making the development of China-Africa relations more complicated than before.[1]

8.1 African NGOs Pay Attention to China-Africa Relations

NGOs are a private force as opposed to the government. The democratic process in Africa and the gradual recovery of African economy after the end of the Cold War boosted the rapid development of the civil society, and the thriving of all kinds of NGOs was particularly eye-catching. The UN Office of the Special Adviser on Africa (OSAA) revised the "Catalogue of African NGOs" (third edition) in 2004, which collected 3,776 influential NGOs.[2] They were engaged in a wide range of areas, focused on poverty alleviation through agricultural development, education

---

[1] Refer to the following articles by Luo Jianbo: "African NGOs and China-Africa Relation," (*Contemporary International Relations*, 4th issue, 2008), "Analysis of NGO's Role in Conflict Management in Africa," (*International Issue Forum*, 2008 (1)).

[2] "Networking: Directory of African NGOs," published online at http://www.un.org/africa/osaa/ngodirectory/index.htm. As a matter of fact, there are much more NGOs in Africa. In 2006, there were about 4,000 NGOs registered at the government of Kenya alone.

and technical training, health and disease prevention and treatment, conflict management, human rights and humanitarian aid, and environmental and resource protection. Typical examples are the Egyptian Organization for Human Rights, Ethiopian Peace and Development Committee, Kenya's Africa Initiative Program and Nigeria's Pan-African Reconciliation Council.

African NGOs see it as their responsibility to perform oversight on the government and to care for the disadvantaged, populations, and participate in the political process quite actively. In recent years, they began to pay attention to the development of China-Africa relations, with a special emphasis on China's trade, investment and aid policies to Africa, as well as the impacts caused by those policies on people's lives and social development in Africa. Many African NGOs hold a positive attitude toward the economic and trade cooperation between the two sides, and fully realize the great significance of China's current development and China-Africa relations for the revival of Africa. While affirming the development of bilateral relations, some people in African NGOs put forth kind expectations regarding China's African policy and Chinese enterprises' behaviors, including sharp criticisms and condemnations. This is a crucial variable that affects the sound development of China-Africa relations today. Negative comments mainly focus on the following aspects.

Democracy and human rights issues in African countries. The African society is generally concerned with how China's African policy may possibly affect its democracy and human rights. Some people in African NGOs associated China's normal relationship with Sudan with the current Darfur crisis, claiming that "China's energy exploitation in Sudan has doubtlessly provided strong financial support for the Sudan government and enabled it to arm itself and conduct military mobilization". Some African public figures blamed the Sudan government and Chinese petroleum companies for the relocation and settlement of people from oil-producing areas. The oil-rich areas in Sudan are concentrated in the upper reaches of the Nile, which is mainly inhabited by the Dinka and the Nuer people. The government of Sudan started a policy of clearance of the local people from the oil areas as the locals were suspected of being subversive and collaborating with the Southern rebels, causing insecurity in the area where multinational oil companies were operating.[3] Some African people even attacked China for developing normal relations with Zimbabwe, saying that the Mugabe regime could linger on the verge of economic breakdown thanks to the aid and investment from countries like China.[4] "While many African societies struggle to further democratic values and strengthen respect for human rights, there is no

---

[3] Daniel Deng Bul, "Oil Exploration and Exploitation in Northern Upper Nile", in Kwesi Kwaa Prah (ed.), *Afro-Chinese Relations: Past, Present and Future*, SED Printing Solutions, Cape Town, 2007, pp. 175–203.

[4] Dani W. Nabudere, "Africa and China in a New Globalised World", in Kwesi Kwaa Prah (ed.), *Afro-Chinese Relations: Past, Present and Future*, SED Printing Solutions, Cape Town, 2007, pp. 204–231.

doubt that Chinese economic assistance is encouraging dictatorship and tyranny in Sudan, Chad, Zimbabwe and elsewhere."[5]

Combat against corruption in Africa. China has always advocated "sovereign equality" and "non-interference in other country's internal affairs", and has carried out mutually beneficial cooperation with other countries on that basis. To support Angola's post-war reconstruction, China agreed to sign a commercial loan contract worth USD2 billion in 2004 to help build a group of large infrastructure, energy and livelihood projects in Angola. Although the cooperation was open, transparent and mutually beneficial, it was questioned and criticized by African NGOs. China doesn't adopt the western approach of providing conditional assistance, which may undermine all the efforts Africa has made in combating corruption and intensifying management.[6] "Following a top-down economic development approach, China's economic assistance to these African countries has encouraged elitism, deepened social and class divisions and widened corruption."[7] They therefore called on African governments to properly manage foreign investment and public assets, and make sure that the economic cooperation could bring more benefits for African people.

Unreasonable structure of China-Africa trade. China maintained trade surplus against African countries for a long time in history, but they generally kept a trade balance in recent years as China imported much more petroleum, timber and other resources from Africa. In 2006, the China-Africa trade volume totaled USD55.5 billion, with China in a deficit of USD2.1 billion; in 2007, their trade volume increased to USD73.57 billion, with China in a surplus of USD1.01 billion[8]; in 2008, their trade volume reached USD106.84 billion, with China in a deficit of USD5.16 billion.[9] However, in terms of specific countries, China was in trade surplus to varying degrees to most African countries except certain big energy exporters, and African NGOs were quite discontented with this. They described the economic and trade relation between China and Africa as unequal "South-North economic relation", meaning that while Africa mainly exported raw materials such as petroleum, copper and timber, it imported from China finished goods such as electromechanical equipment, communication devices and textile.

---

[5] Ali Askouri, "China's Investment in Sudan: Displacing Villages and Destroying Communities", in Firoze Manji & Stephen Marks (eds.), *African perspectives on China in Africa*, Cape Town, Nairobi and Oxford: Fahamu-Networks for Social Justice, 2007, pp. 71–86.

[6] *Star* (Johannesburg), 21 June 2006.

[7] Ali Askouri, "China's Investment in Sudan: Displacing Villages and Destroying Communities", in Firoze Manji & Stephen Marks (eds.), *African perspectives on China in Africa*, Cape Town, Nairobi and Oxford: Fahamu-Networks for Social Justice, 2007, pp. 71–86.

[8] GACC Department of Statistics, "China-Africa trade exceeds USD70 billion in 2007; scope of zero-tariff goods expanded," published online at http://www.customs.gov.cn/YWStaticPage/4370/6a4dc2be.htm.

[9] GACC Department of Statistics, "China-Africa trade exceeds USD70 billion in 2007; scope of zero-tariff goods expanded," published online at http://www.customs.gov.cn/YWStaticPage/4370/6a4dc2be.htm.

Africa's capability of independent development. A topic that African governments, the African Union and the African society are generally concerned with is how to enhance Africa's capability of independent economic development by cooperating with the outside world. In an ideal scenario, the cooperation between African countries and the outside world should be an independent and equal partnership in which they have the initiative; African countries should have sound plans for independent development and manage to incorporate foreign investment and aid in this framework; and they should take the opportunity of foreign cooperation to improve their capability of product production and diversification and cultivate their own technical and managerial talents. Some African people are worried that China's aid to Africa may make the latter more dependent on it rather than depend on its own resources and the wisdom of its own people, and they think the relation between China and Africa is more like the relation between "a giver and a recipient" because "the trend is unilateral. All the cooperative initiatives are mostly undertaken by China and simply followed by African countries."[10] Besides, some Africans also worry that the import of China's cheap products, especially textiles, into the African market in large quantities will seriously affect the manufacturing development in certain countries and cause companies to go out of business and workers to lose jobs, which will undermine the fostering of Africa's independent development capability.

CSR performance of Chinese enterprises. The poor CSR performance of Chinese enterprises is a key point that African NGOs criticize China on, mainly concerning China-Africa three aspects. The first is safety hazards in production. As China is implementing the "Go Global" strategy, Chinese enterprises have undertaken more large projects in Africa in recent years. These projects are mostly in high-risk industries such as construction, mining and chemical industry, with a high risk of production accidents, and require good production conditions and a keen awareness of safety precaution. On April 20, 2005, a gas explosion at the Chambishi copper mine in Zambia killed nearly 50 people. This rare and severe mining accident drew close attention from African civil societies, labor unions and media. The local Labor Union attributed the accident to mistakes on the part of the Chinese investor because the workers involved in the explosion didn't fully grasp relevant production technology, and the Chinese investor wasn't well prepared to deal with hazardous objects.[11] The second is the inadequate provision of jobs. African NGOs believe Chinese enterprises prefer Chinese workers and hope foreign investors can help create more jobs in African countries and tap the local workforce.[12] The third is limited reward for local communities. African NGOs said that although many large Chinese enterprises

---

[10] V. Maurice Gountin, *China's Assistance to Africa, A Stone Bridge of China-Africa Relations,* http://www.cctr.ust.hk/china-africa/papers/Gountin,Maurice.pdf.

[11] Jackie Range of Dow Jones Newswires. *Zambia's Miners Pay High Price For Copper Boom.* http://www.minesandcommunities.org/Action/press791.htm.

[12] John Rocha, "A New Frontier in the Exploitation of Africa's Natural Resources: the Emergence of China", in Firoze Manji & Stephen Marks (eds.), *African perspectives on China in Africa*, Cape Town, Nairobi and Oxford: Fahamu-Networks for Social Justice, 2007, pp. 15–34.

or projects in Africa are aware of CSR, their reward to local communities is negligible compared with the profits they make. In the meanwhile, medium and small enterprises or private operators, which make up the majority of Chinese businesses in Africa, are barely aware of CSR and seldom or never carry out social wellbeing activities.

Impact on Africa's environment because of China's investment and aid programs. These accusations are mainly targeted at China's energy exploitation, logging and dam construction in Africa. Over recent years, China has imported more lumber from African countries such as Cameroon, Congo, Equatorial Guinea, Gabon, Liberia and Tanzania, but its lumber trade is criticized for involving illegal logging and environmental damage. "Gabonese law requires processing before export, yet China's demands are for raw logs". China purchased an estimated 60% of the timber exported from Equatorial Guinea, another country with known illegal logging problems. "Annual timber extraction in Equatorial Guinea exceeds the maximum legally allowed limit by 40–60%".[13] Large projects undertaken by Chinese companies also face serious environmental pressure. The Merowe Dam undertaken by a Chinese company in Sudan has received extensive censure by African NGOs recently, which claimed that the dam has forced local residents living in the abundant Nile valley to relocate to nearby deserts, where the eco-environment is extremely harsh, and the migrants' production and life will undoubtedly worsen the already fragile eco-environment.[14]

African NGOs criticize China's current African policy, especially its trade with, investment in and aid to Africa, partly because they don't really understand China's development and China-Africa relations and have many prejudices and misunderstandings about China due to the long-term influence of western public opinions and ideas. Such negative perceptions greatly affect the international public opinion environment that China is in, affect the African people's opinion and perception of China, and consequently make it more costly and difficult for China to foster soft power in Africa and bring unnecessary uncertainties to the sound development of China-Africa relations. Some westerners, out of prejudices against China or narrow interest considerations, tried to use African NGOs as the tools to instigate and spread the "native" criticism of China from Africa in order to smear China's national image and drive a wedge in China-Africa friendly cooperation. Some media and NGOs from western countries even directly work in African countries and influence the development of African NGOs through a number of ways such as organizing meetings, cooperating in projects and providing financial support. Forces in support of Taiwan Independence and Tibetan Independence also seek to come into contact with African civil societies with a view to conducting political infiltration in African countries. African NGOs are involved in China-Africa relations more deeply and have

---

[13] MichelleChan-Fishel, "Environmental Impact: More of the Same?, in Firoze Manji & Stephen Marks (eds.), *African perspectives on China in Africa*, Cape Town, Nairobi and Oxford: Fahamu-Networks for Social Justice, 2007, pp. 139–152.

[14] Jim Giles, *"Tide of censure for African dams"*, http://www.nature.com/nature/journal/v440/n7083/full/440393a.html.

become an important factor that affects such relations as well as China's overall foreign relations.

8.2 Truth About China's African Policy and China-Africa Cooperation

In our opinion, although China and Africa have similar experience in history and the same demand for development in modern times, they, like all other bilateral or multilateral relations, are not in complete agreement when it comes to interests, and their relations are bound to have new problems amid rapid development. But in general, the China-Africa relationship has withstood the test of time and their current economic and trade cooperation is beneficial for both sides. China and Africa have far more consensuses than divergences and more cooperation than competition. This is a highlight in China's overall foreign relations.

First, the general tone of China-Africa economic and trade cooperation is positive and problems are secondary. China has made remarkable achievements in the African trade, investment and aid in recent years and its influence in Africa has grown rapidly. According to an estimation by the Ministry of Commerce, at present, the economic and trade volume between China and Africa contributes about 20% to Africa's economic growth.[15] However, the fast development of their cooperation has brought some problems that need to be addressed urgently, as represented by the poor social and environmental performance of some Chinese enterprises, but these problems only concern a small number of Chinese companies, and some of the problems are obviously magnified or even artificially distorted.

Second, China's African diplomacy is essentially sincere and friendly, and the bad behaviors of individual Chinese companies don't represent China's foreign policy. Since China and Africa forged diplomatic ties half a century ago, China has provided active support for African countries to fight for political independence and national emancipation, helped them to seek economic development, and preserved their legitimate rights and interests in the international stage. "In the past 50-plus years, China has helped African countries implement more than 900 infrastructure and social welfare projects, provided nearly 20,000 government scholarships to 50 African countries, and dispatched medical staff of 16,000 person-times to 47 ones, treating and curing close to 180 million patient-times."[16] *China's African Policy* declared the kind intention of China's economic and trade policy toward Africa. "China supports African countries' endeavor for economic development and nation

---

[15] "African Development Bank annual meeting held in Shanghai for mutual benefits," published online at http://www.mofcom.gov.cn/aarticle/i/jyjl/k/200705/20070504702076.html.

[16] "Wen Jiabao addresses opening ceremony of 2007 annual meeting of African Development Bank Governing Council in Shanghai," *People's Daily*, May 17, 2007, p. 1.

building, carries out cooperation in various forms in the economic and social development, and promotes common prosperity of China and Africa."[17] When visiting Africa, former Chinese Premier Wen Jiabao said that the label of "neo-colonialism" could in no way be put on China.[18]

Third, the governments and people with vision of African countries mostly comment positively on the economic and trade cooperation between China and Africa, and those negative comments should be analyzed on a case-by-case basis. African countries generally set store by China's role and influence and believe its development has brought opportunities for African people, and that the independent foreign policy of peace upheld by China is an important pillar for protecting the rights of undeveloped countries. It is mostly the US and some European countries that claimed in recent years that China is promoting the "neo-colonialism" and "neo-mercantilism" in Africa, which, in essence, is another edition of the "China threat theory" in Africa. As African NGOs are unfamiliar with China's foreign policy, deeply influenced by western opinions or have all kinds of interest connections with the west, they have joined the hype of the so-called China threat theory. We should see that some African NGOs criticized China with kindness and the hope that the rising China can act differently from western powers and help African countries achieve economic development and social progress on the principle of mutual benefits and common development.

Fourth, the current problems in China-Africa relations are mostly pure economic problems that can be well controlled and solved. "As economic and trade cooperation between China and Africa develops quickly, new situations and problems are unavoidable, but in comparison with the overall situation of China-Africa cooperation, they are problems in the course of progress and development and can be solved through friendly consultation and deep collaboration."[19] Most of the problems are normal economic and trade frictions between the two sides and don't involve political factors. The basic principle on solving those problems is to bear in mind the long-term friendly partnership with African countries, give comprehensive considerations to long-term interests and realistic conditions, adopt a different approach than that for developed countries, and resolve conflicts between China and African countries that arise from trade frictions through friendly consultation. We cannot let the interests of a specific industry undermine our friendly relationship that has been established over long years.

Fifth, the negative comments made by African NGOs on China contain serious misunderstandings and some problems they complained about do not in fact exist or otherwise wildly exaggerated. For example, the China-Africa trade imbalance shouldn't be totally attributed to China. It is partly owing to Africa's irrational economic structure and backward industrial development capability. To fundamentally change the imbalance, African countries should improve their capability of

---

[17] China's African Policy, *People's Daily*, January 13, 2006, p. 3.

[18] Wen Jiabao holds press conferences in Egypt, *People's Daily*, June 19, 2006, p. 3.

[19] Jia Qinglin addresses China-Kenya Economic and Trade Cooperation Forum: "Working Together Towards Win–win Results," *People's Daily*, April 26, 2007, p. 3.

independent development. Besides, the trade between Africa and western countries is also seriously imbalanced, so it's unfair to excessively blame China only. Another example is that China's investment in and aid to Africa has created a lot of jobs and technical training opportunities in local areas, but some African media only made a fuss over the improper behaviors of individual Chinese companies. The Ministry of Commerce and relevant departments issued the *Statistical Report of China's Outbound Investment in 2006*, which showed that at the end of 2006, overseas Chinese companies hired 630,000 people, including 268,000 foreign employees. According to China's official statistics, Chinese investment in Africa in 2006 was equivalent to creating 60,000 jobs for Africa. A survey report by the British Department for International Development also showed that except Angola, 85–95% of the workers engaged in Chinese infrastructure projects in countries like Zambia, Tanzania and Sierra Leone were locals. The report also said China paid close attention to the technical training of African workers, and offered favorable salary to technical and managerial employees. It also sub-contracted some sub-projects to local African constructors.[20] Many Chinese companies in Africa attached great importance to CSR performance and won the recognition and applause of African governments and people. For example, Huawei Group insisted on the "localization" strategy and has set up training centers in Nigeria, Kenya, Egypt, Tunisia and Angola, covering the entire Africa and training more than 3,000 professionals for the African telecommunication industry. Huawei has more than 2,500 employees in Africa, over 60% of whom are locals, making great contributions to local employment, taxation and personnel cultivation. At the Beijing Summit of the Forum on China-Africa Cooperation held in 2006, multiple heads of state from Africa visited Huawei's headquarters in Shenzhen or its research institute in Beijing. They spoke highly of Huawei's localization in Africa, and acknowledged that its training of local telecommunication experts contributed to the development of telecommunication industry in African countries. Angolan Prime Minister Fernando da Piedade Dias dos Santos said that he fully believed Huawei would play an important role in the development of Angola's telecommunication industry, and the two parties could achieve win–win results.[21] Huawei Group, a private Chinese company, has become one of the best partners for African telecommunication service providers and made great contributions to the development of African telecommunication industry.

---

[20] As Chinese and African constructors are not on the same level in terms of technology and experience, they don't have direct competition. China's engagement in African infrastructure projects directly challenged the traditional partners of African countries—western construction companies. DFID, "China's Interest and Activity in Africa's Construction and Infrastructure Sectors," http://www.dfid.gov.uk/countries/asia/China/partners.asp.

[21] "Huawei 2006," published online at http://www.huawei.com/cn/corporate_citizenship/enviroment/standards_regulations.do.

8.3 China's Strategic Planning for Public Diplomacy in Africa

To some extent, China has underestimated the problems that may appear amid the rapid development of its relations with Africa, the new changes that are taking place in Africa today, and the close attention paid by African NGOs to China-Africa relations. As a result, it isn't fully prepared and lacks the proper countermeasures. To respond to the negative voices from the African society more effectively and guide African public opinions to move in the direction favorable for China, China has to establish an African diplomatic strategy that covers African NGOs with great vision.

When making this strategy, China has to give considerations to the interests of all parties. (1) It has to balance the interests of African governments with the interests of the society. African governments and the African society don't always see eye to eye on the China-Africa relation. The former places more stress on the nation's political stability, macroeconomic development and the improvement of international standing, while the latter pays more attention to good governance, democracy and human rights, social harmony, and the improvement of people's lives, especially poverty alleviation for the impoverished population. The former emphasizes the sound development of China-Africa relations and the realistic benefits for both sides, while the latter is more focused on the problems in China's African policy and their negative impacts. (2) China has to balance its own interests with the interests of African countries. Its African policy submits to its general diplomatic landscape and serves the long-term national interests, but African policy should also meet the interest demand of African countries. At present, African countries are in urgent need of external support to carry out economic development plans, handle internal conflicts, and drive the African integration process, particularly the "New Partnership for Africa's Development" (NEPAD). (3) China has to balance the realistic and long-term interests of Africa. China's realistic interests lie in the acquisition of strategic resources, overseas markets and valuable diplomatic support that are urgently needed for boosting economic development, and its long-term interests lie in promoting the rejuvenation of China and Africa, achieving common development of all developing countries, and cementing China's image as a responsible power in that process. Therefore, China's African policy shouldn't be limited to realistic economic gains and temporary diplomatic mobilization, but should aim at China's peaceful rise and the harmonious development of the whole world. There is no doubt that China's African policy is an early test of its global role that is taking shape.

In this diplomatic strategy toward Africa, public diplomacy must be given priority. In a general sense, public diplomacy means that a national government uses official forces or civil resources to proactively influence the public perception and attitude in another country. Public diplomacy toward Africa transcends the traditional intergovernmental exchanges and aims to enhance the African people's perception of China, with a view to deepening mutual understanding and recognition. But for a long time, China attached more importance to official exchanges than diplomatic resources on the public level, and lacked the experience in dealing with scholars, media, NGOs and religious figures in Africa. China's public diplomacy is far from reaching the public society in Africa or the influential African NGOs, so we have to comprehensively summarize our long experience in public diplomacy, and move faster to formulate the public diplomatic strategy with Chinese characteristics. When "traditional diplomacy" and "public diplomacy" are promoted in parallel, they will lead to a firmer public foundation for China-Africa relations.

African diplomacy in the new age should also serve the strategic plan for China's rise and the design and establishment of China's image as a responsible power. As China is rising, it should adopt a broader global perspective, not only focusing on its own economic development, but also paying attention to world peace and development, taking an active part in building the international order and shouldering more global responsibilities, and providing necessary public products for the human society. Going forward, China's diplomacy should be more progressive, open and inclusive. While adjusting the traditional paradigm of national sovereignty and adapting to global demand, China should participate in relevant international activities more actively, selectively meet the international demand for public products from around the world, and effectively protect its expanding global interests in the meantime. China is the largest developing country in the world and a fast-growing power that is merging into the international community. Being such, it is not only a supporter and proponent of South-South cooperation, but also an initiator and participant of South-North cooperation, serving as a "bridge" between South-South cooperation and South-North dialogue. The African continent, on the other hand, is the least developed and most tumultuous region in the world today, and African countries are working hard toward African rejuvenation through integration. China should provide more assistance and support to them within its capacity, in a bid to achieve common development for all developing countries by "doing its best within its power". Realizing mutually beneficial development and common prosperity for China and African countries through cooperation has become an eloquent proof that China's rise is an opportunity rather than threat for the world. The assertion to build a "harmonious world" initiated by the Chinese government in the new age reflected the strategic considerations made by the rising China for the world order and its own role.

8.4 China's Policies and Measures in Public Diplomacy to Africa

Based on the strategic thinking of public diplomacy to Africa stated above, China should timely adjust its diplomatic policies and innovate in diplomatic measures to guide African NGOs to make a turn favorable for China in their comments on and opinions of China.

1. People from African NGOs are invited to China in multiple ways. China has accumulated some experience in this regard. During the Beijing Summit of the

Forum of China-Africa Cooperation, China invited 338 African reporters to cover the summit and 1,030 African entrepreneurs and businessmen to attend the meeting of industrial and business circles. In May 2007, China hosted the annual meeting of the Governing Council of African Development Bank and invited representatives from international and African NGOs. These China-Africa multilateral forums or meetings, while continuing to stress intergovernmental exchanges, could bring in more African public figures and let them feel China's high-speed development and its friendly cooperation with Africa at first hand. The African Human Resources Development Fund was set up under FOCAC in 2000. China should incorporate people from African civil societies and NGOs into this framework at an early date, and organize seminars or training courses for NGOs in areas such as poverty alleviation, education, health, social development and humanitarian aid. To do that, we need to step up front-end surveys and follow-up research, and find out which NGOs are influential in Africa, including civil groups with significant influence on African governments, the African Union and other regional organizations, and civil organizations with extensive international connections or major clout in international public opinions. Tightening the communication with those organizations and changing their old perception of China will have a great bearing on the China policy adopted by African Union and some African countries, and consequently push the sound development of China-Africa relations.

2. Chinese public figures and NGOs are encouraged to "go to Africa". In response to the close attention paid by African society to China-Africa relations, we can mobilize Chinese public figures and NGOs and promote people-to-people exchanges to increase mutual understanding and dispel doubts and concerns, as voices from the people are more easily accepted by the outside world than publicity conducted by the state. It is stated in *China's African Policy* that "China will encourage and facilitate the exchanges between people's organizations of China and Africa, especially the youth and women, with a view to increasing the understanding, trust and cooperation of people on both sides."[22] On October 26, 2005, the Chinese government sponsored the formation of the "China NGO Network for International Exchanges", under the framework of which it began to explore ways to push Chinese NGOs to go to Africa and have direct exchange with African counterparts. China began to send volunteers to Ethiopia in 2005 and planned to send 300 volunteers to African countries in 2007–2009. People-to-people exchange once played a significant role in helping the new China make diplomatic breakthroughs, and the assistant effect of this kind of "track-two diplomacy" should be given more play in the future.

3. China should pay more attention to addressing the trade frictions between China and Africa. To enable Africa to expand its export to China, China cancelled the import duty on 190 goods from 28 African countries in 2005, and enlarged the "zero customs duty policy" on goods from the least developed African countries that had diplomatic relations with China from 190 to 454 entries. The "zero customs duty" policy was not only beneficial for African countries' goods export directly, but also conducive to the sustainable development of China-Africa trade. China also

---

[22] China's African Policy, *People's Daily*, January 13, 2006, p. 3.

encourages capable and creditable companies to invest in African countries to help them improve the capability of industrial development and earning foreign exchange through exports. Particularly, the Chinese government should encourage domestic companies to invest more in the petrochemical industry in major African energy exporters and raise the product's added values through deep processing, in response to the fallacy of China "plundering resources" in Africa spread by western countries. China has set about building overseas economic and trade cooperation zones in Africa, which is a strong measure to boost Africa's economic development while relieving the trade frictions between China and Africa.

4. China should regulate the behaviors of overseas Chinese companies through legal and policy means. In a general sense, the CSR of overseas Chinese companies isn't their individual behaviors, but is part of China's image building efforts. Although only a small number of overseas Chinese companies have poor CSR performance, their misbehavior would easily cause the outside world to misunderstand China's Africa policy and derogate China's national image. This is something China should take seriously in its African diplomacy. Regarding the safe production problems in overseas Chinese companies, relevant departments in the Chinese government jointly issued the *Notice on Strengthening the Supervision and Management of Production Safety in Overseas Chinese Companies* on September 5, 2005, which specified that the investor should perform the duty of production safety supervision and management in overseas companies and improve the production safety regulations.[23] In response to the close attention paid by the African society to Chinese companies' logging projects, the Chinese government released the *Guide for Chinese Companies on Sustainable Afforestation Overseas* on August 28, 2007 to encourage and support them in fostering forests overseas in ways that are "sustainable", "protect bio-diversity" and "promote community development".[24] It was the first policy guide that China issued for a specific industry, and the first management and technical standard in the world concerning the afforestation activities by overseas companies of a nation. When China Development Bank launched the China-Africa Development Fund in 2007, it made it clear that it will gradually formulate the social and environmental impact assessment requirements on investment projects, so as to urge overseas Chinese companies to actively perform their environmental and social responsibilities.

Under the guidance of the Chinese government, Chinese companies in Zambia became more aware of CSR and made more efforts in public welfare activities. In July 2007, the NFC Africa Mining Plc. under China Nonferrous Metal Mining (Group) Co., Ltd. (CNMC) held the launch ceremony of its social welfare program in Zambia, covering a wide range of areas such as infrastructure construction, sports, education, women's employment, and AIDS and malaria prevention and treatment.

---

[23] Four ministries jointly issue "*Notice on Strengthening the Supervision and Management of Production Safety in Overseas Chinese Companies*," http://service.xjftec.gov.cn:7001/DataSupport/Family/Zhengcefagui/guowaiJSHZ/4028c28413d39aca0113de9bc08602fb.html.

[24] "Overseas Chinese companies have guidebook on afforestation," *People's Daily*, September 1, 2007, p. 5.

It was the first social welfare program launched and implemented by a Chinese company in Zambia and it was welcomed by the Zambian government and people. So far the program has invested USD680,000 in local road construction and has made multiple donations. CNMC also built the China-Zambia Friendship Hospital, which is one of the best hospitals in Zambia and has played a significant role in improving the medical care conditions for nearby residents.[25] China should continue to encourage Chinese companies to lay store by the livelihood and development of local areas when exploiting resources in Africa and stress and support the local efforts of environmental protection, education, and health care, thus demonstrating their due moral responsibilities and humanitarian care. We can consider incorporating the CSR performance in the approval and performance assessment of outgoing investment to raise the bar for companies to make overseas investment, so that those with poor CSR performance cannot go out. CSR performance will also be taken as an important reference for the access to favorable state policies in capital, foreign exchange, tax and other aspects. The Chinese government should also timely supervise and restrict certain companies' misbehaviors in Africa through legal and policy means, as the pure market approach of survival of the fittest doesn't completely suit the economic and trade exchanges between China and Africa.

5. China should make greater efforts to increase trust and dispel doubts and misconceptions among the Africans. Some African NGOs are critical of China-Africa relations partly because they don't know much about China's African policy and lack comprehensive knowledge of the history and current status of China-Africa economic and trade cooperation. While solemnly refuting the untrue remarks made by African NGOs about China, China should also actively intensify the dialogue and communication with them through official or nongovernmental channels, strongly publicize the essence of China's African policy and the improvement and adjustment of it (especially economic policy toward Africa), and introduce the positive improvements in Chinese companies' CSR performance overseas, in a bid to dispel Africa's stereotyped opinions and prejudices against China as much as possible. To that end, China published *China's African Policy* in early 2006, taking the initiative to introduce to African countries and the international community the trend of China's African policy in the twenty-first century. It also began to make a point of communicating with African NGOs and public figures and showing them the results of China-Africa economic and trade cooperation. For example, at the annual meeting of the Governing Council of African Development Bank held in Shanghai in 2006, China invited representatives from some African and international NGOs, and the attendees discussed China's investment in and aid to Africa, creating a precedent in Chinese government's proactive communication with African NGOs. Regarding the form of communication, China shouldn't be limited to intergovernmental exchanges and publicity through official channels. It can adopt a "tiered" strategy, mobilize public resources, and encourage scholars, reporters, college students and NGO representatives on both sides to have face-to-face communication, thus enhancing the foreign communication in depth and breadth.

---

[25] "Larger Scale, Wider Scope, Higher Level," *People's Daily*, January 21, 2009, p. 9.

Chapter 9
African Integration and China's African Policy of Multilateral Cooperation

The twenty-first century is a period of strategic opportunities for Africa and China to realize reform and development. African countries are in the course of promoting regional integration and hope to bring peace, stability and development to the continent through collective efforts, while China is accelerating the socialist modernization drive in order to achieve peaceful development of the country and great rejuvenation of the Chinese nation. In recent years, China has conscientiously taken a constructive part in regional and international multilateral affairs, and more proactively displayed its image as a responsible power. Against such a background, the multilateral exchange between China and African countries has made rapid headway, and this new diplomatic form has considerably broadened the scope of cooperation and common interests between the two sides and consolidated the foundation for their cooperation. In-time discussion of the topic of African integration and China-Africa relations is of great importance for enhancing the China-Africa relations in the new age, for China to achieve the strategic goal of peaceful development, and for strengthening the South-South cooperation in the age of globalization.[1]

---

[1] Refer to the following articles by Luo Jianbo: "Africa's Historical Evolution in the Context of Integration," (*West Asia and Africa,* 5th issue, 2007); "African Integration in the Age of Globalization: Ideal, Reality and Way out," (*Contemporary International Relations*, 8th issue, 2006); "Ideal and Reality: Establishing African Union and African Collective Security Mechanism," (*Foreign Affairs Review*, 2006 (4)); "Advancing China's Multilateral Diplomacy in Africa," (*Contemporary International Relations*, 2006 (11)).

9.1 Progress and Historical Achievements of African Integration

In the first half of the twentieth century, African people, which didn't obtain political independence yet, began to pursue a path of self-strengthening through united efforts in their unique way. At that time, the African people, upholding "Pan-Africanism" as their spiritual slogan, called on black people around the world to unite and fight for their emancipation and independence against racial discrimination and colonial oppression.

The Pan-Africanism movement is first and foremost a cultural movement. Those who advocated and disseminated the "Pan-Africanism" ways of thinking in the early stage mostly believed in such concepts as the "national character of black people" or "African individuality". They held that there was a history and culture created by African black people and shared by all black people worldwide, a unique history and culture that was in no way inferior to the western history and culture, that had its unique form and value and a glorious past, and that had made outstanding contributions to the world culture. Based on the common cultural value and historical experience and destiny of all black people around the world, they called on them to be united into an "African force" to rejuvenate the ancient African culture and black nation. The famous American black scholar DuBois devoted himself to the cultural revival movement of black people with great passion, and began to take an active part in the struggles for the full emancipation of black Americans at the end of the nineteenth century, and became an important founder of the Pan-African movement. The revival of African culture and the rights and interests of the entire black nation were the most important topics of Pan-Africanism in the early days. At that time, the tapping and illustration of traditional African culture by Pan-Africanism wasn't to restore the traditions, but to serve the realistic political purpose for all black people because to arouse and emancipate them, the first thing was to free them from cultural and psychological enslavement, restore their cultural and spiritual dignity and confidence, and make the black nation feel proud of their own history, cultural traditions, race and skin color.

Pan-Africanism movement is also a political movement for national liberation. It held five Pan-African Conferences respectively in 1919, 1921, 1923, 1927 and 1945, driving the African national independence movement to a climax step by step. Starting from the second conference, it emphasized every time that African people should enjoy the right of political autonomy. For example, the second Pan-African Conference clearly demanded western countries to give "local self-government for backward groups, deliberately rising as experience and knowledge grow to complete self-government under the limitations of a self-governed world."[2] The third and fourth Pan-African Conference further enumerated the political and economic rights and interests that black people, especially those in Africa, were entitled to. The fifth

---

[2] "London Manifesto of the Second Pan-African Conference," Tang Dadun, ed., *Selected Works of Pan-Africanism and Organization of African Unity (1900–1990)*, Shanghai: East China Normal University Press, 1995, pp. 25–31.

Pan-African Conference held in Manchester in October 1945 could be viewed as a critical turning point or milestone in the development of the Pan-African movement in that the tone it set, especially the resolutions it passed, were far more combative and radical than in previous conferences. The attendees all agreed that Africa should have autonomy and independence, and demanded that "all colonies must get rid of the control of foreign imperialists, both political and economic."[3] From then on, the objective of Pan-Africanism movement had new historical connotations—to unite all forces in Africa to fight against imperialism and colonialism and achieve the complete independence and liberation of the African continent.

In a standard sense, the regional integration movement centered on economic and trade relations and integration is a modern phenomenon with its own attributes and contents of the time, so the "Pan-African movement" that lasted 100 years on the African continent in the twentieth century didn't have the attributes of a modern regional integration movement in the early period. However, in terms of Africa's historical development, the existence and development of early Pan-Africanism largely aroused the national awareness and dignity of African people, gave rise to the special regional awareness and sense of historical mission on the African continent, and provided the ideological foundation and practical experience for Africa's integration in the future. Therefore, the fast-growing African integration after WWII wasn't an imitation or reproduction of the regionalization of Europe or other regions, but had its own logic of historical development and special mission. When Africa was still under colonial rule, the colonies that hadn't obtained political independence yet already began political coalition to fight for national independence and emancipation, a special way of the African continent to begin regional integration. This was an important feature that set African integration apart from the regional integration elsewhere.

African integration in the modern sense didn't begin until the second half of the twentieth century. The foundation of the Organisation of African Unity (OAU) in 1963 marked the formal beginning of African integration based on independent sovereign countries. As the most important political achievement of Pan-Africanism, the OAU provided the necessary organizational foundation and institutional guarantee for modern African integration and cemented the institutional and long-term unity and collaboration of African countries through legal means.

With the OAU as a carrier, the primary task of African integration was the complete liberation of African continent. The organization stated in its Charter that it is committed to eradicating all forms of colonialism in Africa, and called on all African countries and nations to stay more closely together and dedicate themselves to national emancipation on the African continent. For the better part of the second half of the twentieth century, the most lasting and effective political campaign of all Pan-Africanism activities conducted by OAU was the consistent support to the national liberation movement in Africa that was still under colonial rule. First, it

---

[3] "Resolution of the Fifth Pan-African Conference," Tang Dadun, ed., *Selected Works of Pan-Africanism and Organization of African Unity (1900–1990)*, Shanghai: East China Normal University Press, 1995, p. 43.

conducted political mobilization and publicity for struggles of national liberation to secure moral and material support from the international community. Till the late 1980s, almost all Assemblies of Heads of State and councils of ministers of the organization emphasized and discussed decolonization and full liberation of Africa. They expressed through declarations sympathy and support for the independence movement by people in some colonies, published resolutions against colonialism, racism and apartheid, and worked out documents and guidelines for the liberation struggles. Those declarations and resolutions immensely inspired the African people who were fighting for independence and stirred up international public opinions and mobilized the democratic and progressive forces in other countries to exert pressure and sanction on forces that stubbornly insisted on colonial rule. Second, they set up the African Liberation Committee to make plans and coordinate independent African countries in providing assistance to the liberation struggles of the non-independent countries and regions. Through the African Liberation Committee and the Front States Organization that was formed under its influence, the OAU provided a lot of weapons, capital, living materials, medical equipment and training bases for the liberation organizations in relevant regions. Thanks to its support, the national liberation movement thrived in Africa, and a large group of African countries claimed independence successively in the 1960s and 1970s. With Namibia's claim of independence in 1990 and the birth of new South Africa in 1994, the historical mission of the national liberation movement in Africa was finally accomplished.

Another task of the African integration then was to preserve the political unity of the newly formed countries. To realize the political dream of Pan-Africanism for African unity, Africa not only needed thorough national liberation, but also required a regional political and security order featuring the unity, cooperation and good-neighborliness among African countries, and had to promote political coordination and integration on that basis. Since Africa achieved independence, the OAU has taken unity and stability on the continent as an important cooperation topic and has taken a series of measures for that purpose. First, it specified in the Charter the modern sovereign and diplomatic principles that all countries should observe, such as sovereign equality and non-interference in other country's internal affairs. It also passed the *Declaration on the Problem of Subversion* in 1965 prohibiting subversive activities among African countries and opposing those conducted by foreign forces against OAU and its member states. These efforts by OAU could be regarded as a kind of collective compensation for the inadequate sovereign principles and diplomatic rules among African countries, and played an important role in establishing normal international relations in the region.[4] Second, it set the principle that the borderline was unchangeable to prevent territorial conflict between countries. OAU's consistent stance of maintaining the current border of African countries set the ground rule for solving their border conflicts and ensured the general stability in African border and territory. Third, it set up the regional conflict control mechanism. The first Assembly

---

[4] Robert H. Jackson and Karl G. Rothberg, "Pan-Africanism and Its Problems", in Richard E. Bissell & Michael S. Redu (eds.), *Africa in the Post-Decolonization Era*, New Brunswick: Transaction Books, 1984, p. 163.

of Heads of State of OAU held in July 1964 passed the resolution on forming the Commission of Mediation, Conciliation and Arbitration, and stressed that all member states pledged to solve state-to-state conflicts in peaceful ways and within the scope of Africa. Thanks to the principle laid down by OAU on solving Africa's conflicts within Africa, most African countries considered mediation within the OAU framework when handling conflicts.[5]

Since the 1990s, the high-tech revolution with information technology in the center has developed by leaps and bounds, largely boosting the global flow of production, trade and financial activities. In the globalized world today, as opposed to the world system before the mid-twentieth century, the relation between the western world and the African continent has undergone many structural changes, and equality among nations and countries has been achieved at least on surface, but the interest distribution and risk flow in the process of world economic and cultural exchanges is uneven. Developed countries in the west seem to benefit while backward countries in Africa suffer some of the adverse consequences. The African economy suffered deeply from colonial exploitation and was marginalized in the world economic landscape, so when African countries participated in the globalization process as independent nations, they had "innate handicaps". Starting at a much lower level and being subject to unfair game rules, African countries find it very hard to achieve normal economic development in a relatively favorable environment, not to mention make leapfrog progress. In the course of globalization, the development crisis of African countries is very likely to worsen, and Africa is very likely to be further marginalized in the world. This vicious tendency is prominent even in comparison to some countries and regions in Asia and Latin America. For African countries, how to avoid the adverse factors of globalization and make full use of development opportunities to realize economic growth and social progress quickly has become a momentous political issue concerning their national survival and development.

Against such a background, the African Union formally replaced the OAU in July 2002, bringing African integration to a new stage. The formation of the African Union indicated that Africa, having completed the task of national liberation, began to seek national modernization and regional revival, and the theme and historical mission on that continent shifted from "independence" and "liberation" to "peace" and "development". If the appearance of OAU symbolized that the African continent was about to be freed from colonial rule, the birth of African Union marked a new starting point for African rejuvenation. It reflected African people's ways of thinking about the historical development trend, Africa's political and economic situation and future in the new stage, displayed African countries' new understanding of collective development and self-reliance, and fully demonstrated Africa's progress toward a higher level of integration.

The African Union has taken a range of new measures in recent years to promote peace and development in Africa.

---

[5] Olatunde J. C. B. Ojo, D. K. Orwa and C. M. B. Utete, *African International Relations*, London: Longman Group Limited, 1985, p. 40.

First, it made many innovations and breakthroughs in regional security governance. It set up the Peace and Security Council (PSC) that is specifically responsible for peace and security for the first time in African history. According to the African Union Charter, the Union and its PSC have the right to enforce intervention, including the use of armed intervention, when serious situations (e.g. crime of war, of race and against humanity) appear in its member states or when one member state invades another; and the right to impose sanction when unconstitutional change of regime happens in a member state, in order to restore normal national order and governance. African Union's breakthroughs in security principle pushed Africa's collective security principle from "non-interference" to "non-ignorance" and gave the union the right to proactively intervene in potential or realistic crisis and conflicts. That was the biggest difference between African Union and OAU in security principle, and this change, for the first time in history, enabled an African regional organization to intervene in the domestic crisis of member states legally, thus solving the long-term legal contradiction between collective intervention and national sovereignty in Africa's collective security mechanism and laying the necessary legal foundation for African Union to implement its peace mission. Since 2003, the Union has applied direct intervention in multiple conflicts and wars, including the civil war in Burundi, the conflict in Sudan's Darfur, the political crisis in Togo, the civil strife in Cote d'Ivoire, and the civil war in Somalia, making a contribution to keeping those conflicts within control and facilitating an early solution.

Second, it actively pushed for the comprehensive operation of the "New Partnership for Africa's Development (NEPAD)". The long-term goal of NEPAD is eradicating poverty in Africa, promoting its sustainable economic development, and preventing its "marginalization" in the course of economic globalization, and its specific goal is maintaining the average GDP growth rate of African countries at 7% in the next 15 years and halving the impoverished population by 2015. NEPAD listed the following priority areas: infrastructure construction, especially, road, railway and traffic and communication systems connecting with neighboring countries; HR development, especially the training of health and education talents; and production and export diversification, especially the export to developed countries. NEPAD aims to achieve Pan-African collaboration through integration within and among sub-regional economic communities in Africa and eventually build a mature African economic community.[6] To advance African revival, the NEPAD creatively established the African Peer Review Mechanism (APRM), a mutual supervision and restriction mechanism for African countries that demanded the member states to open up their government administration, economic policy and human rights situations and accept the inspection and evaluation of other member states according to preset standards. The purpose is to restrict African countries' political and economic behaviors with collective rules and the supervision by public opinions, urge them

---

[6] For details of NEPAD, see "The New Economic Partnership for Africa's Development," published online at http://www.nepad.org/2005/files/documents/inbrief.pdf.

to realize sound governance, and consequently bring political stability and fast economic growth to them.[7] By September 2008, 25 African countries had joined the APRM.[8]

Third, it called for "speaking in one voice" on major international issues. At present, economic cooperation, conflict management and common diplomacy are the three pillars of African Union's integration efforts. Regarding common diplomacy, integrating the resources and forces on the African continent and raising its international standing through active diplomatic participation is one of the Union's important missions. In its Constitutive Act, the African Union enumerated in detail the goals it wished to achieve on the international stage: promoting and maintaining a joint stance of African people on issues concerning their interests; encouraging international cooperation and fully respecting the UN Charter and *Universal Declaration of Human Rights*; creating necessary conditions for Africa to play its due role in global economy and international negotiations; promoting collaboration in all aspects of human activities to improve the lives of African people; and working with international partners to eliminate preventable diseases and improve the health care in Africa.[9] In sum, the African Union is currently focused on the following international topics and goals: (1) working with major countries in the world to secure more external support for Africa's peace and development; (2) integrating political and economic forces and diplomatic resources of Africa and raising its international standing; (3) working to reform the irrational international order to safeguard the common interests of Africa and developing countries.

The African Union has primarily set up the institutional platform for African countries to conduct foreign exchanges in a collective identity.

(1) African Union participated in international organizations. African Union and its member states make a point of joining international organizations such as the UN, WTO and IMF, with a view to pushing for the revision and improvement of relevant international rules through the united "African forces" and raising their status and influence in the international system as a collective group. For example, regarding the reform of UN Security Council in recent years, African Union made assertions for the rights and interests of Africans in one voice. In March and July 2005, it successively issued the *Ezulwini Consensus* and *Sirte Declaration*, calling for a comprehensive reform of the United Nations on the principle of universalism, equity and regional balance, demanding the assurance of Africa's legal rights in that process, and requesting two permanent

---

[7] "About APRM", http://www.nepad.org/aprm/.

[8] The 25 countries are: Algeria, Angola, Benin, Burkina Faso, Cameroon, Democratic Republic of Congo, Egypt, Ethiopia, Gabon, Ghana, Kenya, Lesotho, Malawi, Mali, Mauritius, Mozambique, Nigeria, Rwanda, Senegal, Sierra Leone, South Africa, Sudan, Tanzania, Uganda, Zambia. "Participating Countries," published online at http://www.nepad.org/aprm/.

[9] For details, see "Constitutive Act of the African Union", "Protocol on Amendments to the Constitutive Act of the African Union," published online at http://www.africa-union.org/root/au/Ducuments/Treaties/treaties.htm.

seats to Africa with all the privileges, including the right of veto, and five non-permanent seats on the Security Council.[10] African countries reached a basic consensus on the UN reform and made a common motion in the name of African Union, something that has never been seen anywhere else in the world.

(2) African Union adjusted relations with western countries through NEPAD. As the Union's guideline on economic and social development, NEPAD's goal is eradicating poverty in Africa and leading African countries toward the path of sustained growth and development, either individually or collectively. African countries demanded that all programs concerning African development should be based on their own will of development and strategic arrangements, and the international community, especially western countries, should lighten or re-arrange Africa's debts to create conditions for its new development. NEPAD is the leading collective development mechanism for Africa at the moment, which provides a basic framework for African countries to build a new model of partnership with the outside world. NEPAD has received positive responses from the international community, and the UN, World Bank, IMF and EU have expressed support for it many times.

(3) African Union utilized the G8 Summit to hold South-North dialogue. In the twenty-first century, with the positive turn in the political and economic situations of African countries and the rebound in their international strategic status, western countries, particularly the G8 bloc, began to reevaluate their African strategy. Pushed by African countries, the G8 Summit initiated many times to hold the South-North Dialogue conference on African development. For instance, at the 2003 G8 Summit held in France's Evian, the five founding states of NEPAD—Egypt, Senegal, Nigeria, Algeria and South Africa—were invited to attend the first North–South informal dialogue meeting and discuss African development and aid to Africa. The 2008 G8 Summit at Toyako, Japan's Hokkaido, made "African development" one of the main topics again, at which the G8 leaders held dialogue meeting with leaders of the African Union as well as seven African countries—Algeria, Ethiopia, Ghana, Nigeria, Senegal, South Africa and Tanzania, and also with leaders of five developing countries—China, Brazil, India, South Africa and Mexico. During the 2009 G8 Summit in Italy's L'Aquila, the G8 leaders met with leaders of a number of African countries, including Algeria, Angola, Egypt, Ethiopia, Libya, Nigeria, Senegal and South Africa, as well as heads of the African Union and other international organizations. The G8 countries pledged to provide assistance in enhancing African countries' basic capability of executing water and health plans, strengthening their coordination in solving water and health problems, and other aspects.

---

[10] "Sirte Declaration on the Reform of the United Nations," published online at http://www.africa-union.org/root/au/Documents/Decisions/hog/Decisions_Sirte_July_2005.pdf.

(4) African Union encouraged African countries to create multilateral cooperation mechanisms with the outside world. So far the African continent has formed a number of cooperation mechanisms with the U.S., EU, Japan, India, China and other countries and blocs, and has set up important cooperation platforms like the US-Africa Economic and Trade Cooperation Forum, Africa-Europe Summit, Tokyo International Conference on African Development (TICAD), India-Africa Summit and Forum on China-Africa Cooperation (FOCAC). In particular, the development of FOCAC in the twenty-first century has considerably expanded the contents and forms of China-Africa cooperation and created new ways of South-South cooperation, having great importance for China's rise, Africa's rejuvenation and the world's harmonious development.

In the course of Africa's historical development, after nationalism flourished in Africa in the beginning of the twentieth century, the Pan-African movement aiming for the revival and unification of the African continent and its modern edition—the African integration movement—constituted the centerline of Africa's centennial campaign of awakening and rejuvenation, and represented African people's lasting efforts to recognize their rights, interests and values, and confirm Africa's position in and relation with the world. Through arduous struggles for more than a century, the united Africans not only awakened their national consciousness and the awareness of racial equity and overthrew the colonial rule and political oppression of western powers, but also, after gaining political independence and national sovereignty, committed themselves to economic independence and cultural reconstruction, in the endeavor to achieve the complete liberation and thorough rejuvenation of the African continent. As a matter of fact, the Africa history in the twentieth century was a history of African people fighting for independence and collective self-reliance through united efforts. From this point of view, integration was a key content of African history in the twentieth century and an inevitable historical stage that Africa had to pass on its way to modern revival. The ups and downs of this movement had a significant bearing not only on the political and economic changes and cultural transformation on the African continent in that period, but also on the international landscape on the continent and its relation with the outside world. In this sense, African integration is bound to influence the development, changes and future direction of China-Africa relations. In return, China-Africa relations, as an important foreign relation for African countries, also influence their political and economic development as well as their cooperation and integration process to some extent and in some way. Therefore, the mutual effect and influence between African integration and China-Africa relations, or the interpretation of the history, reality and future of China-Africa relations from the perspective of African integration, is a topic of major significance that hasn't been well studied and addressed yet.

9.2 Birth and Development of Multilateral Exchanges Between China and Africa

Before the formation of OAU, China actively supported African people in fighting for national independence against foreign aggression with a united front. In April 1958, Premier Zhou Enlai sent a telegram via Ghana Prime Minister Nkrumah to the Conference of Independent African Countries, expressing his warm congratulations on its success in fighting against colonialism, striving for the national independence of African countries, opposing racial discrimination, deepening the friendly cooperation among African countries and their peoples, and preserving world peace. When the All-African Peoples' Conference was convened on December 5, 1958, Premier Zhou Enlai also sent a congratulatory telegram, wishing the Conference greater accomplishments in the righteous undertaking of uniting all African people to fight against imperialism, striving for national independence and preserving world peace. After the OAU was formed in 1963, China actively bolstered its efforts to acquire national liberation and preserve sovereign independence, and expressed its support to African people's righteous cause on multiple international occasions. The premier of Chinese State Council sent a congratulatory telegram to every Assembly of Heads of State of the OAU (except in 1966–1969). Chinese leaders and foreign ministers visited Africa many times, met with OAU representatives and discussed African and international situation as well as China-Africa relations. When then Chinese President Jiang Zemin visited Africa in May 1996, he, upon the invitation of OAU, delivered an important speech titled "Setting A New Monument to China-Africa Friendliness" at the OAU Headquarters, and held talks with OAU Secretary General regarding the new ways and forms of China-Africa cooperation in the new period. OAU leaders also visited China many times to seek cooperation. From March 30 to April 4, 1974, Omar Arte Ghalib, Executive Chairman of OAU Liberation Committee and Foreign Minister of Somalia, headed a delegation to visit China, the first time after OAU was founded. From October 22 to 26, 1990, Salim was the first OAU Secretary General who paid a formal visit of friendliness to China at the latter's invitation. China also provided long-term assistance to African people's anti-imperialism and anti-colonialism struggles, supported OAU and its Liberation Committee, and offered a huge amount of economic, material and military aid to African countries.

Although China has paid attention to OAU for a long time, it was mainly in the form of congratulatory message and expression of support in both ways, while more substantial and diverse cooperation contents and channels were lacking. For a very long time after the People's Republic of China was founded, China's diplomacy to Africa was focused on the bilateral level, and the attention paid to African integration was just a supplement.

As African integration deepened in the twenty-first century, the regional integration of African continent was increased, and regional and sub-regional organizations represented by African Union had growing power and played a bigger role in Africa's political and economic development and foreign relations. In the meanwhile, China has conscientiously participated in regional and international affairs through multilateral diplomacy in recent years, trying to establish its image as a responsible country. On the international level, China more actively and responsibly engaged in the work of UN Security Council and the UN reform, joined the WTO and began to play an important role, and tried to communicate and cooperate with the G8 bloc. On the regional level, it took an active part in the APEC integration, strongly pushed for the establishment and development of China-ASEAN free trade area, continuously promoted the deepening of SCO, and successfully forged the comprehensive strategic partnership with the EU. Multilateralism gradually became an important value orientation for Chinese strategic and diplomatic circles, and multilateral diplomacy has become an important approach and means for China to handle the relationship with the outside world. Against such a background, the traditional model of bilateral diplomacy with Africa could no longer adapt to the political and economic changes on the African continent and China had to adjust its diplomatic strategy. Multilateral diplomacy with Africa, as an increasingly independent diplomatic model, was quickly put on the agenda of China's African diplomacy and acquired growing historical significance. China obviously attached more importance to the African integration process. It took African Union and other integration organizations as important objects of diplomatic work on both the strategic and tactical level, and, along with African countries, creatively initiated the new cooperation model of FOCAC. The successful introduction of multilateral diplomacy has brought about substantial changes in China's African diplomacy and exerted positive impacts on China-Africa relations.

First, the exchanges between China and African Union developed across the board. Compared with OAU, China has closer exchanges with the top level of African Union both in form and frequency. On July 9, 2002, Yang Wenchang, a special envoy of the Chinese government and Deputy Foreign Minister of China, attended the first African Union Summit held in South Africa's Durban as a non-voting special guest. On July 9, 2003, former Premier Wen Jiabao sent a congratulatory letter to the convention of African Union Summit, saying that the Chinese government will continue to support African integration and the implementation of NEPAD, and will make unremitting efforts together with African countries to realize peace and development in Africa and build a new model of China-Africa partnership that is lasting, stable, equal and mutually beneficial. In March 2005, China assigned a representative to African Union. In June 2006, the Chinese government, upon the invitation of African Union, assigned a delegation to attend the African Union Summit to be held in early July as an observer, marking a great step forward in tightening the bilateral connections and friendly relationship between China and the Union. On the other hand, the rotating chairman of African Union and president of Nigeria Obasanjo, Chairman of African Union Commission Konare and other African Union leaders have visited China successively since 2005.

The Chinese government repeatedly expressed its staunch support for the development of African Union and the cause of African integration. The *Declaration of the Beijing Summit Of the Forum on China-Africa Cooperation* stated, "China commends Africa's progress in safeguarding regional peace, promoting regional cooperation and accelerating economic and social development, appreciates the active role played by the African countries, the African Union and other regional and sub-regional organizations in this regard, reaffirms its support for the African countries in their efforts to strengthen themselves through unity and independently resolve African problems, supports the African regional and sub-regional organizations in their efforts to promote economic integration, and supports the African countries in implementing the 'New Partnership for Africa's Development' (NEPAD) programs."[11] In the field of traditional security, China intensified the multilateral cooperation with African Union in solving regional conflicts and hot-button issues in Africa, and encouraged and supported the Union and other sub-regional organizations in playing an important role in safeguarding Africa's peace progress. In 2001, the Chinese government donated USD200,000 to the OAU Peace Foundation for its peacekeeping operations in Democratic Republic of Congo (DRC). After that, China actively supported the independent peacekeeping operations led by African Union. In July 2003, it provided military logistics materials worth RMB2.5 million to the African Union peacekeeping troops in Burundi; in 2005, it provided USD400,000 spot exchange to support African Union in expanding its peacekeeping operations in Darfur, Sudan; in 2006, it increased this assistance to USD1.4 million spot exchange, driving the total donation for African Union's Sudan mission to USD1.8 million; in June 2007, it decided to provide two donations of USD300,000 each to support the Union's own development and its peacekeeping operations in Somalia. China also made a special point of discussing with African countries the coordination in various non-traditional security issues, such as supporting African countries' efforts to prevent the infection of AIDS, and endorsing the measures they took to prevent and combat terrorism, including reaching anti-terror agreement and building terrorism research and investigation center. *China's African Policy* expressly pledged to promote the China-Africa cooperation in non-traditional security fields, "in order to enhance the ability of both sides to address non-traditional security threats, it is necessary to increase intelligence exchange, explore more effective ways and means for closer cooperation in combating terrorism, small arms smuggling, drug trafficking, transnational economic crimes, etc."[12] In the field of economic and social development, the Chinese government paid close attention to the special challenges and difficulties faced by the African continent and gave stronger support and help to the governments and people of African countries in the priority areas designated by NEPAD, such as infrastructure construction, HR development and agriculture.

Second, the initiation and development of FOCAC is the most important form of multilateral exchange between China and Africa today. In October 1999, former Chinese President Jiang Zemin sent a personal letter to OAU Secretary General and the heads of state of some African countries, formally putting forth the initiative to hold the FOCAC conference, and received positive responses. In October 10–12, 2000, the Forum on China-Africa Cooperation Ministerial Conference Beijing

---

[11] "Declaration of the Beijing Summit Of the Forum on China-Africa Cooperation," *People's Daily*, November 6, 2006, p. 4.

[12] China's African Policy, *People's Daily*, January 13, 2006, p. 3.

2000 was grandly held in Beijing and caught global attention. It was a significant moment for China and African countries at the turn of the new century, the first multilateral collective dialogue on the basis of equality and mutual benefit, and a milestone in the history of China-Africa relations. The FOCAC was the first intergovernmental mechanism of multilateral consultation and collective dialogue between China and African countries, which marked China's successful introduction of multilateral diplomacy into its diplomacy with Africa. From October 2000 to the present day, FOCAC has successfully held four ministerial conferences, whereby the two sides had substantive dialogues and consultations on how to promote the establishment of an equitable and rational international political and economic new order to safeguard the common interests of developing countries, and how to further enhance the China-Africa cooperation in economy, trade, culture and education. During the third FOCAC conference in 2006, a China-Africa Summit was specially held, indicating the great importance attached by both sides to multilateral exchanges. The FOCAC has notably enriched the contents and forms of China-Africa relations and largely pushed their development in the new century.

9.3 How to Further Promote China's Multilateral Diplomacy to Africa?

In the new century, multilateral exchanges between China and Africa have developed by leaps and bounds and achieved remarkable diplomatic results. But China's multilateral diplomacy to Africa is still in the early stage and should be deepened further. (1) In China's overall multilateral diplomacy, its multilateral diplomacy to Africa lags behind its activities on global multilateral platforms and its multilateral diplomacy with other regions like the Asia Pacific and Europe. For instance, while FOCAC is mainly a ministerial meeting mechanism, China's multilateral cooperation with the Asia Pacific and Europe has long risen to the level of heads-of-state meeting, and its multilateral cooperation with Asian-Pacific countries took the form of the more substantive regional integration from the very beginning. In particular, China and ASEAN are building a comprehensive free trade area. (2) For a long time in the past, multilateral diplomacy played second fiddle to bilateral diplomacy between China and Africa. Its historical role wasn't fully brought into play and its position and value was underestimated. Therefore, formulating a basic framework for China's multilateral diplomacy to Africa in a timely manner on the basis of the current initial foundation and promoting the multilateral exchanges between China and African countries on all fronts is an important topic faced by Chinese diplomacy today.

1. Basic strategic ways of thinking

To carry out multilateral diplomacy, the first and most important thing is establishing a strategic ways of thinking on the conceptual level. Nowadays when multilateralism is flourishing, multilateral diplomacy has acquired a more independent position, value and effect, the traditional diplomatic landscape where bilateral diplomacy is dominant and multilateral diplomacy is ancillary has seen substantial changes in some areas and on certain occasions, and many international, bilateral and even domestic issues have to be solved through multilateral channels. Conducting multilateral diplomacy doesn't mean the mere introduction of a new diplomatic approach or means, but is more about the change of ideas and thinking about multilateralism. Theoretically speaking, multilateral diplomacy is usually aimed for longer and deeper cooperation among different nations, and requires a nation to restrain or even give up unilateral or short-term interests in certain fields in order to safeguard the interactive common interests of multiple parties. Under the framework of China-Africa multilateral cooperation, the two sides can continue to deepen consultation and cooperation in the UN, WTO and other international organizations, and support each other on major issues of principle such as international order, regional security and the rights and interests of developing countries, in a bid to jointly protect their due interests. China's multilateral diplomacy to Africa has diversified the contents and forms of their economic and trade relation, and helped them to pay timely attention to and address the serious problems encountered in economic and trade contact. It also provided a fine diplomatic channel for China to illustrate its diplomatic stance. Compared to China's bilateral diplomacy with African countries, multilateral diplomacy features extensive space of activity, large number of participants, and diverse forms of implementation, and is helpful for China to showcase to African countries and the international community its African policy and the principles and standpoints of handling international issues. Since the 1980s, some Africans deemed that China's diplomacy was inclined toward western countries and its Africa policy was focused on economic interests with little regard to the development and interests of African countries. This biased viewpoint once affected the diplomatic relation between China and Africa. China's multilateral diplomacy with Africa, especially the creation of FOCAC, demonstrated to African countries China's political attitude and resolve to help with Africa's development and largely changed some African countries' one-sided perception of China's diplomatic adjustment. Moreover, intensifying multilateral diplomacy with Africa will also contribute to the joint efforts by China and African countries to foil the attempt of Taiwan separatist forces to meddle in China-Africa relations in that by uniting the African countries closely and coordinating their common standpoint through multilateral mechanisms, we can considerably squeeze Taiwan's space of activity and consequently safeguard the general stability in China-Africa relations.

The multilateral cooperation between China and Africa concerns the cooperative relation between China and a whole continent. Since there are a large number of African countries and their diplomatic strategy differs widely, it is more challenging and complicated and takes more diplomatic wisdom and political patience for China to develop multilateral relations with them than to develop bilateral relations with individual countries. Therefore, China should adopt a new mindset when fostering the strategic foundation for the multilateral diplomacy with Africa.

First, it should continue to expand the contents and strategic direction of China-Africa multilateral cooperation. When thinking of their multilateral cooperation, both

9.3 How to Further Promote China's Multilateral Diplomacy to Africa?

sides should think beyond their own interests and give considerations to the common interests of the international community, especially of developing countries. When dealing with the relation with developed western countries, they should shake off the ideological limitations and the restriction imposed by traditional political concepts, neither labeling them as "enemy" or "friend" nor taking sides with the "east" or "west". Although China and Africa both emphasized over and over that they are opposed to power politics and hegemony and committed to the establishment of a new international political and economic order, they have no intention of creating an actual or potential enemy or rival. They are just opposed to the irrational old international order and hegemonistic behaviors in the world, not to specific countries. On the way of pursuing economic development, developed western countries and the international market system dominated by them constitute the principal international environment faced by China and African countries. Therefore, correctly and properly handling the relation with developed western countries is of great importance for China and Africa to achieve their development goals.

Second, it should fully realize that China-Africa multilateral cooperation is a continuously developing process. This has twofold meanings. On one hand, China and Africa should not be contented with their cooperation achievements in history, but should keep their eyes on the future and push their friendly relationship to a new level; on the other hand, the contents and forms of China-Africa relation are also changing and evolving all the time. Political, economic, cultural and security cooperation proceeds in parallel, official and people-to-people exchanges complement each other, and multilateral and bilateral diplomacy develops in balance—this will be the biggest characteristic of the multilateral relationship between China and Africa for a long time to come. FOCAC began to hold the Conference of Chinese and African Entrepreneurs in 2003, in order to boost the people-to-people exchanges and economic and trade relation on the government level. This is a strong step taken in recent years to coordinate intergovernmental communication with people-to-people exchanges and political cooperation with economic and trade cooperation, and will help deepen the China-Africa relationship. Besides, China has paid much more attention to the regional security in Africa in recent years. It not only supported the African Union and other sub-regional organizations, both politically and materially, in conducting independent peacekeeping operations, but also participated in UN peacekeeping missions in Africa within its ability, making security cooperation an important agenda in the China-Africa political cooperation in the new period.

2. Specific diplomatic strategy

In view of the strategic ways of thinking for China-Africa multilateral cooperation, the tremendous political and economic changes in China and the African continent, and China's traditional diplomatic practices with Africa, China should take account of the following points when carrying out multilateral diplomacy with Africa in the twenty-first century.

Prioritize the relation with African Union. African Union is the largest comprehensive inter-national organization in Africa and the most important organizational carrier of African integration. In an age when globalization and regionalization pick up speed and African countries actively pursue development, African integration will be further intensified and the position and role of African Union will be further reinforced. Therefore, tightening the cooperation with African Union is an important part of China's African work in the time to come, which can be implemented on three levels. (1) Strengthen the direct communication with African Union, including following its development, paying attention to the activities carried out by its major organizations such as the African Union Summit, Governing Council, Peace and Security Council and Pan-African Parliament, and providing timely political, diplomatic and economic support when necessary; carry out direct contact with the rotating chairman of African Union and chairman of African Union Commission, either inviting them to visit China or holding meetings or consultations when Chinese leaders visit Africa, so as to promote multilateral relation. (2) The FOCAC mechanism is an important means of China's multilateral diplomacy with Africa and the most significant outcome of China's cooperation with African Union. Deepening this multilateral mechanism will generate effects that cannot be replaced by other bilateral relations. (3) Intensify the consultation and cooperation with African Union on international multilateral stages, secure African countries' diplomatic support by coordinating with African Union in diplomatic standpoint, and jointly safeguard the interests of developing countries.

Develop the relation with sub-regional organizations in Africa. Sub-regional organization is the most basic unit through which African countries conduct political and economic cooperation, and an important foundation for African countries to eventually realize unification. Sub-regional organizations represented by the Southern African Development Community (SADC) and Economic Community of West African States (ECOWAS) have displayed strong political ambition and certain operating capability in mobilizing and integration regional forces. For a long time, China didn't have a close relation with most sub-regional organizations in Africa, and that obviously didn't suit the trend of African integration. In conducting multilateral diplomacy with Africa, China must set store by sub-regional cooperation, conduct multilateral cooperation on the regional, sub-regional and international platforms in parallel, and form an all-round cooperation situation covering all tiers and fields. The current priority is to intensify the relation with relatively mature sub-regional organizations such as SACD and ECOWAS, with a view to forming a cooperation network covering the whole Africa. For example, China should tighten the economic and trade relation with SACD, actively tap the southern African market centered on South Africa, and leverage on its radiating effect to further increase the share in the African market, so as to form a network with the economic links already established in the north, west, middle and east of Africa and cover the entire African continent. Moreover, China should place stress on ECOWAS' contributions to safeguarding regional peace and actively reinforce the cooperation with it. Since the West African peacekeeping troops began to carry out regional peacekeeping operations in the early 1990s, the Chinese government has shown its support to ECOWAS' efforts for restoring peace in West Africa through the UN and other international organizations, and assigned military observers to Liberia and Sierra Leone to participate in UN peacekeeping missions. To adapt to the changing situation, it's necessary for

9.3 How to Further Promote China's Multilateral Diplomacy to Africa?

China to give more importance to ECOWAS, work with the international community to support its active efforts for promoting regional economic integration and peacekeeping, and continue to intensify the friendly cooperation with its member states. *China's African Policy* clearly stated that China appreciates and supports the positive role played by African sub-regional organizations in promoting regional political stability, economic development and integration, and is willing to intensify the friendly cooperation with them.

Enrich the contents and forms of FOCAC. From the very beginning, FOCAC isn't a talk shop, but a multilateral platform of practical cooperation between China and Africa. In addition to political consultation, the two sides mainly enrich the contents and forms of bilateral exchanges through economic and trade contact and cultural communication. First of all, economic and trade factor plays a more prominent role in international relations today, and economic relation has a growing weight in China-Africa relations. Therefore, well implementing the economic and trade work toward Africa, including trade, investment and aid, is key to further consolidating the friendly relations with African countries. The FOCAC has not only provided an occasion for China and Africa to discuss major issues such as economic and trade cooperation, investment policy and aid to Africa, but also successfully introduced the "Conference of Chinese and African Entrepreneurs" to enrich the contents of China-Africa economic and trade cooperation. Second, China and Africa have also reinforced their cooperation in such fields as education, technology, cultural exchange and HR development on multilateral occasions like this, diversifying the contents and forms of their substantial cooperation. In today's world where international connections are closer and the humankind has come to the information age, diplomacy has long evolved beyond its narrow concept and become a general concept covering a range of fields, including politics, economy, technology, culture, military and people-to-people exchange. Other than the traditional "hard power" such as economic and military strength, "soft power" such as political system and cultural and ideological influence is also playing an increasingly important role in international relations. Due to loose historical connections and remote geographical distance, the Africans today know and recognize the western civilization and Islamic civilization much more than Chinese civilization, a situation that won't change fundamentally for a very long time to come. Besides, African civilization and Chinese civilization are two different civilizations with long history. Their exchange and mutual learning is not only conducive to their respective development and evolution, but also of special significance for deepening the friendly relation between China and Africa and the mutual understanding between their peoples, and promoting cultural prosperity in the world and the harmonious development of the human society. Therefore, through the multilateral forum of FOCAC, we should strengthen the cooperation with African countries in education, culture and other fields, strongly disseminate China's good image, and enhance the influence of its soft power in Africa.

Strengthen the consultation and cooperation with African countries on international multilateral occasions. Especially in major international multilateral organizations or conferences such as the UN and WTO, there are many opportunities and topics for China and Africa to cooperate on and their viewpoints are quite similar.

For instance, on relevant occasions of the UN, China repeatedly called on the international community to respect African countries' right of independently choosing their own development path, supported African regional organizations' efforts to prevent and solve conflicts, and provided African countries with material and financial assistance without any political conditions. African countries also gave China diplomatic support on international multilateral occasions, such as supporting China in restoring its legitimate position at the UN, opposing Taiwan's re-admission to the UN or other important international organizations in support of that, and opposing certain western powers' groundless accusation of China on the human rights issue. According to *China's African Policy*, "China will continue to strengthen solidarity and cooperation with African countries on the international arena, conduct regular exchange of views, coordinate positions on major international and regional issues and stand for mutual support on major issues concerning state sovereignty, territorial integrity, national dignity and human rights. China supports African nations' desire to be an equal partner in international affairs. China is devoted, as are African nations, to making the UN play a greater role, defending the purposes and principles of the UN Charter, establishing a new international political and economic order featuring justice, rationality, equality and mutual benefit, promoting more democratic international relationship and rule of law in international affairs and safeguarding the legitimate rights and interests of developing countries."[13]

The multilateral cooperation between China and Africa is continuously developed and improved. Compared with the bilateral cooperation model, mature multilateral diplomacy to Africa should have the following characteristics. (1) It should be more institutionalized. Multilateral diplomacy consists of temporary multilateral meeting and institutional multilateral conference or organization. Regarding temporary meeting, China had frequent contacts with the OAU, African Union and other African countries on international multilateral stages and coordinated with and supported each other on major international issues. Meanwhile, the FOCAC is an institutional form of cooperation from the very beginning, whereby the two sides meet frequently to discuss issues of common concern, thus sustaining and deepening the existing substantial cooperation. Continuously expanding and deepening the China-Africa multilateral cooperation mechanism will be a significant institutional guarantee for further development of China-Africa relations in the future. (2) It should be more practical in contents and broader in scope. The current China-Africa multilateral cooperation doesn't just pursue a consistent political slogan or publicity, but pays close attention to the actions and effects of win–win cooperation. Since 2000, China and Africa have had fruitful cooperation in a wide range of areas, including high-level exchange, political dialogue, economic and trade cooperation, technological and cultural exchange, and development aid and debt reduction for Africa, making practical cooperation a main feature of the current China-Africa exchanges. Their cooperation not only concerns international order, major international issues and intercontinental topics, but also the bilateral cooperation between China and African countries and some domestic issues that have to be solved through

---

[13] China's African Policy, *People's Daily*, January 13, 2006, p. 3.

9.3 How to Further Promote China's Multilateral Diplomacy to Africa?

joint efforts. Going forward, the multilateral exchange between China and Africa should continue to place more emphasis on such aspects as economy and trade, education, science and technology, culture and health care. (3) It should have more diverse participants. Multilateral exchange between China and Africa should shift from central governments playing the dominant role and people-to-people exchange playing second fiddle to the diversified situation where the central and local governments, enterprises and social groups all play a part. The more extensive participation of NGOs, enterprises and the general public will further broaden the scope of China-Africa cooperation, enrich the forms of their communication, and boost mutual understanding and trust between Chinese and African peoples. It has a potential yet significant bearing on the lasting and steady development of the friendly relationship between China and Africa.

In China-Africa relations, multilateral and bilateral diplomacy should be two important means for China to intensify relations with African countries. They complement each other and are both indispensable. The future development of China-Africa relations will depend on better coordination between these two diplomatic approaches.

Lightning Source UK Ltd.
Milton Keynes UK
UKHW020432211122
412554UK00008B/542